Sandhurst

A TRADITION OF LEADERSHIP

Sandhurst

☙ A TRADITION OF LEADERSHIP ❧

EDITED BY
VAUGHAN KENT-PAYNE,
CHRISTOPHER PUGSLEY AND
ANGELA HOLDSWORTH

Third Millennium
Publishing

Contents

PART THREE: SERVE TO LEAD

PART FOUR: A TRADITION OF LEADERSHIP

Foreword

Major General Paul Nanson CBE

When I commissioned in 1986, the furthest thing from my mind was that thirty years later I should return as the Commandant. Even further was that I might be asked to write the foreword to the revised edition of this book, which was first published in 2005. A lot has changed since then and new combat uniforms now give the original a rather dated feel. However, many of the changes reflect not just the cosmetic, but also the way in which the British Army, and Sandhurst, has adapted to a rapidly changing world.

The Skill at Arms wing has been retitled Dismounted Close Combat, reflecting the lessons learned on operations in Iraq and Afghanistan. Short Courses, once seen as a backwater for instructors, are now inextricably linked to the life of the Academy with an increased emphasis on the Reserves and the long-overdue training of our officers commissioned after a career in the ranks. So too the chapter on Women at Sandhurst reflects the fact that much has changed since the days when women trained in a separate location to now, with mixed platoons and the first female Officer Cadet commissioned into the Royal Armoured Corps.

However, some aspects of life at Sandhurst have not changed in my career. The backbone of the Academy is still the NCO instructors and the experience and guidance they bring to the cadets. They are still the worthy successors to the legendary Academy Sergeant Major Jack Lord. The sense of comradeship remains, reinforced now that the regular courses are a year long. The international cadets continue to be an integral part of life and it was an honour to recently accompany the Sovereign's representative, King Abdullah II of Jordan (a Sandhurst graduate, son of and father to a Sandhurst graduate), as he inspected the parade. Finally, the fabric of Sandhurst remains a jewel in the nation's architectural crown. The recent refurbishment of Old College has restored it to its former glory, and both the original colour and the many magnificent new photographs in this edition showcase the history of the site.

This book, edited by Vaughan Kent-Payne, Director of the Sandhurst Trust, our alumni charity (another change since the original edition), captures life at the Academy today and intertwines it with the Sandhurst of generations past. It is a splendid addition to the story of Britain's great military academy.

Opposite: RMAS Commandant Paul Nanson with the Sovereign's representative, King Abdullah II of Jordan, at the Sovereign's Parade.

Major General Paul Nanson CBE
September 2017

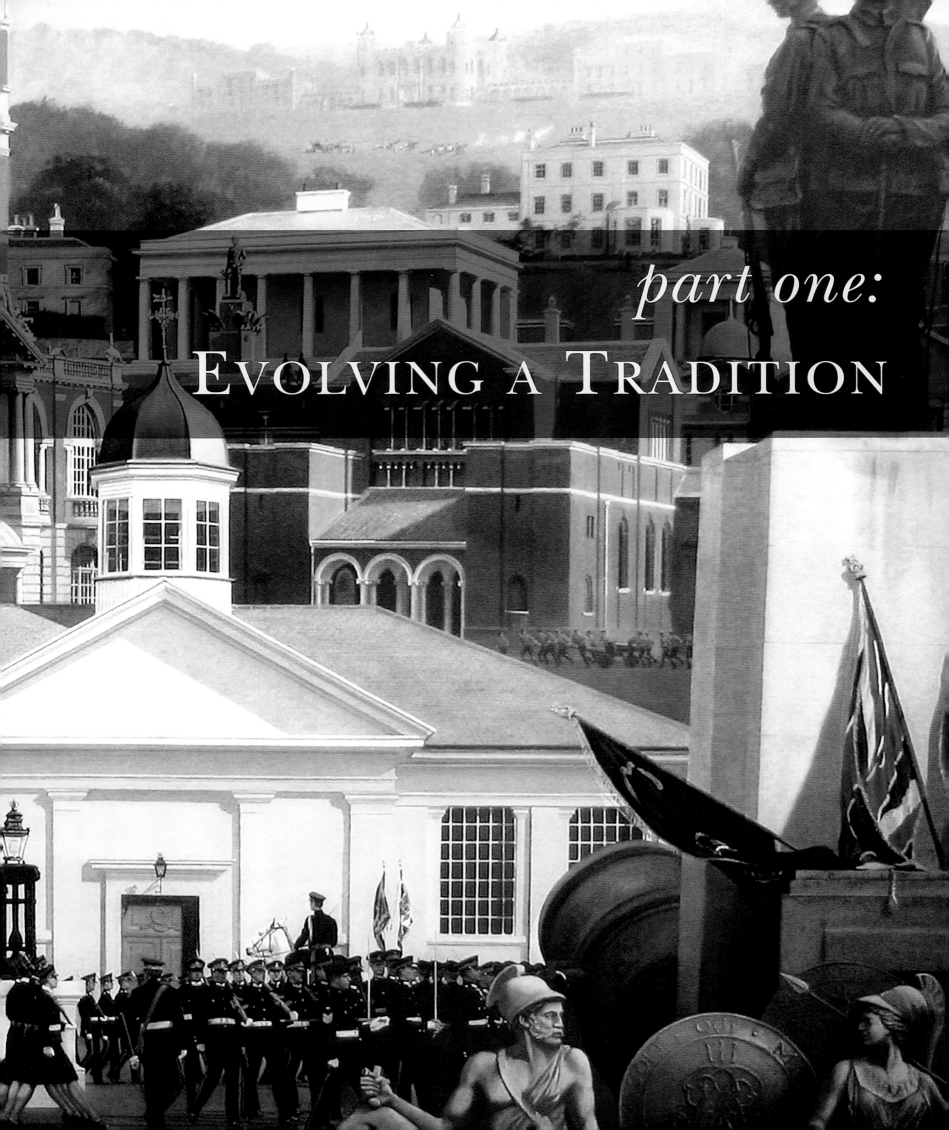

part one:

EVOLVING A TRADITION

chapter one:

The Royal Military Academy Sandhurst: An Introduction

SEAN McKNIGHT

Opposite: The Grand Entrance, Old College, RMAS.

Below: The Royal Military Academy Crest.

'*Ironing Board Sunday' seems like a lifetime ago now when a Colour Sergeant, standing at least eight foot tall, looking particularly intimidating in his dress uniform, greeted me. I am glad to say I did not transition from civilian to soldier alone. Twenty-seven other men and women stood by me from the start and we quickly became a family. Like a family, we obviously had our arguments and differences, especially in such stressful circumstances. However, we learnt to communicate as a group, work for each other and help each other out. Without my platoon behind me, I do not think I would have got through the first five weeks of training. Look to the people to the left and right of you and look for their support. The best part of being in the Army so far has been that sense of comradeship and loyalty you get from living and working with each other through the good and the bad.*
Officer Cadet Mackay, 2016

The Royal Military Academy Sandhurst was formed in 1947 with the primary purpose of training officer cadets to become Regular officers in the British Army. It was the successor of two earlier establishments, the Royal Military Academy Woolwich (the RMA), and the Royal Military College Sandhurst (the RMC). The title of the new academy combined the official name of the original RMA with the familiar one of the former RMC, whose college buildings at Sandhurst it took over. Since 1947, officer education and training has become solely focused at Sandhurst, with the transfer and absorption of the Mons Officer Training School for Short Service Commissioned Officers in 1972 and the Women's Royal Army Corps College in 1984. Nowadays officers with all types of engagement, be it regular, reserve, professionally qualified or late entry, pass through the remarkable institution which is Sandhurst.

Previous page: Carl Laubin, A Sandhurst Fantasy, 1998, oil on canvas. Commissioned to commemorate the fiftieth anniversary of the Academy, this painting is a potpourri of wishful images and history, centred around the buildings; the working sketches showing the various options the artist experimented with can be seen in the corridors of Academy Headquarters. Note that Mars' sword is missing its blade. This reflects a prank that went awry during the gnome craze that swept RMAS in the late 1990s. An officer cadet abseiled from the roof to place a gnome behind Mars and steadied himself by gripping the sword which duly came away in his hand. Although he decamped quickly with the gnome the jungle drums eventually found him out!

In the early 1970s, WO1 Huggins, encapsulated his views on Sandhurst in four simple words: 'Sandhurst is about standards'. However clearly we define Sandhurst's mission and with whatever degree of sophistication and complexity we set out its objectives, WO1 Huggins' words express an enduring ethic. Standards of personal behaviour and integrity remain at the core of what it is to be an Army officer, and such standards are in no way diminished because they are difficult to define. Today one must add the standard of professional competence, for if ever it was possible to justify the existence of the (gifted) amateur, it is not so now. Soldiers rightly demand more of their commanders, Officers must have professional competence, professional awareness, knowledge and understanding, forged in their time at Sandhurst.

Sandhurst remains a timeless and traditional institution, set in beautiful grounds graced by magnificent neoclassical buildings with everywhere reminders of the triumphs, tragedies and sacrifices of the British Army. This is a deceptive image because the modern Academy is also a place where the pace of change is ferocious. Recent conflicts, and an unfolding increasingly complex twenty-first century, are challenges for Sandhurst in preparing officers for the demands of their chosen profession. From introducing mixed-gender platoons, to coping with the demands of an era of contingency – rich with unknowable unknowns and wicked problems – Sandhurst continues to adapt and improve in order to deliver the agile-thinking, capable officers of character that the British Army needs.

It is a sobering thought that the men and women who commission from the RMAS are entering a career where they voluntarily put their lives on the line for their fellow citizens. In taking up the challenges of this career our officers draw strength from both the living past and the demanding months of the Sandhurst commissioning courses. The Sandhurst motto 'Serve to Lead' remains at the heart of what makes the Academy such a unique and extraordinary place.

chapter two:

The Evolution of the British Army Officer, 1600–1871

DUNCAN ANDERSON

Officers' commissions were originally commercial, an early sort of public–private partnership. A general or king would engage a colonel to raise a regiment, paying him a lump sum to recruit, train, clothe, feed and pay about a thousand men (in the infantry, fewer in the cavalry). Infantry colonels would raise one company themselves, and subcontract nine other men to raise further companies. Each colonel would also hire a sergeant-major (later just called the major), a surgeon, chaplain, a captain-lieutenant to command the colonel's own company, and ten lieutenants to be second-in-command of companies. Ensigns were hired to carry regimental and company colours. Cavalry regiments were similarly organised: captains of cavalry commanded troops, and were assisted by lieutenants who were put in charge of squadrons, and by cornets rather than ensigns.

Part of the general's prerogative, specified in the colonel's contract, was to approve the colonel's choice of sergeant-major, captains, lieutenants, ensigns or cornets. The colonel or captains at discretion could appoint other officers such as sergeants and corporals. When Parliament created the New Model Army in 1645, it took away from generals the right to approve 'commissioned' officers. Officers were vetted for political reliability by Parliament, and approved by the same vote that approved the tax to raise the Army's money. The idea of national commissions for officers survived the Restoration, but while the Army's money came to be controlled by the Secretary at War (easily confused with the Secretary of State for War) from his offices in Pall Mall, commissions came to be controlled by the Commander-in-Chief's Military Secretary and were administered from the old cavalry barracks at Horse Guards.

Most government jobs in early modern England were bought. The officer-holder paid a fee for the job and expected to earn back the money plus a profit from the ordinary operations of the job. The profit centre in the Army of the seventeenth and eighteenth centuries was the company. Captains were paid slightly more than the paper strength of their companies and were expected to cream off the difference. Until the creation of the New Model Army, captains were paid the same no matter how few soldiers were left in their companies. This increased the potential profit for captains (which is why colonels were also captains of companies). It also perversely encouraged them to keep their companies under strength so that they could pocket the money intended for the missing soldiers' pay, rations and uniforms.

After the Jacobite rebellions of the early eighteenth century, however, it became clear that neither the King nor Parliament could afford to have officers whose loyalty to the Crown was anything but firm. Yet during the same era the size of Britain's empire increased, requiring an ever-larger army for operations in places like India and North America. A larger army meant a larger officer corps, and more operations meant still more officers to replace those killed in action. During the Napoleonic Wars, commissions were given without purchase to gentlemen who could never have afforded to buy in; once the emergency was over the poorer officers were squeezed out by a deliberate policy of requiring officers to spend lavishly: for example smart regiments wishing to cull the less wealthy ran up the officers'

China figurines on display in Old College.

Above: Oliver Cromwell (1599–1658), Lieutenant General of Horse, New Model Army and Lord Protector of England, oil on canvas, artist unknown.

Above right: HRH The Duke of Cambridge, Commander-in-Chief 1856–95.

tailoring bills by changing uniform patterns and colours more than once a year.

In the nineteenth century the Military Secretary had to find reliable officers for 109 Infantry regiments of the line plus the Brigade of Guards and the Rifle Brigade, including some regiments of two battalions – and for thirty-one regiments of cavalry (including four regiments of Household Cavalry), as well as for the Indian Army. Officers also had to be found for the Royal Artillery, Royal Engineers, Royal Marines (including the Royal Marine Artillery) and the Royal Navy. As the number of regiments in the army increased, it became harder for the Military Secretary to vet each of the potential applicants. Over the years, officers' pay was allowed to stagnate, while the amount they paid for their commissions increased significantly. The technically illegal practice of selling commissions for higher than their paper value was tolerated. Holding commissioned rank had been permitted to become a very bad financial bargain.

Giving commissioned rank greater social prestige was one compensation for this decline in financial value: members of the royal family lent their patronage to regiments, accepting appointments as colonels-in-chief and adopting some regiments as 'royal' or 'the King's Own'. Though English kings had long since ceased to accompany their armies on operations, they began to wear army uniform in public, proclaiming their martial prowess and lending royal prestige to the forces. While Beau

Brummell put the Prince Regent's court into simple, elegant dark suits, he, the Prince Regent and their fellow officers of the 10th Hussars covered their dark blue uniforms with silver lace, and wore trousers so tight they could not dance in them.

The militia and yeomanry, important in the event of a French invasion or social unrest in the days before civilian police, were likewise given social cachet. The militia officers at Meryton we hear about in Jane Austen's *Pride and Prejudice* are an example. Country gentlemen were drawn into the fringes of the armed forces by the offer of a share in the army's social cachet. In the colonies, a well-to-do tradesman's son would never be presented to the Governor General, but when he took a militia commission he was invited to a New Year's levee in Government House.

An army commission was no money-maker, but it was a sound investment in that it could be sold at a career's end for at least as much as it cost to buy, and for many officers selling their commissions was a pension plan. (The only risks were promotion to major general or death in service, either of which lost the officer his investment.) It became attractive for a father or elder brother to buy a commission for a younger son who would not inherit land. Because army pay was low, however, officers still required at least some private income to meet their day-to-day expenses. The result was that officership was largely confined to men from families with significant income from land or business.

It is worth noting the comparatively small number of officers who required technical ability; naval officers, gunners and engineers did not buy their commission. Rather, from an early date, they were trained from a young age (The Royal Navy took midshipmen from age twelve or fourteen) and promoted on seniority or even merit. In addition, a very small number of Army officers were commissioned or promoted for personal bravery or competence.

Britain's army was never the main arm of defence of the realm. The home islands and Empire were defended first by the Royal Navy. This meant that Britain and the Empire could afford to risk the weaknesses of disconnected administration and an officer corps selected by pounds, shillings and pence rather than ability and professional competence.

Through most of the nineteenth century the combination of purchase and vetting by the Military Secretary ensured that all officers were in social status gentlemen. The phrase 'officer and gentleman' was in common use by the 1810s, the model of gentlemanly behaviour being the Duke of Wellington. Historians have lavished attention on the cult of Napoleon, but in Britain there was an equally strong cult of Wellington, which was arguably of more long-term significance. Accounts of the Duke's character – his lack of flamboyance, his coolness under fire, his politeness, reticence and modesty, his acerbic wit, his paternalistic care for his men – filled the columns of the press and quarterly journals. They were transmitted to future generations by the historians of the Peninsular War and disseminated into the educational system in the didactic works of the Chaplain General of the Forces, George Robert Gleig. From here, they were picked up by Thomas Arnold and a host of reforming headmasters until they became the model of behaviour expected from boys at Britain's public schools.

It is still widely believed that in 1871 Gladstone's Liberal government abolished purchase so as to allow young middle-class men to become officers in the infantry and cavalry. In fact, the opposite is nearer the truth. The younger sons of rich business and professional men had been buying commissions with increasing frequency, forcing out the sons of impoverished gentry and rural clergymen, the descendants of officers who were themselves younger sons of aristocratic families. The abolition of purchase gave young men from 'traditional' military backgrounds a chance to compete with the newcomers. In place of purchase came a military education at the Royal Military College Sandhurst, with rigorous entrance examinations.

The effect on Sandhurst was dramatic. Before this, the College had resembled a highly disciplined private school, its syllabus orientated towards polishing the gentleman's polite accomplishments, although many of these – for example, the study of the French language, drill and sketching – had obvious military utility. Within a few years Sandhurst had become a military university, with an eighteen-month course for the gentleman cadets, adopting some of the professionalism and attention to detail already practised at RMA Woolwich.

General Lord Edward Somerset 1836, oil in canvas by Andrew Morton – displayed in Old College.

chapter three:

The Royal Military Academy, 1741–1939

ANTHONY MORTON

Since I have been at the Academy I have drawn a cannon and a mortar-bed by a scale, and have begun a landscape after the mezzotinto manner; the French master has been ill ever since I came, so I have not seen him.

I have written all Mr Muller's Artillery, *which is forty octavo pages; I am now constructing the plates with Mr Simpson; I am in multiplication of fractions …*

Letters to his parents from Robert Sandham, Gentleman Cadet 1750

Command was assumed to come easily to gentlemen, but technical matters involving battering down walls with artillery fire or building bridges to keep armies moving were more difficult, involving more skill than breeding provided. Commissions in the Ordnance Corps, comprising the two specialist arms of artillery and engineers, were therefore not open to purchase like the infantry and cavalry but were granted by the Master General of the Ordnance after proof of competence in the necessary skills. In 1721 a short-lived elementary school was set up at the Royal Arsenal in Woolwich for officers, NCOs and men of the Ordnance Corps who required a high standard of general education, particularly in mathematics. This education was added to the intensely practical work of making explosives.

Two expressions from the old RMA have passed into the language. 'Talking shop', meaning to discuss subjects not understood by others, derives from the RMA being commonly known as 'The Shop'; as its first building was a converted workshop in Woolwich Arsenal. A former cadet of the RMA invented 'snooker', the tabletop game, which takes its name from the fact that members of the junior intake were known as 'snookers'.

On 30 April 1741 the Duke of Montagu obtained a Royal Charter from King George II 'for instructing the raw and inexperienced people belonging to the Military Branch … in the several parts of mathematics necessary to qualify them for the service of the artillery, and the business of engineers'. The cadets joined at the age of twelve and studied for five years. They were commissioned following a simple oral examination at the end of the course. Imposing discipline and education taxed the staff. A gentleman cadet writing to his mother in 1751 spoke of 'a set of young fellows whose most honourable epithet is wild, the generality of them bear the worst of characters, being ever engaged in riots and drunken broils'.

The structure of the Royal Academy was formalised in 1764 by the Marquis of Granby, Master General of the Ordnance. The Royal Military Academy, as it became known, taught mathematics, classics, French and fencing, but also the 'Art of Science of War'. In 1765 the first formal graduation examinations were introduced and the school was split into a Lower Division for boys between the ages of twelve and fifteen, and the Academy proper for young men of between fifteen and nineteen.

Names of artillery officers of distinction grace the halls of Old College.

Woolwich flourished in crisis and was neglected in peace. An increase in the demand for officers occasioned by the Revolutionary and Napoleonic Wars (1793–1815) did little to improve the standards of education or the conditions of cadet life. In 1794 examinations were suspended and were only permanently reinstated in 1816. During this period the number of cadets under training increased, reaching 248 by 1806. For a few years following Napoleon's defeat in 1815 the Royal Military Academy Woolwich found it difficult to attract candidates, and in 1828 there were only fifty-eight cadets. Due to financial stringency, fees were introduced for the first time in 1831, when the minimum age for entry was raised to fifteen.

In 1855, when the Ordnance Corps was abolished, nominations for places by the Master General ceased, and public examinations were introduced to decide who could attend the Academy. As this quite radical change was introduced at the same time as the demand for officers increased substantially due to the outbreak of the Crimean War, it took some time before the new system of admissions was able to operate as intended. Discipline was very strict and this led to cadet mutinies in 1861 and 1868, but conditions gradually improved and the Academy enjoyed a period of relative calm. During the following decade two prizes were introduced for high-achieving cadets. In 1876 General Lord Napier of Magdala, RE, presented a sword as a reward for the best essay by a cadet on the Waterloo campaign. In the following year an annual cash prize was introduced to be presented to the senior artillery cadet of each intake in honour of Major General Sir Henry Tombs, Bengal Artillery who had won the Victoria Cross during the siege of Delhi in 1857 and had died in 1874.

All officers of artillery and engineers had to attend the Academy as gentleman cadets and were only granted their commission after completing the course. On passing out, they were placed in order of merit. Promotion in the various ordnance corps was by seniority, not by purchase. This was a great incentive to study. A difference of one or two places in the final order of merit at the RMA could result in many years' difference in later promotion, as the career pyramid narrowed in the higher ranks. An immediate effect was to limit a gentleman cadet's choice of arm. When there were more candidates than there were vacancies in the Royal Engineers (which formerly offered better pay and wider prospects of employment than the Royal Artillery), the places were offered to cadets in order of merit.

My term at the Shop pass out after eighteen months, instead of two years, because there was a sudden shortage of officers for some reason. The syllabus of training included 'square-bashing' gun drill, gym, riding, ordnance, field engineering, including bridging, 'scotch-up', military history, with maths and French as the only non-military subjects. There was plenty of 'spit and polish' and meticulous cleaning for Sunday church parade … Incidentally, 'scotch-up' was the art, necessary for coast defence guns in those days, of moving pieces of ordnance with the aid of gins, rollers and levers. There were several old cannon lying about the Shop which we used to move from place to place.

A gentleman cadet, 1908

As the new century began the RMA Woolwich offered cadets a two-year course geared towards commissions in the Royal Artillery or Royal Engineers. The syllabus with its continued emphasis on mathematics and science, strong discipline and a tradition of sporting achievement, had been firmly established and the RMA had secured a reputation for professionalism.

Top left: Interior of a barrack room at the RMA 1810–12 showing the different costumes in those years, watercolour and ink.

Above: HRH The Duke of Cambridge presenting prizes in the Dining Hall at the Royal Military Academy Woolwich, 1860, watercolour, by Geo B. Campion.

The 'scotch-up', or moving a coastal defence gun with gins, rollers and levers, 1861, watercolour, artist unknown.

The need for officers increased with the war against the Boers in South Africa, and in later 1900 the Woolwich course was reduced to one year. The lessons of war were reflected in the syllabus with new emphasis on fieldcraft, signalling and practice firing. In 1902 the Woolwich course reverted to two years, the entrance age was raised to seventeen and a half, and the entrance examination was made stiffer. During the next decade competition for places at the Academy became very stiff.

Work was long, hard and all-pervading. As far as I can remember, it began at 6.30am and went on to the same time in the evening. We future field-gunners dashed about the front parade pulling 1-pdrs. with and without drag ropes, pedalled out to Eltham in the pouring rain to do map-reading and sketching, leapt lightly over horses (wooden) in the gym, and drilled like guardsmen when there was any time to spare.
A gentleman cadet at RMA Woolwich in 1915–16

In the summer of 1914, as Britain went to war, the senior term was recalled from leave and immediately commissioned. The course was reduced to six months of practical training and the entry age was widened to from sixteen and a half up to twenty-five. By November 1918, the RMA had produced 1629 wartime officers, of whom 860 lost their lives during the conflict.

After the Great War, the RMA reverted to its two-year course which now included, under the heading 'car mastership', instruction on the internal combustion engine and driving instruction. Fom the 1920s commissions were also granted in the newly formed Royal Corps of Signals and the Royal Tank Corps. For the first time some cadets were drawn from the non-commissioned ranks of the British Army.

Amongst the cadets I myself instructed there was Orde Wingate, a very lone and reserved type, And King Farouk, who was very charming and very lazy but did exactly as he was told. The King of Siam we reckoned was the best vaulter we ever had. Possibly the nicest horseman among

Far right: View of the Royal Military Academy Woolwich. Engraving of a drawing by Major Cockburn, 1816.

Below: Riding at the RMA repository in the 1930s.

them was the Maharajah of Jaipur, who offered me Master of Horse to Jaipur at the end of his year at RMA. He later came over to England with the Jaipur Polo Team, which consisted of four Jaipur princes who were during their stay unbeatable.
John Lynch, Riding Instructor, RMA Woolwich, 1936

As early as 1858 a Select Committee on Military Education had proposed an amalgamation of the RMA Woolwich and the RMC Sandhurst as it seemed wasteful to have two separate institutions training cadets. Although the proposal was rejected at the time, it reappeared regularly over the next eighty years. In 1933, the Financial Secretary at the War Office suggested that £42,000 could be saved if the two institutions were amalgamated. In 1938 the Macdougall Committee again suggested the amalgamation, and in June 1939 the proposal was accepted. The official announcement stressed the need in modern warfare for officers of all arms to have the same basic training. The decision was taken to close RMA by August 1940, with the cadets being transferred to a new, amalgamated establishment at Sandhurst.

The outbreak of war in September 1939 accelerated the closure of the RMA. At 4.20pm on 1 October the Academy was mobilised. By 10pm the cadets had been transferred to separate special to-arms schools for further training. Postings were based on the order of merit, with the top GC (Gentleman Cadet) going to the 'Sappers', the next to Signals, the rest to the Gunners. After 198 years of officer education, 'The Shop' had ceased to exist in less than six hours.

James Wyatt's design for the Royal Military Academy at Woolwich was very different from his designs for the Royal Military College at Sandhurst. At Woolwich the new building for the Academy had a central structure linked by arcades to an outer range of barracks, with a complex of gardens and courts behind.

The cadets lodged in rooms opening off a central corridor which continued through the arcades to the school where stone stairs led up to the four main teaching rooms. This he modelled on the Tower of London, the Ordnance's original home. The style Wyatt chose was the Gothic of Fonthill … It was completed by 1806.
James Douet, *British Barracks, 1600–1914*

chapter four:

Establishing the Royal Military College, 1799–1812

DUNCAN ANDERSON

T hat we have plundered the whole country is unquestionable; that we are the most undisciplined, the most ignorant, the worst provided Army that ever took the field is equally certain … [O] ut of fifteen regiments of cavalry and twenty-six of infantry which we have here, twenty-one are literally commanded by boys or idiots … we do not know how to post a piquet or instruct a sentry in his duty; and as to moving, God forbid that we should attempt it within three miles of an enemy.

Major General Craig to Sir Hew Dalrymple, 1793, quoted in Hugh Thomas, *The Story of Sandhurst*

At the heart of the history of the Royal Military College is the towering figure of John Gaspard Le Marchant, a visionary who transformed the British Army by his pursuit of military excellence. His lasting memorials are the systems of training for officer cadets and staff officers that have evolved to become the present-day Royal Military Academy Sandhurst and the Joint Services Command and Staff College, Shrivenham.

Born in Amiens of Guernsey stock on 9 February 1766, Le Marchant was a gifted, strong-willed child who was easily bored, leading his headmaster to declare him 'the greatest dunce I ever met'. Le Marchant joined the York militia at sixteen and made his mark by challenging his commanding officer to a duel within days of arriving. He spent four years in Gibraltar and was granted a lieutenant's commission in the 2nd Dragoon Guards by King George III in 1789. He served with distinction as a cavalry squadron commander against the French in the Flanders Campaign of 1793–94, when he despaired of the universally poor standards of leadership and command and staff skills of British officers, which were matched by the poorly trained and ill-equipped soldiery.

Restlessly innovative, Le Marchant redesigned the cavalry sword and instituted a system of sword drill to utilise it effectively. This brought him to the attention of George III, who awarded him a lieutenant-colonelcy in the 7th Light Dragoons,

and won him the lifelong backing of the King's second son and Commander-in-Chief, the Duke of York. The ever-active Le Marchant then devoted his time to improving regimental procedures and practices and rewriting the Standing Orders for the Army, all of which increased his standing with the Commander-in-Chief at Horse Guards.

Gentlemen cadets of the 1930s in cadet uniform of the early nineteenth century.

In 1798 Le Marchant concluded that the system of officer training he had introduced into his regiment should be universally applied to the British Army. He saw the need to train cavalry and infantry officers in the art of war in the same manner that artillery and engineer officers were trained in the skills of their profession at the Royal Military Academy Woolwich. Le Marchant recommended a military college of three divisions. The First Division would consist of fee-paying boy students between the ages of thirteen and fifteen, who would receive a general education for entry into the Second Division, where the students would be educated for commissions into the cavalry or infantry at the age of eighteen. The Third or Senior Division would be open to officers with at least four years' regimental service and would train them in staff duties. He also saw the need for a school for the sons of soldiers to be trained in the art of soldiering – a Legion, as he termed it, which would provide a demonstration battalion for his military college.

This aim was pre-empted when the Commander-in-Chief, Prince Frederick, Duke of York, established the Legion at the Royal Military Asylum at Chelsea, which later became the Duke of York's Royal Military School. (This institution later moved to Dover, but its portico, visible from King's Road Chelsea, resembles that of Old College at RMAS, both buildings being the design of John Sanders, architect to the Barrack Master General's Department.)

The scheme of a military college where commissions were awarded without purchase was seen as a threat to the social structure and was subject to intense criticism from an establishment faced with the threat of Revolutionary France. Nevertheless Le Marchant persevered, and with Britain in the tenth year of war and the traditional sources for recruiting officers becoming exhausted, he gradually won royal approval and the grudging consent of the Government.

On 20 November 1800 a committee set up by the Duke of York reported that 'a suitable piece of ground has been found near Blackwater' and that 'the proprietor is disposed to sell the same for about £8,000'. Six days later a memorandum from the War Office made clear that William Pitt, the Prime Minister, was fully committed to the project: 'HRH [the Duke of York] desires you will, with all possible despatch, carry Mr Pitt's and Mr Dundas's intentions into effect by making the purchase in question'. In one of his last acts before resigning as Prime Minister over the question of Catholic emancipation, Pitt secured parliamentary approval for a vote of £147,000 for the project. The choice of Sandhurst as the site for the College was justified on the grounds of 'the uncircumscribed character of the land which admitted of the buildings being so placed as to avoid a neighbourhood which might corrupt the morals of the cadets and which allows space also for military movements' and 'the opportunity afforded for military instruction of large encampments of troops which, when in this country, are generally situated in the neighbourhood of Bagshot and the low price of the land, with the vicinity of water carriage by the Basingstoke Canal'.

Le Marchant's proposals coincided with an approach to the Adjutant General from General François Jarry, a French emigré, to conduct a course of lectures to officers seeking Army staff appointments. This was approved on the understanding that Le Marchant would be Commandant and the sixty-seven-year-old Jarry would be Director of Instruction.

Le Marchant's school for the Third or Senior Division, responsible for training regimental officers in staff procedures, opened on 4 May 1799 with thirty officer students in temporary

Inspection Day, Marlow, 1804, hand-coloured print.

accommodation in The Antelope inn in High Wycombe. A Royal Warrant of 24 June 1801 formally established the school as the Senior Department of the Royal Military College. It would remain at the inn for fourteen years before moving to further temporary accommodation in Farnham, eventually transferring to Sandhurst in 1821. The department was renamed the Staff College in 1858 and moved into its own building on the Sandhurst estate in 1862. The two establishments finally became separate bodies in 1902, but continued to share a number of facilities, including the hospital and the Royal Memorial Chapel, until in 1997 the Staff College was subsumed into the Joint Services Command and Staff College.

The success of the Senior Department in producing staff officers was demonstrated soon after its foundation when three instructors of the Senior Division were attached to General Abercromby's staff commanding the British expeditionary force sent to eject the French from Egypt. The work of these three 'Wycombites' in Egypt was highly praised and in March 1802 led to the granting of a Royal Warrant for a Junior Department to be established. This college of gentlemen cadets opened in 'Remnantz', a rented private house in Great Marlow. General Sir William Harcourt was appointed as its first Governor with Le Marchant as Lieutenant Governor and Superintendent General.

On 17 May 1802 Le Marchant oversaw the entry of sixteen Gentlemen Cadets to a two-year course for future officers. Their number increased to forty-two by the end of the year, five of them being destined for the private army of the Honourable East India Company. In 1803 a Royal Warrant approved the gradual expansion of the course to a maximum of 400 cadets, divided into four companies. Of these 100 should be 'orphan sons of officers who have lost their lives in His Majesty's service'

GENERAL FRANÇOIS JARRY

England was never fully aware of his abilities, nor did we make the most of them.
– Colonel John Gaspard Le Marchant

General François Jarry was a French emigré who served with the Prussian Army on the staff of Frederick the Great. Ge returned to France and served as Adjutant General and maréchal de camp in the Revolutionary Army. Disenchanted, he fled into exile in England arriving with a reputation as one of the finest staff officers in Europe. Penniless, and with a family to support, the opportunity to instruct in staff procedures in the Senior Department offered him both an income and the prospect of a pension. Jarry taught tactics with an emphasis on applying key principles on the ground in a series of comprehensive outdoor exercises, along with skills of rapid military sketching. He instructed in French and was regarded as something of an elderly, eccentric curiosity by the student officers. In failing health, he retired on 16 August 1806 after a final lecture on 'supplies and movements' in the field'. He died on 15 March 1807 having established the principles that underpinned British staff training.

and educated free; eighty should be 'sons of officers actually in His Majesty's service' paying £40 per annum; 100 'sons of noblemen and gentlemen', sixty were to be cadets of the Royal Artillery and sixty cadets of the East India Company, all paying ninety guineas per annum. Their ages ranged between thirteen and sixteen years. *The Times* commented on 25 February: 'The

Military College at Marlow promises to prove a powerful rival to that at Woolwich. Its system is formed upon the most economical and correct principle.'

Despite the establishment of the Junior Department, these were unhappy and frustrating years for Le Marchant. He found himself in conflict with Lieutenant Colonel James Butler, the Commandant at Marlow, over the running, discipline and standards of the Junior Department and was isolated when the Governor, Sir William Harcourt, sided with Butler against him. His one pleasure was the building of the permanent home of RMC on the grounds purchased by the Crown near the village of Sandhurst. This project had been beset by delay after delay as the Treasury looked for a cheaper option, but finally in 1808 with the war going badly a decision was made to build at Sandhurst.

In June 1811 Le Marchant, newly promoted Major General, could see his life's ambition realised in the substantial building that was growing brick by brick on the open heathland east of Blackwater:

Above: Frederick Duke of York (1763–1827), painting in oil by Sir Thomas Lawrence. The Duke of York was an inept tactician but an important military administrator who played a major role in the creation of the Royal Military College.

Right: An aerial view of Government House (once Governor's House) and the original manor house built in the period 1762–99, surrounded by its grounds and rebuilt in 1811. The King Hussein Pavilion stands on what was the Lieutenant Governor's field, and the outline of Oak Grove House can be seen in the grove that gives it its name immediately above it.

They stood on a wild and barren heath, which had been partially cleared, to admit of a few plantations recently made under his superintendence. The walls just rose above the surface, and extended along an eminence that commanded an immense expanse of bold open country. Immediately below were numerous groups of huts and tents for the protection of the stores and the accommodation of the workmen. The constant stir of men and the ceaseless hum proceeding from such a concentration of human and mechanical industry, on a spot that bore every mark of having been condemned by nature to perpetual solitude and sterility were singularly impressive.'

Denis Le Marchant, *Memoirs of the Late Major General Le Marchant 1766–1812*

Le Marchant was not to remain at the College, however: in 1811 he was appointed to command the Heavy Brigade of Cavalry under Wellington in the Peninsula. A year later he was dead, killed at Salamanca on 22 July 1812 after his brigade's charge had broken the French centre in the course of one of Wellington's most brilliant victories of the Peninsula Campaign. He was the first staff member of the Royal Military College to be killed in action.

Le Marchant's achievement is more than the 200 officers who had been 'educated to the duties of the General Staff' and proved their worth in the Peninsula and Waterloo campaigns, or the 1,500 former members of the Junior Division sent into the Army as regimental officers during his tenure as Lieutenant Governor. It lives on in the Academy that has inherited the traditions and standards of the College he founded.

chapter five:

Creating Sandhurst

Edward R. Flint

The College is situated in the corner of Berkshire where Surrey and Hampshire meet it, and is an extensive E-shaped building with two stories of a dirty white colour. Behind it is a chapel and riding school and on the right-hand side a gigantic gymnasium. In front on either side of the broad road leading up to the entrance is a football ground that on the right for Rugby and the one on the left for Association. Golf links also are marked round these two grounds. The cricket ground is to the right in front of the Gymnasium with a Pavilion. There is a swimming lake in the woods a short distance to the right of the cricket ground with a spring-board. In front of the College on the far side of the football and cricket grounds are two large lakes, on which the cadets skate in winter and row and sail in summer.

This was the description of the Royal Military College main building, now Old College, by Gentleman Cadet Arthur William Donnelly Harrington in his cadet journal titled *Sepia Sketches of Life at the Royal Military College Sandhurst* (1890–91). Viewed

James Wyatt (1746–1813), the most celebrated architect of his day, submitted plans for the building of the Royal Military College but was not involved in the final detailed work, which was the responsibility of John Sanders. His concept for the Royal Military College contains the essential elements incorporated into the final building. Watercolour, location of original painting unknown.

from the front, apart from the addition of the Gymnasium (now the Library), the Cricket Pavilion and sports grounds, this description differs little from how the College would have looked on opening in 1812. Behind the College, the two trident accommodation wings, Chapel and Riding School had yet to be built.

Driving or walking through the 600 acres of the grounds immediately surrounding the College buildings at the Royal Military Academy Sandhurst, it is clear, by virtue of two large man-made lakes, the sweeping lawns, the type of walls either side of Old College and the layout of the other colleges, that one is looking at a designed landscape that goes beyond mere practical training function into the deliberately aesthetic. It is possibly the only combined landscape garden and military training facility in Europe. The landscaped grounds of the Academy were almost certainly designed to create an establishment atmosphere for learning and reflection for a Royal Military College. Yet, it is also a landscape that has not stood still, evolving as new building has taken place and as new sporting and training needs have developed.

In 1802 when the Crown purchased the estate it comprised mostly of open heathland with a small farm close to Blackwater. From the College, one could view south to the line of the London Road to the Golden Farmer public house and beyond to the rising ground of Surrey and Black Hill. To the southeast an obelisk was evident, in the time before the creation of Camberley the only visible manmade structure. The small farm centred on the manor house (now Government House), its surrounding farm buildings and cottages, a mill, and the grove of oak trees that still stands between Government House and Oak Grove House.

The first architect to draw up plans for the College was Sir James Wyatt (1746–1813). Wyatt submitted drawings and estimates in 1802, 1804 and 1805, 'according to different Designs for the Royal Military College, at that time proposed at

Enlarging the Mill Pond to create the Lower Lake, c.1812, watercolour, one of two versions, artist unknown but possibly William de la Molle, Drawing Master at RMC 1803–43. Despite the impressive façade the building was still unfinished and unpainted and would remain so after the financial cuts imposed after the end of the Napoleonic Wars.

Queen Victoria's statue was sculpted by Mr Henry Price and unveiled at RMA Woolwich by HRH The Duke of Connaught on 27 July 1904, three years after the Queen's death. The statue was brought to Sandhurst from Woolwich in 1947. It stands guard over King's Walk (named after Queen Victoria's grandson King George V), which leads towards Old College Parade Ground, the scene of each year's three Sovereign's Parades and other important ceremonial occasions.

Blackwater'. However, despite Copland, the builder, occupying Government House and setting up a brickworks on site, little was done other than some preliminary planting of trees on the estate. The appointment of Lord Castlereagh as Minister of War broke the deadlock, and his intervention in 1808 led to the reluctant approval by Treasury for the erection of a building that would house the College Headquarters and the Junior Department of 412 cadets.

THE COLLEGE LAYOUT 'ACCORDING TO A DESIGN SUBMITTED BY MR SANDERS'

The College design became the responsibility of John Sanders (1768–1826), Principal Architect to the Barracks Department, who was closely monitored by the Supreme Board of the Royal Military College chaired by the Duke of York in his role as Commander-in-Chief. It is Sanders who decided on the principal details we see today. These included the Grand Lodge (now Staff College Gate), the access way, the contour of the lake and the planting of trees in what became the American Gardens. The plan included a 'Bathing Place and Open Shed for undressing'. The Board decided on the layout of the planting 'with public Walks, bordering the Plantations on the South, also on the line to the Professor Houses, and round the Northern Boundary'. The Old Building has some similarities with Wyatt's layout for Woolwich – 'a long spine passage linking separate sections with colonnades in between – but stylistically it is quite different: a long calm, Classical front broken only by a large central portico'

(James Douet, *British Barracks: 1600–1914*). The Grand lodge was joined by others of which only Yorktown Gate survives that encircled the estate and reflected the landscape design style of domesticating the surrounding environment.

The Board directed that the Hospital (the East Wing between the Main Building and what is now Old College Headquarters) should not be of three storeys but should be symmetrical to the West Wing. They also directed that the 'General Parade in Front of the College be left unenclosed, and the Ground formed in a Gentle Slope towards the Lake'. The basement was planned as kitchen and stores areas as well as being living quarters for servants, soldiers and bandsmen and their families, with the 'Housekeeper's and Purveyor's Apartments' located at each end of the main building. Sanders' design also allowed sunken access ways at the back of the building so that the movement of servants and staff running of the College would not be visible from the officers' quarters in Chapel Square.

The Board confirmed that the main buildings be linked by colonnades and that houses be erected, '[f]or the Paymaster [Oak Grove House] on the Western extremity of the Plantation continued from the House of the Lieutenant Governor, and for the Surgeon [Lake House] on the Eastern extremity of the Plantation continued from the House of the Commandant … corresponding in dimensions and Elevation for those for the Captains', and linked by a wall to the main buildings. These sweeping walls ascend to the higher ground of the College and are a purely aesthetic feature. The ground level in front was raised and the subterranean part of the wall was built in the form of arches to save on brick. In what is now Chapel Square, colonnades to the main building link the houses.

The initial tree planting was the responsibility of Mr Edward Bracebridge, whose headstone can be found in the cemetery. His later appointment as College Porter from 1812 until his death in 1825 suggests his role was that of foreman or superintendent rather than landscape designer, as is sometimes suggested. Most of Bracebridge's work was completed between April 1801 and August 1802, with further planting on the Camberley side of the Lower Lake in 1808 together with the fencing-in of the estate that was determined by Sanders' designs. Behind the College and its flanking walls trees were planted to follow the landscape fashion of creating a backdrop. Altogether the vast sum of £20,000 was spent on trees, fencing and bridging in the construction of the RMC.

CHAPEL SQUARE

When completed, the original RMC building dominated the landscape. Looking north from Chapel Square one would have had clear views beyond the ménages (outdoor riding arenas) across to the largely treeless and scrubby bushes of lowland heathland. The square is not merely the back yard of a country house. The captains, Adjutant and Quartermaster were in the terraced houses whose dimensions equated to those permissible for an officer of captain's rank. The detached house at No. 4 Chapel Square was for the Major of the Junior Department, and its mirror image opposite at No. 5 was for the Chaplain, whose status equated to that of a major. Both these appointments were entitled to two horse stalls and an outhouse at the rear of the buildings, while the captains in the terraced houses were entitled to 'Outhouse Accommodation for each of 18 feet by 15 feet'.

Chapel Square from the Chapel of Christ the King.

The Square RMC, *pencil drawing by Gentleman Cadet B83 Northey, 1852.*

The gardens at the centre of the square were of a symmetrical design, with an outer belt of trees and railings, a circular walk, linking paths to the entrances and a central feature of a fountain raised over the mound formed by the water tank that served as a reservoir for the College. The water feature was not a success. The supply pipe from Barossa quickly became silted up with the local sandy soil, costing much to keep it clear. The tank was also blamed as the source of cholera that swept the College shortly after opening, and the noise of the running fountain became a cause of complaint by Chapel Square residents. Today the mound can still be seen but the original outline of the gardens has gone. The Old College dining room, built in 1912, cuts into the garden, as does the Royal Memorial Chapel built in 18787–9 and further enlarged between the two world wars.

THE AMERICAN GARDENS

The American Gardens and a bowling green ran along the Wish Stream below Lower Lake. The gardens took advantage of the bog-like conditions on either side of the stream to provide the right conditions for the spectacular autumn colours of trees from the North-Eastern United States – a feature that was very popular at the end of the eighteenth century. The gardens later fell into disuse and have been encroached on by the horse paddocks, but the area is still a pleasant public walkway running between the houses in the Terrace and the area around Government House. Across the road was located the College laundry, which gave the road its name. The laundry itself is where the retail store now stands and was built from materials dismantled at Marlow and re-erected with the construction of the College. In 1887 the laundry employed thirty-five women.

TEA CADDY ROW

To overcome Treasury concerns about the lack of local accommodation for the staff, Alexander Copland (one of the largest building contractors of his day and who became known as Barrack Master to the Empire) together with the contract to build the Royal Military College built thirteen houses. They are known variously as The Terrace, the 'Professors' Houses' and 'Tea Caddy Row'. The latter was the name given by coachmen who drove past them on this otherwise deserted stretch of road. Their cost – a considerable £42,258 over and in addition to the £89,770 budgeted for the main building – was to be recouped from the rentals charged to the professors who occupied them. In laying out the grounds Sanders was directed to ensure that each house had the same relative amount of land to avoid any petty jealousies. The four principal professors occupied a complete house, while the eighteen junior or assistant instructors had semi-detached houses far superior to anything available to the NCOs and College staff, who had to be satisfied with living in the basements of the College until the first servants and other ranks quarters were built in the 1870s and 1880s.

Top right: The layout of Chapel Square showing the linking colonnades to the terraced houses and the layout of the formal enclosed gardens and walks around the fountain in the centre. The grounds and stables allocated to each of the houses in the square can be seen as well.

Right: Map showing the layout of the American Gardens and Tea Caddy Row, and their relationship to the Government House Gardens.

Bottom right: No. 12A, 'Tea Caddy Row', or more properly, The Terrace.

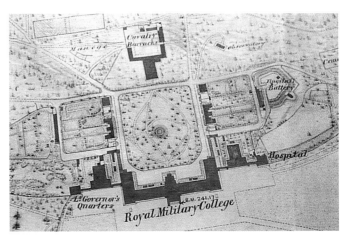

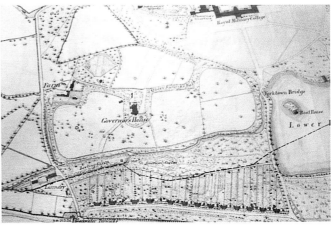

GOVERNMENT HOUSE GARDENS

The Board agreed by 1816 to the rebuilding of the Manor House as the Governor's House with its own pocket park, tree-lined approach road, paddocks and walled garden. They also determined the site and gardens surrounding the house of the Lieutenant Governor (now Le Marchant House) and that of the Superintendent (now Old College Headquarters). The Lieutenant Governor was allocated a field where the athletics

Far left: The College buildings and the Lower Lake as depicted from the York Town side of the Lake in the mid-1800s, oil on board, artist unknown.

Left: Gentleman Cadet Austin's sketch of Flagstaff Battery, also known as Fort Royal, and the Surgeon's House, now known as Lake House.

track is today 'for the maintenance of such Stock as may add to the comfort of their Families – Further that a Field should be given without Rent, to the Commandant, and another to the Major of the Junior Department, as also that a common Pasture should be set apart in which every Commissioned Officer should have the Right of Pasturing one Cow, free from Expense'.

The nearby Oak Grove was known as 'Gymcracks' because it was used as an outdoor gymnasium until the first gymnasium was completed in 1862. It was here that cadets settled differences of opinion with bare-knuckled bouts overseen by one of the permanent staff.

THE LAKES

The Board determined the excavation and damming of the three millponds on the Wish Stream to create the Lower and Upper Lakes and also the Bathing Lake (completed in 1818). The Royal Staff Corps carried this out, and the bridge next to

the present Academy Headquarters was named after them to record their efforts. The North Gloucester Regiment of Militia, who had been mobilised against the Napoleonic threat, were kept busy landscaping the grounds, transporting the 3,000 cartloads of spoil at 6d a cart and depositing them as part of the lawns that sweep down from the College to Lower Lake. By 1816 the area had been transformed by the creation of two large landscape lakes, the lower with two islands, and the laying out of the plantations and drives one sees today. In the area of the grass tennis courts near Government House it is evident that either money or soil ran out as the sweeping lawns from the College stop abruptly and the otherwise subterranean arches of the walls are exposed. Lower Lake is a reflecting lake and is designed to have the image of the College reflected when viewed from the circular walk on the far shore.

To the east the Wish Stream formed a series of brooks cutting through heathland and merging under a Chinese

Interior of Fort Royal showing saluting cannon, 1883.

Above: Print of York Town Gate, c.1842, artist unknown. York Town Gate, now closed except for access for parades, was built in 1831. York Town was the nearest centre and location of bootmakers, tailors, baker's shops and, for many years, Ma Hart's pawnbrokers.

Top right: A trophy of the Crimean War at York Town Gate.

bridge before flowing past the Pontoon Shed and under Staff Corps Bridge (rebuilt in 1933 and now known as Academy HQ Bridge) to Lower Lake. Looking from the steps of the College to the northeast it would have been possible to have seen the heathland and early tree-lined tracks on Barossa together with one of the entrance lodges. Today this view is blocked by trees and the Wish Stream is reluctantly channelled through concrete channels past Churchill Hall, Victory Building and Academy Headquarters.

Also to the east of Old College were once a maze of batteries, redoubts (including a moated fort in the vicinity of the polo field), forts, permanent and practice field works, including a massive zig-zag trench system modelled on the lines of Torres Vedres in the area just east of the hospital, military bridging sites, an observatory, several ménages and ranges. To the northeast of the College was built a Flagstaff Battery (also known as Fort Royal) that comprised a training field work, a saluting battery and if contemporary drawings are correct a huge flagstaff.

FORT NARRIEN

Close to what is now College Town Gate was once the site of a major earthwork used for practical fortification exercises throughout the nineteenth century. The earthwork was star-shaped, moated and had its own complement of troops. By 1898 Fort Narrien had begun to disappear, although traces of it still existed up to the development of the married quarters for other ranks in 1959. Today its name is remembered by the six concrete houses and an electricity sub-station that stand on its site.

The name commemorates John Narrien (1782–1860), the son of a stonemason, who was apprenticed as an optician. His skill in mathematics led to his appointment as an instructor in mathematics in the Junior Department at RMC Sandhurst from 1814. He was appointed as Professor of Mathematics and Fortifications in the Senior Department from 1820. Due to financial stringencies, he was compelled to tutor himself in practical fortifications to add to his skills as a mathematician and astronomer. Narrien was the author of a series of textbooks used at the College. His involvement in astronomy led to the establishment of an observatory on the treed mound to the northeast of Chapel Square and from where he observed the partial eclipse of the sun on 6 May 1845. The onset of blindness led to his retirement in 1858. After the observatory fell into disuse the building became a staff sergeant's quarters, but now the only evidence of where it once stood are remnants of brick foundations.

EXPANSION

As the College expanded and new facilities (covered in more detail in following chapters) were built including 'Fives Courts' (now Mons Hall), a gymnasium (now the Library), an isolation hospital (to the east of the present hospital and then rebuilt in the area of the Slim Mess in the years following the 1919 influenza epidemic), New College, Montgomery Gymnasium, wartime Nissen huts, Victory College, Academy HQ and the Faraday Hall what is remarkable is how the original atmosphere has been retained. Viewed from Lower Lake the 'arc of the colleges' allows each building to co-exist, with a backdrop of trees to enhance the key buildings or in other cases to conveniently hide the functional or less fashionable. What is kept is an atmosphere for learning and reflection that sits as part of an estate designed as much for its utility and amenity.

chapter six:

The Early Years at Sandhurst, 1812–1900

TONY HEATHCOTE

I was a Gentleman Cadet there in 1854 when I was 14 years old. We always wore a red-tailed coat like an ordinary civilian evening coat, tightly buttoned up, and a stiff and high horsehair stock. We had milk and rancid butter for breakfast, mutton, shoulder one day, leg the next, which smelt and tasted like a sheepfold, with rice or baked plum pudding afterwards, for dinner. We had tea and bread and butter in our bedrooms – 5 boys in each. There were no baths, only a cold water tap in a cemented room, one for each company, whither in the early morn each boy ran down the long passages in the primitive garb of Eden, each with his foot pan in his hand, which he presented filled from the tap and dashed over his head and body. Wasn't it cold! Wasn't it pandemonium let loose! I wonder what the modern boy would say? The food was the worst part of it all, and to this day I can taste that awful mutton …
RMC Magazine, Vol. 12, Easter Term 1921

In August 1812 the cadets were transferred from Marlow into the unfinished and unpainted buildings, while the militia laboured over digging out the lake; the soil from this operation was used to build up the exercise ground in front of the main steps and workmen were still busy with the building itself. The cadets came to a home consisting of the main building flanked

Left: New College, as viewed down King's Walk, c.1895.

Right: The Duke of Cambridge's last Inspection Parade, 1895.

by the two wings – the east and west wings, the former housing the hospital and then the two houses, all linked by colonnades. The west building (now Le Marchant House) was home to the Lieutenant Governor, with the east building (now Old College Headquarters) housing the Superintendent. When the post of Superintendent was abolished this building became part of the hospital. The semicircular wall connecting the home of the College Surgeon (Lake House) and that of the Paymaster (Oak Grove Lodge) was still being built. The Governor occupied the Manor House, with the professorial staff in residence in Tea Caddy Row.

From the gravelled parade ground, two tiers, each of five steps, lead up to the portico, appropriately known as Grand Entrance, composed of eight massive Doric-style pillars, with the pediment containing a sculpture. This consists of a roundel bearing the monogram of King George III, surmounted by a crown and surrounded by a circlet with the Garter motto 'Honi soit qui mal y pense'. It is flanked by figures of Mars and Minerva, the classical deities of War and Wisdom respectively.

Visitors then, as today, would have been conscious of the ironwork lamp holders, ornamented with lions' heads and claws, and the railings, which are actually pike rests, used to hold the pikes carried by infantry and artillery sergeants until the early nineteenth century. The brass door handles and the foot scrapers at the entrance pick up the lion motif. The ornamentation inside the entrance hall has changed over the years, except for the great iron lantern surmounted by a crown. The Brown Bess muskets either side of the door into what was the original chapel, now the Indian Army Memorial Room, are cadet pattern, especially light versions made for the use of the early gentlemen cadets, whose average age until the 1850s was fourteen.

The anterooms and display rooms downstairs acted as dining messes served from kitchens in the basement. The basement also housed the soldiers and the servants and their families in

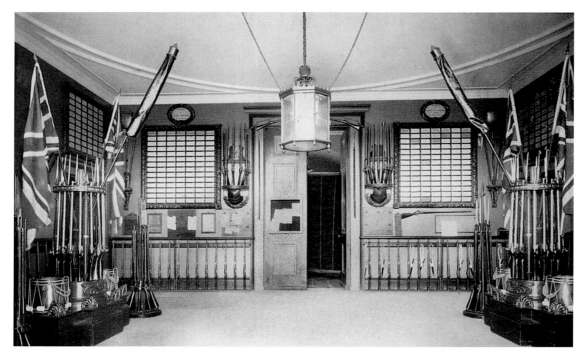

Left: The Grand Entrance in 1901.

Below: The lion head doorknobs of the Grand Entrance.

Below left: Drain head at Old College.

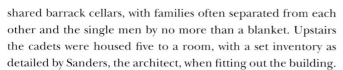

shared barrack cellars, with families often separated from each other and the single men by no more than a blanket. Upstairs the cadets were housed five to a room, with a set inventory as detailed by Sanders, the architect, when fitting out the building.

In wartime money was no object. In the Annals of Sandhurst, Major A.F. Mockler-Ferryman records: 'the war had made the Army popular with the nation, and Sandhurst was training officers for the Army; expense was nothing and, so long as the money was forthcoming, it was readily spent'. In 1817 the final accounts for the principal buildings, fencing and work on the estate came to almost £370,000. Napoleon was in exile on St Helena and retrenchment was the order of the day. It would be another eight years until in 1825 the College received £6,000 to complete the riding school buildings which, because of lack of stabling, could only operate in the summer months.

Cadets in the Junior Department completed a four-year course with two terms each year of nineteen or twenty week's length divided by a six-week summer and a seven-week winter vacation. Professors and instructors gave lessons in drill, fortification, topography and military surveying, as well as the more general subjects of mathematics, classics, French or German, history, geography and English. Life was similar to boarding school but with more severe discipline. Progress from Lower to Upper School was governed by examination, the final hurdle being an examination of senior cadets by a Board of Commissioners, held in the room above the Grand Entrance (now Topper's Bar). If the cadet passed, he received a certificate recommending him for a commission without purchase in cavalry or infantry regiments. The Senior Division was moved into the main building from Farnham in 1821 and took over the west wing, with the officer students taking up houses in Tea Caddy Row and the overflow moving into the growing village of York Town.

Le Marchant had sold the concept of the College to the Crown on the basis that RMC would be financially self-sufficient, but after the war financial stringencies saw the decline in facilities and standards. Conditions were poor: accommodation was crowded and cold, the food unappetising, and the cadets, always dressed in uniform, were subject to petty restrictions. Staff numbers were reduced and fees increased, with the number of places for orphans being finally reduced to ten. Self-sufficiency was the catch-cry: after the Parliamentary Vote was completely cut in 1832, the College had to survive on fees alone.

On the outbreak of the Crimean War in 1853 there were 178 cadets at Sandhurst. The teaching staff was reduced to John Narrien, Professor of Fortification, and one other professor; the College, in the words of its historian Alan Shepperd, was 'half empty, understaffed and paralysed through lack of funds'. The purchase system remained the primary means of obtaining commissions, but gentlemen cadets who completed the course and were recommended by the College were granted their first commissions without purchase. Moreover, when there were more candidates than vacancies, RMC cadets were given priority. Despite these advantages, the RMC gained a reputation for disorderly behaviour, rioting and bullying comparable with

Above: Breastplate from the Royal Armouries stamped Toiras, the name of the French commander who successfully defended the Île de Ré against an English army under the Duke of Buckingham in l627.

Right: Stained glass detail, Indian Army Memorial Room. Image of Gentleman Cadet George Ascough Booth, who died in 1868 whilst at RMC, dressed in uniform of the day.

Above: The Grand Lodge in 1840, pencil drawing by Gentleman Cadet B68, F.M. Callinghan. This was the main entrance to the Royal Military College and is now the Staff College Gate; Cambridge Town, now Camberley, grew up outside it with the opening of the railway in 1878. This was one of a number of gates controlling entry into the College grounds: Forest Lodge at what is now the York Road Gate (built in 1831 to quarantine the College in response to a cholera epidemic), Barrossa Lodge on the east and the Windsor Ride Lodge on the north. A gatekeeper – gatekeepers were known as 'Bluebottles' because of their blue serge uniform jackets – manned each of these. The lack of other ranks housing saw the lodges used as living accommodation. In 1884 in the single-room building on the right was home to an NCO, his wife and two children aged ten and fifteen. The larger building on the left housed the gatekeeper, his wife, seven children and his mother-in-law. The third building (out of sight) contained a kitchen, a washhouse and a toilet.

unreformed public schools of the period, with the average age of the cadets being about fifteen.

THE EAST INDIA COMPANY'S MILITARY SEMINARY, 1809–60

The East India Company maintained its separate military establishment until 1858, when the government of British India was transferred to the Crown. In 1798 the Company had begun to send cadets to the RMA to train as officers in the Indian artillery and engineers; cadets were also sent to the Junior Division of RMC when it opened at Marlow. The Company consulted Le Marchant on officer training and in 1809 it set up a military seminary at Addiscombe House, Croydon, based upon the RMA and RMC. After the Mutiny of 1857–8 it was decided that, for security reasons, all artillery and engineers in India should be part of the British Army. The establishment of the Royal Artillery and Royal Engineers was increased accordingly. Addiscombe was closed and its functions were taken over by an enlarged RMA.

It was then decided that the new Indian Staff Corps should provide officers for the Indian Army. All candidates had first to serve for two years on probation as subalterns in the British Army. Those who did not wish to purchase commissions in the British Army prior to joining the Indian Staff Corps were able to attend the Royal Military College at Sandhurst instead. Thus both the RMA and the RMC continued the link with the Indian Army established by the EICMS at Addiscombe.

THE CRIMEAN WAR, THE INDIAN MUTINY AND THE EXPANSION OF THE RMC

The crisis of the Crimean War (1854–56) followed by that of the Indian Mutiny in 1857–58 reinvigorated the RMC. The transfer of the governance of India from the East India Company to the Crown and of the 24,000 British soldiers in the Company's army to the Army of the Queen had major implications for officer numbers. The addition of a second battalion to twenty-four regiments, together with the need to find British officers for the 150 Indian cavalry regiments and infantry battalions, plus eighty-six batteries of artillery and fifteen companies of sappers and miners, could not be met within the existing capacity of either RMA Woolwich or RMC Sandhurst. The number of staff was increased and a separate building for the Senior Division was planned. In the Main Building, gas was installed, the kitchens improved, and rooms

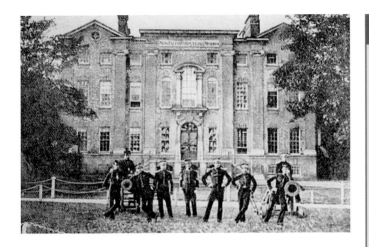

Honourable East India Company cadets at Addiscombe House.

at the ends of the two dormitory corridors were fitted for baths and lavatories with cold water. In 1858 the entry age was increased to between sixteen and nineteen, with a competitive examination to gain admission to what was now a two-year course. Sandhurst cadets were given priority of appointments to commissions with and without purchase. This represented a move to greater professionalism within the Army.

THE TRIDENT BLOCKS

The closure of Addiscombe saw growing pressure on accommodation at RMC. The West Trident Block was completed in 1863, replacing the Colonnade Walk that connected the Main Building to the officers' quarters in Chapel Square. The date 1862 can be found on the drain heads of the building.

It is said that the Bandmaster's house, which housed the young Arthur Sullivan when his father Thomas was Bandmaster at RMC, was one of the houses demolished to complete the West Trident Block. However, a study of the maps of the time shows that no houses were demolished in Chapel Square and that the colonnades linking the main building to the houses were the only casualties of the wing's construction. It is more likely that the Bandmaster and his family lived in the College basement

Swink's Folly, marked on the map as Redoubt, was occupied by the cadets in the Great Siege of 1862 and is now where the lawn is in front of Old College.

THE GREAT SIEGE OF 1862

Despite the increased age of the gentlemen cadets the College authorities failed to lift the more irksome petty rules intended for schoolboys rather than young men. This led to the Cadet Mutiny of 1862, when the cadet battalion withstood a three-day siege at Swink's Folly, one of the earthworks used for fortification training, before finally surrendering to the Commander-in-Chief, HRH The Duke of Cambridge, who came down in his coach from London to restore order.

Swink's Folly bears the nickname of the Professor of Fortification, Major W.H. Adams, who used the cadets to lay out a square redoubt southeast of the cricket ground where the rugby ground is now. It was finished and revetted and a palisade gate erected that was entered over a small footbridge. Although Fort Narrien and Fort Royal are usually cited, it was Swink's redoubt that the cadets used in the siege of 1862. Major A.F. Mockler-Ferryman records the events in his *Annals of Sandhurst*:

The redoubt was secretly provisioned to withstand a siege, and on 10 October, when warned for extra drill, the cadets refused to attend, but fell in and were marched by their corporals to the redoubt. The authorities, seeing that matters had assumed a serious aspect, endeavoured to talk the mutineers into reason. Colonel Scott proceeded to the redoubt to open up negotiations, but the parapets were manned by cadets armed with loaves of bread, and he was warned to say what he wanted at a distance. No sooner did he open his mouth than he was received with hoots and jeers and he retired discomforted. Colonel Napier then tried his hand, but with little success, though he was received in a friendly spirit and his speech lustily cheered. Eventually the Governor, Sir Harry Jones, agreed to listen to their grievances if the cadets would surrender and come on to parade. This they did, but the next day, before any redress had been offered all the corporals were arrested; and the cadets furious at the breach of faith, returned forthwith to the redoubt. They now refused all terms, and they remained in a state of mutiny until the arrival of HRH the Duke of Cambridge, who, after dressing them down in his own inimitable style, saw that justice was done to them, and ordered the corporals to be restored to their rank.

Detail of George William Frederick, 2nd Duke of Cambridge, 1819–1904, as Lieutenant General commanding the Guards Division at the Battle of Alma, 20 September 1854 during the Crimean War, artist unknown.

before moving to Albany Terrace on the London Road, where McDonald's now stands. The East Trident Block that extended from the Hospital Wing was completed and handed over in January 1877. The College could now accommodate ten divisional officers living among the cadets and 250 cadets based on a single room per cadet, or 300 if they were doubled up in the larger rooms. The new buildings provided single rooms for under-officers but cubicles for cadets, partitioned to within 2′ 9″ of the ceiling. Plumbing and heating were installed on the cheap and were not finally fixed for six or seven years, condemning the cadets to bitterly cold nights, freezing showers from jugs of water poured over them, and the families in the basements having to endure a constant stream of waste water pouring down the stairs from the cadet quarters above.

THE ABOLITION OF PURCHASE

I have got three gentlemen to valet. I have to wait at breakfast, at lunch and again at Mess at night. I do not have anything to do between Lunch and Mess. I have the afternoon to myself without I am what they call Orderly. That is to answer all bells and do anything that the gentlemen want but that don't come but once in eight days because there are eight of us and we take it in turns … We wear livery. It is dark blue with a red collar and brass buttons with the letters R.M.C. on them.
Alf Hayes, Servant, RMC, 14 February 1875

The abolition of purchase led to the temporary closure of the RMC because commissions in the Line became obtainable through an open competitive examination, and so there was no point in parents paying the fees charged by the RMC. The new scheme evolved, however, to include a short period of initial training for all young officers, or sub-lieutenants as they were termed, which saw the reopening of Sandhurst as the venue for this training. This scheme proved unpopular and unwieldy. In 1877, therefore, the competitive examination was used for

the appointment to a cadetship rather than a commission, and gentlemen cadets were reinstated at the RMC. Further facilities were installed to cope with the increased number of cadets arising from this decision, including a new chapel, Christ Church, built in 1878–79. In practice, the cost of the College fees was much the same as that formerly charged for an ensign's commission and this, plus the school fees required in preparation for the entry examinations, meant that the social composition of the Army's officers remained unchanged. The RMC was not large enough to train all the subalterns needed by the Army, so an alternative route, favoured by those who failed entry to the College, was to obtain a commission by nomination in the militia. It was then possible to transfer to the Regular Army after a period of full-time service and passing the College's final examination. Throughout the 1880s there was constant pressure on both the Royal Military Academy and the Royal Military College to increase the numbers of cadets available for commissioning.

In 1893, when Winston Churchill entered the College, a one year course was offered:
At Sandhurst I had a new start. I was no longer handicapped by past neglect of Latin, French or Mathematics. We had now to learn fresh things and we all started equal. Tactics, Fortification, Topography (mapmaking), Military Law and Military Administration formed the whole curriculum. In addition were Drill, Gymnastics and Riding. No

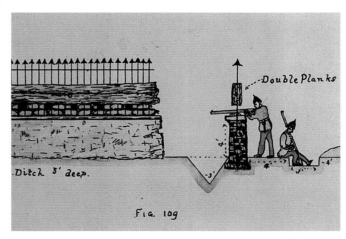

Winston Spencer Churchill as a gentleman cadet and his performance details from the Register.

one need play any game unless he wanted to. Discipline was strict and the hours of study and parade were long. One was very tired at the end of the day. I was deeply interested in my work, especially Tactics and Fortification. I did not much like the drill and indeed figured for several months in the "Awkward Squad", formed from those who required special smartening up. But the practical work in field fortification was most exciting. We dug trenches, constructed breastworks, revetted parapets with sandbags, with heather, with fascines, or with 'Jones' iron band gabion'. We put up chevaux de frises and made fougasses (a kind of primitive land mine). We cut railway lines with slabs of guncotton, and learned how to blow up masonry bridges, or make substitutes out of pontoons or timber. We drew contoured maps of all the hills round Camberley, made road reconnaissances in every direction, and set out picket lines and paper plans for advanced guards or rear guards, and even did some very simple tactical schemes. We were never taught anything about bombs or hand-grenades, because of course these weapons were known to be long obsolete. They had gone out of use in the eighteenth century, and would be quite useless in modern war.

Winston S. Churchill, *My Early Life*

The practical side of fortification being exercised at RMC. Where New College stands was once a maze of trenches dug in the nineteenth and early twentieth centuries. A replica of the lines of Torres Vedras from the Peninsula War can still be traced on Hospital Hill in the out-of-bounds area behind the rifle ranges.

THE PRINCE IMPERIAL STATUE

'Where is the Prince?' 'I fear he is killed!'
'Then,' said Colonel Buller, 'you ought to be shot!'

The Prince Imperial statue stands at the eastern limit of New College Square. It was erected in honour of the French Prince Imperial, Louis Napoleon Eugène Jean Joseph, son of the exiled Emperor Napoleon III and great-nephew of Napoleon Bonaparte.

After France's defeat by Prussia in 1871, Napoleon III took up residence in Chislehurst and was eager that his son should have military training. Louis Napoleon was an honorary gentleman cadet at RMA Woolwich from 1872–75, when he was offered a commission in the Royal Artillery. Four years later, Prince Louis, having persuaded Queen Victoria to give him permission to take part in the Zulu War, died in an ambush in Zululand on 1 June 1879. The commander of the escort, Lieutenant Carey, who fled the scene only to chance upon Colonel Redvers Buller VC, was court martialled. The death of Napoleon Bonaparte's only remaining descendant meant the end of his dynasty.

The statue by Count Gleichen (1833–91), whose daughter followed his path and was the sculptor of the War Memorial trio of soldiers in Chapel Square, was unveiled at RMA Woolwich in January 1883 by HRH The Prince of Wales (The future King Edward VII) and later inspected by Queen Victoria. It was moved to RMA Sandhurst in 1955, and it is said that its removal was delayed until the London Transport bus timetables were reprinted, as the bus stop close by was known as The Prince Imperial.

Dr Anthony Morton

Moving the Prince Imperial into position at RMA Sandhurst in 1955.

chapter seven:

The RMC Adapts to the Twentieth Century

ANTHONY MORTON

*W*e lived in the old buildings, the new ones were not even contemplated, and the battalion was organised into six companies, lettered A to F … Outwardly also we looked quite different from the Gentleman Cadet of today. Our full dress was a scarlet tunic, blue overalls with a narrow red piping, cloth helmet with badge, spike and chain, white pipeclayed belts and gloves …

Our instruction was based on the Franco-Prussian War of 1870 and the Russo-Turkish War. For instance, we formed square to receive cavalry, the front rank kneeling, the rear rank standing, and each side of the square fired volleys at the imaginary horsemen, exactly as did the British squares at Quatre-Bras. The drill sergeants remained inside the square, not equipped with halberds, as in Marlborough's time, but with pacing sticks (large wooden compasses; I do not know if they are still in use).

Lord Carnock, 'Sandhurst 30 Years Ago',
***RMC Magazine and Record*, Spring 1933**

With the arrival of the twentieth century came many significant changes at Sandhurst. The initial disasters suffered by British professional officers and regular soldiers at the hands of a few thousand Boer farmers in the South African War of 1899–1902 shocked public and military opinion. It was realised that there were serious shortcomings in the organisation and training of the Army. The subsequent reforms included improvements in cadet training and the enlargement of the RMC. By 1907 the syllabus had been revised to include combined arms and night operations, use of the magazine rifle and quick-firing artillery and annual month-long camps on Salisbury Plain. In January 1904 the course was extended to eighteen months to allow for the month of instruction lost to the annual camp. Eventually though the dramatic increase in cadet numbers that resulted from the Haldane Reforms of 1906–12 meant that the logistics of organising the Salisbury camp became too onerous, and from 1913 onwards the camp would be moved to the College's own training area on Barossa Common and last from one to three days. The period leading up to the First World War was far from

settled, and the expansion of the Army in light of the perceived threat from Imperial Germany saw ongoing pressure to increase the number of cadets.

NEW COLLEGE

In 1911, having passed in eighteenth out of a very big field, I was admitted to the Royal Military College Sandhurst. I was then eighteen … Shortly after I joined the RMC it had been nearly doubled in size by

MONTGOMERY REMEMBERS

In the realm of work, to begin with things went well. The custom then was to select some of the outstanding juniors, or first term cadets, and to promote them to lance-corporal after six weeks at the College. This was considered a great distinction; the cadets thus selected were reckoned to be better than their fellows and to have shown early the essential qualities necessary for a first class officer in the Army. These lance-corporals always became sergeants in their second term, wearing a red sash, and one or two became colour-sergeants carrying a sword; colour-sergeant was the highest rank for a cadet.

I was selected to be a lance-corporal. I suppose this must have gone to my head; at any rate my downfall began from that moment. The Junior Division of 'B' Company, my company at the College, contained a pretty tough and rowdy crowd and my authority as a lance-corporal caused me to take a lead in their activities. We began a war with the juniors of 'A' Company who lived in the storey above us; we carried the war into the areas of other companies living farther away down the passages. Our company became known as 'Bloody B', which was probably a very good name for it. Fierce battles were fought in the passages after dark; pokers and similar weapons were used and cadets often retired to hospital for repairs. This state of affairs obviously could not continue, even at Sandhurst in 1907 when the officers kept well clear of the activities of the cadets when off duty.

Attention began to concentrate on 'Bloody B' and on myself. The climax came when during the ragging of an unpopular cadet I set fire to the tail of his shirt as he was undressing; he got badly burnt behind, retired to hospital and was unable to sit down with any comfort for some time. He behaved in an exemplary manner in refusing to disclose the author of his ill-treatment, but it was no good; one's sins are always found out in the end and I was reduced to the ranks.

Viscount Montgomery, *The Memoirs of Field-Marshal The Viscount Montgomery of Alamein*

Field-Marshal Montgomery at the unveiling of the Luneburg Heath Memorial which commemorates the surrender of the German forces in North Germany and Denmark but had suffered from vandalism soon after its erection. In 1958, just before the British Army handed over Luneburg to the German Army, Montgomery had the memorial taken down and re-erected at the RMAS where, in his words, 'all that it records is very welcome'. The memorial stands on the edge of New College Square, opposite the Officers' Mess.

the addition of the so-called 'New Building', a large red brick structure, not nearly so picturesque as the old college, but far lighter, more sanitary and up to date. The new building had its own lecture rooms, dining halls, and parade ground, so we were quite independent of the other half of the college and only went there to take part in battalion parades. A, B and C Companies were located in the old building and D, E and F in the new. I was posted to E Company which, for the second year running, had earned the honourable distinction of being 'Champion Company at Arms'. This title of Champion Company had only recently been introduced and was much prized. Every cadet played his part in it by the number of marks he was awarded in all the various activities which went to make up our life at the College. The keenness was intense: as we marched onto the battalion parade, after all the other companies, and took our place on the right of the line, it was quite a thrill and we really did throw a chest … The life was hard and the discipline strict. Very great importance was attached to drill – rigid barrack-square drill – and the drill and discipline of the cadet battalions at Sandhurst was second to none in the British Army.

Sir John Smyth, VC, *Milestones: A Memoir*

The Haldane Reforms that had resulted from the experience of the Boer War included creating a new Territorial Force to support the regular army in time of war. Large numbers of trained regular officers were needed to train the new Territorial Divisions and so the RMC had to expand to cope with the increase of cadets required. The decision was taken that Old College was no longer sufficient for the RMC's needs and that a new building was needed. New College was designed by Harry Bell Measures, Director of Barrack Construction, and built between 1908 and 1911, at a cost of £105,000. A light railway was constructed from Blackwater station through the Oak Grove, and a railway shed was built behind the 1862 College Gymnasium for the three million or so bricks needed to complete the task. (This temporary railway shed has since been incorporated, as Marlow Hall, in what is now the Central Library.) The New Building was designed to house 424 cadets and also contains classrooms and offices. New

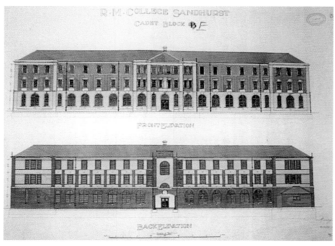

Top left: The new Royal Military College in the course of construction, July 1911. Cox Collection.

Left: Building plan for the New Buildings, RMC, 1911, ink and watercolour.

Above: New College buildings in the 1950s, watercolour, Dennis Flanders.

Building or New College is said to be the longest military building in Britain and, according to James Douet in his history of British barracks, Measures completely rethought British barrack design and construction: 'Stylistically, Measures threw much of the vocabulary of Free Imperial Baroque into a lively and highly eclectic design, with polychromatic effects in brick and stone'; the building 'represent[s] the culmination of a brief but luxuriant flowering of richly decorated military quarters'. The building of New College in 1911, in an area previously used for practice fieldworks, helped the process of consolidating the appearance of the Academy as one sees it today, as it takes forward the feature of the 'arc of the colleges' which was later completed with the opening of the contentious Victory College in 1970.

Each of New College's six cadet blocks was built to contain a single self-contained company. Two companies remained in Old College, and two more were raised and accommodated there on the outbreak of the First Word War. The staff consisted of the Commandant, Second-in-Command (also of colonel's rank), the Adjutant, a major, Quartermaster, Riding-Master, Surgeon, Assistant Surgeon, Chaplain, Accountant and Nursing Sister. There were four academic professors, for English, French, German and Hindustani, as well as three instructors in French.

A major who had passed Staff College commanded each company, his staff numbering four officers of captain's rank. The cadets provided an internal structure of three divisions for the three terms, with cadet ranks above that of gentleman cadet being from lance corporal to sergeant and then under-officer. There was one staff sergeant posted to each company and in the autumn term of l912 the Guards provided three of the six staff sergeants postings. In 1912 the RMC was increased in size to eight companies, six of which were accommodated in New College, completed in that year. Another two companies were added during the First World War. The first two years of the First World War saw the RMC given the additional responsibility of providing 'temporary officers' (orginally university graduates given a

Above: Old College showing the Dining Room chimney stack which was erected in 1913 after the completion of New College buildings.

Above: G Company, raised on 4 September 1912, had to be accommodated in tents for the first few days of its existence while Old College was being refurbished.

temporary commission for the duration of the war) with short one month training courses. By April 1916 when these courses came to an end, 2,700 temporary officers had passed through Sandhurst.

SANDHURST IN THE FIRST WORLD WAR

Sandhurst in 1915! … Everything was of course telescoped, as the War Office wanted all the young officers it could get. I had come straight from Wellington, aged just over 17, and the policy for people of my age was to put us through in 5 months …

    Obviously it was impossible to fit into so abbreviated a course all that we needed to know. But it was more than doubtful whether the authorities knew what a young officer needed to know in World War I. One had a strong impression that, on a basic scheme of training designed to fit us for

the Boer War, all sorts of extras were tacked on as the World War showed itself to be following a disquietingly different line of development. I have a vivid recollection of my company receiving careful instruction on forming a square, fixing bayonets and preparing to receive a cavalry charge, (we were formed up shoulder to shoulder, rear rank standing, front rank kneeling on one knee, so that I rather fancy this particular item dated back to pre-Boer times …). On the other hand, we spent a number of evenings defending trenches against another Company, lighting flares and throwing imitation bombs at the attackers.*

**Gentleman Cadet Douglas Lockhart,
RMC April–September 1915**

By August 1914 there were nearly 700 cadets under training and the Commandant was ordered to prepare for a total of 960. On the outbreak of war, the Senior Term received immediate commissions and all those who completed half the course were put on tactics refresher courses and sent to their units. On mobilisation the course shortened to three months but after 1916 it was steadily increased in length until it reached the pre-war length of 18 months, and it was then extended to two years. In January 1917 the addition of two extra companies saw the College strength reach 920, the additional companies were disbanded in August 1918 and the strength was reduced to the normal establishment of 700. One certainly needed to be physically fit at the Royal Military College in those hectic months early in that War. Long before it was light in the early mornings we were doing Recruits Arms Drill indoors. Long after it was dark in the evenings, we were each locked in our rooms, or study bedrooms, mugging up, say, 'Tactics' for the morrow. During the day we were never still. We changed our clothes and uniforms at least six times a day, always at top speed. First uniform, then PT kit, then dungarees for digging, for Field Engineering as it was called, then uniform again, followed by Games Kit for compulsory games, and last Dinner Jackets for Mess, as Mess kit had gone out with the War. Any spare time, during the week, I ever had, I lay on my bed just resting for what was coming next.

Gentleman Cadet Douglas Wimberley, RMC 1914–15

Between the outbreak of war and 19 December 1918, a month after the signing of the Armistice, 5,131 gentlemen cadets received their commissions through the Royal Military College. The roll of honour up to 30 June 1919 was 3,274, with thirty-five VCs awarded to former gentlemen cadets.

THE WAR MEMORIAL

The bronze group of three soldiers that stands on the lawn outside the West Door of the Royal Memorial Chapel is a copy of an original monument located at Monchy-le-Preux in France. The original cast was sculpted by Lady Feodora Gleichen as a memorial to the British 37th Infantry Division in the First World War (her brother, General Lord Edward Gleichen, was the first commander of the division). The 37th Division captured the town of Monchy-le-Preux during the First Battle of the Scarpe in the first phase of the Arras offensive (9–14 April 1917). It later took part in the Third Battle of Ypres, the Passchendaele battles and the battles of the Hindenburg Line. The division suffered 29,969 casualties during the war.

    After the sculptress's death, her sister Lady Helena Gleichen presented this replica, exhibited at the Royal Academy, to the Royal Military College, Sandhurst. HRH Prince Edward, Prince of Wales, unveiled it on Sunday 18 June 1927. In his speech he referred to the statue as a memorial to the rank and file of the British Army who fell in both world wars, and is a permanent reminder to all who enter the Chapel of the devotion and sacrifice of the other ranks and the undying bonds of loyalty between the officer and the men he leads and serves.

Dr Anthony Morton

Ben Pearce painstakingly retouches the detail of the regimental memorials in the Royal Memorial Chapel to Officers commissioned from the RMC who died in the First World War.

GENTLEMEN CADETS

Rough and rude as we often were, we gentlemen cadets – and I still relish the old-fashioned ring of the phrase, which some booby in the War Office abolished soon after the war broke out – had an element of the romantic in us, as all good soldiers must.

There were few of us without close army connections already. I was impressed only lately, when reading a book about the Duke of Wellington, by the fact that many of the names of his officers in the Peninsula and at Waterloo were represented in my generation at Sandhurst: Fane, Luard, Paget, Vandeleur, and so on. We warmed to the history of individual Regiments, to which a generous amount of time was given in the Syllabus, as much as to any of the subjects we were taught. Why did the Glosters wear their cap-badges aft as well as fore? Why did the Royal Welch wear black flashes at the back of their collars? Why did the West Yorkshires have Ca Ira as their regimental march? Why was this regiment called 'Pontius Pilate's Bodyguard', and another the 'Pompadours', and another the 'Moonrakers', and another the 'Dirty Half-Hundred'? We drank in such lore, and never forgot it.

Gentleman Cadet Bernard Fergusson,
The Trumpet in the Hall 1930–1958 (1930)

Saint Cadet, 1930s.

1918–39

From September 1919 the course was extended to two years. The company structure was also reorganised from the old linear structure based on ten companies each of four sections to a system of four large companies each of four platoons, in line with the infantry company organisation within the infantry battalion organisation of the time. This was done 'in order to make the company at Sandhurst an exact representation of an Infantry Company, and in order to make the platoon the unit for training as it is in the infantry'. Courses were updated to include the lessons learnt in the First World War, and to cope with the demands of the new technology, including the internal combustion engine. The College also saw an influx of overseas cadets from India and China, and the first cadets selected from serving NCOs.

The issue of amalgamating RMA and RMC had been raised on a number of occasions and at various levels during the interwar years. It emerged again in the late 1930s, and Sandhurst became the chosen site for an amalgamated academy due to its new accommodation and its ease of access to training areas. This was scheduled to take place in August 1940 but the war intervened. The RMC Sandhurst formally ceased to exist on 4 September 1939, the day after war was declared, and became the Sandhurst Officer Cadet Training Unit.

The Sandhurst term is a long one: there are only three during the eighteen months' course. That first term was never dull. Apart from the novelty of everything, there was the Munich crisis of 1938, and we were not among the least affected by it. Bookwork was abandoned, and we turned our hands to digging trenches, sandbagging, and finding A.A. guards. For three days we dug up the lawns of the Royal Military College and made

trenches among the lovely shrubberies known as 'Fisher's Follies'. While sweating at a particularly hard piece of ground I remember my company commander walking up and ordering me to get myself a haircut by that time to-morrow. I think I got into more trouble at Sandhurst over my hair than over anything else. Once, in a temper, I had it practically shaved off, and as a result was told by my S.U.O. [Senior Under-Officer] that it was too short!

After the crisis life reverted to normal – or perhaps not quite to normal. There seemed more punch behind the lectures and the tempo seemed a little sharper. In spite of the assurances of politicians there were few of us who did not believe that war would come within two years; and the thought made us take our training seriously.

Anon, 1938, *Infantry Officer: A Personal Record*

Air-raid shelters in front of the Old College buildings dug in response to the Munich Crisis.

Above: Cadets on parade in blazers and 'pillbox' hats, 1938.

Far right: Room 2, Blenheim Company – a sketch by OCdt Hugh Naismith, Intake 15, 1954.

Cavalry. Training, under the eagle eye of our sergeant major, Mr Leckie of the Irish Guards, was hard, discipline on the square positively cruel and the level of 'bullshit' required, in terms of both personal kit and the rooms which we occupied, little short of ridiculous. However, we co-operated with enthusiasm and worked very hard at everything they gave us to do. Unfortunately, our exposure to armoured vehicles, gunnery, wireless and driving was minimal. Our exercises were carried out in trucks or on foot, and looking back on it all, we learned very little of technical or tactical value … Despite my boredom and frustration with the drill, the polishing and the scrubbing, I put my heart into it all and undoubtedly left Sandhurst with a more informed and adult approach to problems and their solution.

Officer Cadet Bill Bellamy, 1942,
Troop Leader – A Tank Commander's Story

At the outbreak of war in September 1939 Government House, the residence of the RMC Commandant, became the staging post for Lord Gort, Commander-in-Chief of the British Expeditionary Force and some of his staff. It was here that both Lord Gort and HRH The Duke of Gloucester stayed the night before they left for France. On 4 September, the day after war was declared, the RMC became the Sandhurst OCTU. The gentlemen cadets of the RMC, like those of the RMA, were attested as Territorials, to bring them under military law. Those who were not commissioned at once remained at Sandhurst and joined either 101 (Royal Armoured Corps) Officer Cadet Training Unit, or 161 (Infantry) Officer Cadet Training Unit. All subsequent arrivals were officer cadets rather than gentlemen cadets, and were men conscripted into the ranks under the National Service Acts. 161 OCTU drew its instructors from the RMC and was allowed to use the subtitle Royal Military College; its cadets were entitled to wear the RMC cap badge during the intensive sixteen-week infantry course. This continued after 1942, when 161 OCTU moved to Mons Barracks,

Students at the RMA and RMC were known as Gentlemen Cadets (GCs). Their equivalents in the other colleges of the other two Services were Naval Cadets and Flight Cadets respectively. Unlike modern officer cadets, who are technically private soldiers and as such are paid and clothed by the Ministry of Defence, gentlemen cadets were not subject to military law. Their parents paid tuition and boarding fees, in the same way as at a public school or university, and also paid for uniforms (of the same pattern as worn by subaltern officers, but without badges of rank), books and mathematical instruments. Fees were reduced for the sons of serving or former officers, and there were also a number of cadetships (comparable to scholarships). Admission was by competitive written examination in a variety of academic subjects, and candidates passed in, in order of merit, according to the number of marks they achieved. There were no practical tests of aptitude for leadership: these were first introduced during the Second World War and continue to form the basis of the present-day Regular Commissions Board (RCB). This had the effect of confining entry to the RMA and the RMC to public schoolboys, often from families with a military connection.

THE OFFICER CADET TRAINING UNITS AT SANDHURST, 1939–47

On arrival at Sandhurst, I was posted to 24 Troop, quickly known as 'The Lords Troop' because it contained so many cadets with titles. I was in 'C' Section, commanded by Captain Julian Ward of the Household

Aldershot, and it seems that after the move the first two or three courses returned to the Old College parade ground for the graduation ceremony.

By contrast, 101 OCTU drew its staff from the Inns of Court Regiment. In 1942 this amalgamated with the Reconnaissance Corps OCTU, and the new OCTU (100) RAC remained as the only unit at Sandhurst until the end of 1945. It then moved to Bovington Camp and 161 OCTU reoccupied the Sandhurst site until it was disbanded in November 1946. The armoured course was twenty-four weeks, with an intake passing out every fortnight.

Two companies of Auxiliary Territorial Service (ATS) were posted to Sandhurst in September 1939 and expanded to include the Staff College and Minley Manor, providing cooks, orderlies, clerks and drivers. Lake House became the ATS sick bay and No. 4 Chapel Square the Officers' Mess and company office, with the other ranks accommodation in spare soldiers' married quarters. No. 4 was out of bounds, but two bottles of beer inside one's battledress would get one invited inside on Wednesday evenings. On the Sunday Church Parade the ATS found themselves marching past to 'They'd Be Far Better Off in a Home'.

Although the College was a recognisable target there were only two recorded instances of night bombing on Sandhurst. The first was on Wednesday 29 January 1941, when a single bomb hit the end of D Block of New College. It was a bright clear night and the lake was an obvious landmark. The bomb demolished the end of the wing killing five cadets, three of whom are buried in the cemetery. A landmine was dropped towards the end of the war in the area of Lake House and blew out many windows, including the Chesney Memorial windows in the Chapel. The existing gap in the wall between Old College and Lake House shows where the landmine impacted.

The only other invasion was when Squadron Leader Reynolds, RNZAF, arrived at Sandhurst by parachute in the early hours of 7 December 1942 when he and another crew member baled out of a badly damaged bomber returning from Germany, and he found himself balanced dangerously on the parapet above the Grand Entrance to Old College, leading to both men being arrested and held under guard.

THE NIGHT THE BOMB HIT NEW COLLEGE

It was January 1941 and it was a dining-out night for my company except for those on duty of which I was one. It must have been about 10.30pm and I had my bath and was on my way back to my room in my pyjamas on the second floor. I heard a hefty crump which I didn't think much about as we were used to German aircraft jettisoning their bombs at random. However what happened next was almost like a freeze-frame. I saw the bomb come through the ceiling in the corridor ahead of me and pass through the floor, and then everything blew upwards and outwards. I was quite aware initially and then blacked out. I landed on the grass about 30 yards from the building along with bricks, stone, glass and wood. The impact of landing woke me up and I felt all wet and was quite angry, but I did not appear to have any bones broken.

I was conscious that I was one of the duty cadets so I scrambled to my feet and made my way through the rubble back into the long corridor that linked the wings. A chap came towards me with a torch and when he saw me he threw up. The wetness that I felt on me was not water but blood and I was covered in it from head to toe. I was covered in puncture wounds, some quite serious and over the following days, various bits and pieces made their way to the surface and were extracted and the holes plugged up again. However I could not feel a thing. A couple of cadets helped me to the hospital, which had all its windows blown out. I was laid out on a stretcher in the hall, given a cigarette and a jab of morphine.

Officer Cadet Richard Todd, 1941

FROM FOREIGN FIELDS: THE POLES AT SANDHURST

Among the earliest wartime overseas cadets to be admitted to the then Royal Military College, Sandhurst was a group of ten Polish soldiers. They joined the Officer Cadet Training Unit (OCTU), Royal Armoured Corps course at Sandhurst in spring 1943. With the formation of the 1st Polish Armoured Division (*Pierwsza Dywizja Pancerna*) in Britain, there was a pressing need for armour-trained junior officers. The selection of this particular group of Poles to come to Sandhurst was based in part on their ability to speak English. For the ten young men representing Poland at Sandhurst, however, much more in the way of expectations rested on their shoulders. These men would be thoroughly tested at Sandhurst and, later, in the more demanding school of wartime operations. From both experiences emerged leadership qualities of the first order.

Representative of this group of Poles was Ryszard Zatorski. Assigned with six other Poles to Troop 73 on the OCTU course that ran between May and October 1943 (the other three Poles were distributed between Troops 78 and 80), Zatorski's outstanding performance saw him finishing not only the top of Troop 73 but as the best officer cadet of the entire OCTU course. Zatorski earned the much coveted belt of honour.

After commissioning at Sandhurst, Zatorski returned, along with two of his Polish colleagues, to serve as instructors in tank tactics on the OCTU course. Later he joined the 1st Polish Armoured Division on operations in Northwest Europe. While commanding the reconnaissance platoon of the 2nd Armoured Regiment (2 *Pulk Pancerny*) he earned a *Virtuti Militari*, Poland's highest military decoration in April 1945. In the course of the war he also received a *Krzyz Walecznych* (Cross of Valour). Indeed, of the ten Poles who marched up the steps of Old College in October 1943, half of them earned the Virtuti Militari and between all of them were awarded eleven Crosses of Valour.

Dr Paul Latawski

A smiling Lieutenant Zatorski wearing the belt of honour (front row, second from right) photographed with his Polish colleagues of Troop 73. The impressiveness of the group at Sandhurst was matched by their wartime records.

chapter eight:

Sandhurst 1947–2017

Robert Pellow

The Royal Military Academy Sandhurst emerged in 1947 from the merger between the Royal Military Academy, Woolwich and Royal Military College, Sandhurst. Perhaps apocryphally the origins of the Royal Military College at Sandhurst lie in the poor British performance in the Flanders campaign during the Napoleonic Wars. Major-General John Le Marchant was so enraged by an Austrian officer comparing British sword technique to a 'farmer chopping wood' that he persuaded parliament, already concerned with the poor leadership displayed by officers who had purchased their commissions, to grant him £30,000 to establish a Royal Military College dedicated to the training of officers.

Whatever the case RMAS was intended to carry on the best traditions of both its legacy institutions and has maintained its strong commitment to equipping officer cadets with the necessary tools to be strong and effective leaders. Indeed the motto of the 'new' Sandhurst became 'Serve to Lead', replacing

Above: In 1970 Victory College moved into the new East Building. This had been designed in the contemporary style at the express wish of the then members of the Army Council, who wanted Sandhurst to have a modern image.

Right: Aerial view of New College with Faraday Hall left rear and the medical centre right rear. The Nissen huts housed the cadets of Victory College until the completion of the building in 1970.

LOSING ONE'S NAME

Each company was headed by a Senior Under-Officer, with a Junior Under-Officer for each intake, supported by cadet sergeants and corporals. Throughout my junior term Normandy 42 was run by JUO Denis Pead and Cdt Sgt John Patchett. So, when not being 'beasted' by the training NCOs we were chased from pillar to post by the cadet government. I discovered that I was one of a number of service-entrants who, more than most, managed 'to enjoy' the junior term. We had all completed basic training; two were trained parachutists and found ourselves repeating most of what we had already learned. The majority, however, were school entrants with no military experience who were starting from scratch. This put the onus on the trained soldiers among us to make sure that we all achieved the required standards so once we had sorted ourselves out we would help the others. To put the need for camaraderie into context, there was a semi-formal disciplinary process referred to as 'losing one's name'. This meant that for whatever reason, you could be placed on report to receive minor punishment decided by the Senior Under-Officer. The trouble was that once you had lost your name the chance of repeating the exercise was very high – this became known as the 'Dripping Shit' for once shit drips it's hard to stop it! The normal punishments were Extra Parades in the morning before the formal Breakfast Roll Call or BRC and in the evening before dinner. For really heinous crimes it was Extra Drill for one hour on a Wednesday and/or Saturday afternoon. This was when the shit really dripped for it was quite common to lose one's name during this drill period thus perpetuating the punishment process!

Officer Cadet Iain Powrie, 1967

the Latin of its two predecessor institutions. This represented the spirit of the age, with the new Sandhurst being open and accessible to all rather than being seen as a gentleman's finishing school, reflected in the change of terminology from 'Gentleman Cadet' to 'Officer Cadet'. The new Sandhurst was to have equal weighting between academic and military studies with an aim to provide 'a proper balanced educational

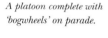

A platoon complete with 'bogwheels' on parade.

Temporary accommodation –
cold outside and cold within.

background, so that after leaving the Academy the cadet may advance to full officer status', as Cathy Downes wrote.

The Courses at Sandhurst

The length and nature of the course taught at Sandhurst has changed and adapted over the last 80 years in response to both the changing nature of the people becoming officer cadets and the British Army's requirements. The original course in 1947 took place over 18 months, rising to two years in 1955. This increase was to give cadets more practical training without reducing the academic half of the course. The range of subjects was broad including science, mathematics, languages, and military history to highlight a few: drawing upon the long tradition of academic excellence at the 'old' RMC Sandhurst which had taught subjects as varied as Latin, English composition, and military drawing. The greater amount of time for teaching and instruction from a two year course meant there was a more relaxed feel to life at the College, with the result that there was a lively extra-curricular life. Officer Cadets could engage in activities such as amateur dramatics, musical societies, a literary society (the intriguingly named 'Polished Bun Club'), a Russian Circle, a debating society, a film club, among many others. There was also a strong sporting culture including the standard trio of rugby, football and cricket, but also slightly rarer activities like deep-sea sailing in the yacht 'Wish Stream' and the 'Rupert Bear Club' for those who wished to become parachute-qualified.

However in 1972 there was a significant remodelling and shortening of the course. With the end of National Service in 1960 and the general tightening of military resources, the 1971 Army Review decided that training should take the form

The company plaques of RMAS which line the New College Dining Room.

of the accelerated model favoured by the Mons Officer Cadet School. Mons had been responsible for not only training Short Service officer cadets but also territorials and those entering the army from university. It had been increasingly favoured by those looking to join as officers given the much shorter course in comparison to the longer and more rigorous standards demanded by the Sandhurst course, the intensive course granted all the benefits of commission in six months whilst Sandhurst cadets would still have another 18 months before becoming officers. In 1972 the school at Mons was closed and moved into New College, leading to a relatively confusing two-tiered system of training. All cadets had to enrol on the now six month course of basic military training at New College in order to turn them into officers. If they wished to have a regular commission they then had to do a further six months at Old College which consisted of the academic studies that had previously been spread over two years, in order to 'ensure they are officers'. However the academic component was now focused on war studies, international relations, British politics and communication. Short Service commissions did not have to proceed onto this academic course. Meanwhile existing officers could go to a separate course at Victory College, whilst some cadets could become officers by doing this and also going to university for three years. These more compressed courses differed starkly from the collegiate university style of the previous twenty-five years.

There were however concerns within the military establishment about the 'quality of the product' emerging from the compressed Mons-style course, notwithstanding the illogical course structure which had led to a breakdown of cohesion and camaraderie in the cadet corp. It was also felt that the course didn't provide a progression for leadership, one of the key attributes meant to be taught at Sandhurst, given the lack of time for the development of leadership responsibilities. Therefore the Common Commissioning Course was introduced in 1992 in order to both streamline the process, since all cadets now did the same course, and to lengthen the course to forty-four weeks to add more content. This also reinvigorated the course as being modern and professionally focused with a

strong military flavour. A modern focus was achieved through better assessment over all three terms in order to ensure that all cadets were encouraged to do better and maintain a consistent high standard of attainment. There was also a shift in course focus from simply training cadets to be ready for command at platoon level to wider horizons like preparation for combined arms battle. The structure that has been retained since 1992 divides the year into three terms. The first five weeks of the first term is devoted exclusively to military training and instruction, before the academic element gradually escalates throughout term two and three. There is some discussion as to whether the five weeks of military training should be turned into a pre-Sandhurst course in order to devote the entirety of the Sandhurst programme to specific training for potential officers, although for now there is no major change on the horizon.

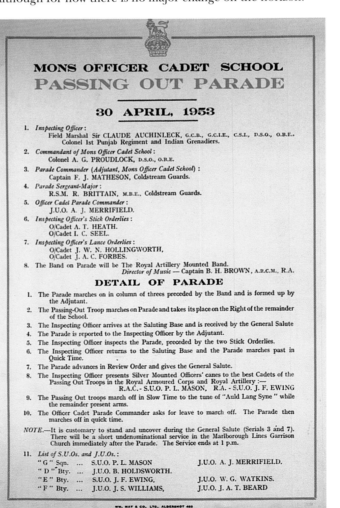

However the syllabus of taught material has continued to shift and adapt to the more pressing operational needs of the army. Rather than being static and fossilised the syllabus at Sandhurst has adapted with the times to provide relevant military skills, knowledge and information: the nuances of Cold War geopolitics gave way to a focus on the Middle East and counter-insurgency tactics and with major operational commitments in Iraq and Afghanistan Sandhurst's military training became increasingly influenced by the demands of these specific conflicts. Of greater importance than this background knowledge was teaching officer cadets how to think critically and be able to adapt to whatever situation comes there way. With the British Army so operationally engaged the RMAS commissioning course became increasingly focused on military skills and preparing new officers for the high likelihood of an operational commitment early in their careers. Although it remained the case that the Academy used infantry tactics as a vehicle to develop leadership the commissioning course acquired a considerable focus on 'the war today'.

Despite the criticism of many militaries that they are always preparing to fight the last war, Sandhurst's course attempts to equip its cadets with the tools needed for a complex and changing world with a variety of threats and risks that the British Army may be deployed to in the near future. This has been accompanied in recent years with a shift back towards using infantry tactics to inform leadership rather than teaching infantry tactics for use in the field, one of the concerns being that Sandhurst had simply become a pre-deployment centre for those officers going to serve in Iraq and Afghanistan. Indeed, even prior to the draw down in Afghanistan the RMAS course

was responding to the British Army view that the UK was entering a period of contingency where the exact nature of near future operations was very hard to predict which puts stress on developing agility, flexibility and adaptability.

In 1947 the RMAS was not the only British Army establishment that awarded a commission, but it is now the case that all officers in the British Army have a 'Sandhurst Experience'. Professionally Qualified Officers and Reserve Officers not only have commissioning courses at Sandhurst but they now parade and march up the famous steps of Old College. This not only recognises the requirements that all commissioned officers face in their careers but also that their commissioning courses have become more challenging. The three weeks of the old Sandhurst course for professionally qualified officers became the eleven-week Professionally Qualified Officers course in 1988 and Reserve Officers now complete their commissioning course with a final two weeks at Sandhurst.

In modern times the British Army has systematically commissioned highly experienced NCOs. In 2003 a four-week course was introduced at the RMAS for Late Entry Officers and although they have already attained the rank of captain before arriving they now all have a Sandhurst experience.

Officers of the Standard Graduate Course march onto Sovereign's Parade 1974.

Captain Robert Nairac, Grenadier Guards, commissioned in 1972. He was on his fourth tour of Northern Ireland and conducting covert operations when he was abducted and murdered by the IRA. He was posthumously awarded the George Cross in 1979.

That the Academy has become more central in developing officers with the character, professional expertise and intellectual agility required to lead is without doubt a good thing. It is particularly important that all those who are required to face the leadership challenges of being an officer have the common experience of RMAS with its unique sense of history and ability to both capture the timeless verities of the profession of arms and its endless need for adapting to a dynamic, ever changing set of demands.

Changing Nature of the Cadet

These changes in the length and nature of the course at Sandhurst post-1947 have in part been driven by the need to adapt to the changing educational profile of the officer cadets passing through. The modern cadet is older and significantly more likely to hold a university degree or other post-eighteen qualification than a cadet of 1947. In 1947 the average age of a cadet was nineteen, being in general men who had joined straight from leaving school without any other form of higher or further education. However by the late-1980s the average age had risen to twenty-three with many having attained a degree. It was for this reason that the separate, shorter commissioning course was introduced since these degree-holding cadets were considered to already have some of the skills and education taught by the standard commissioning course. This practice ended in 1992 with the introduction of the Common Commissioning Course, which was designed to treat all cadets as mature and intelligent adults rather than as teenagers straight out of school. Now 85% of contemporary cadets have attended university, and a small but growing number also hold post-graduate qualifications. This perhaps makes the contemporary cadet less malleable than the nineteen-year-olds of the 1940s due to their diverse range of life experiences, but it also means they are more adaptable, mentally resourceful and able to think independently – all of which are key skills required for the modern army and the changing nature of contemporary hybrid warfare.

The most obvious change from the RMAS in 1947 in many ways is the introduction of female officer cadets to the Sandhurst commissioning course. Originally women were trained at the Women's Royal Army Corps College in Bagshot but when that closed in 1984 responsibility was shifted to Sandhurst. Female cadets were organised into separate platoons and put straight onto the shorter graduate course. With the introduction of the Common Commissioning Course women did the same course as men but remained in separate platoons. It was recognised that significantly higher injury rates resulted among female cadets put on the identical course due to differing physiologies, so Sandhurst became committed to gender-fair training, whereby female officer cadets do as much as they are realistically capable of doing. In 2015 women-only platoons were abandoned in favour of fully integrated platoons. Whilst this has posed some problems for the more conservative-minded foreign cadets, as of late 2016 this change

General Sir Michael Carver, GGS, inspecting the last Commissioning Parade at Mons, Aldershot, 4 August 1972.

appears to be a resounding success. The full integration of women into the commissioning course also fits the evolution of the wider role of women in the Army which in 2016 has seen the first women officer cadets apply for commissions with the Royal Armoured Corps and it seems very likely that in the near future that all gender restrictions will be removed.

Sandhurst also takes overseas cadets from around the world and they make up around 10% of the current intake. The countries from which they come have varied over time, with many 'new' nations such as Kazakhstan, Bosnia and Ukraine sending their officers. Although there is a constantly changing international community at RMAS there are some traditional friends such as Jamaica, Pakistan, Jordan and the Gulf States who have a long association with the Academy. In recent years cadets from the USA, Germany and the People's Republic of China have taken the Sandhurst commissioning course. Although undoubtedly these cadets have benefited from the outstanding training Sandhurst offers it is also the case that their presence on the course hugely enriches the experience of their British cadet colleagues. These cadets bring an interesting extra dimension to Sandhurst due to the diverse backgrounds that such a broad geographical and cultural spread of people brings. Sandhurst alumni include monarchs and political leaders but all our overseas cadets face the formidable task of adapting to the very challenging environment of the course – not least the vagaries of our weather – and they all take huge pride when they successfully complete the course.

Unique Characteristics of Sandhurst

Despite all these changes there a number of enduring characteristics which add to the uniqueness of Sandhurst. First among them is the rigorous focus upon instilling effective leadership qualities within the cadets, a tradition stemming from the earliest days of the RMC Sandhurst, although strangely a specific course on leadership was only introduced in 2004. The greater historical military lineage and traditions of Sandhurst and its predecessor organisations help to instil a professional military culture. Of course taking your commissioning course at such a historic place surrounded by pictures and objects that remind everyone of the proud past of the British Army reinforces this culture on and throughout the commissioning courses.

More important is the major role that NCOs play in officer cadet training, using colour sergeants with operational experience to assist cadets in their training. This is a system unlike most other military academies in the world and in many ways it is these very able NCOs who are the custodians of the tradition of leadership at Sandhurst. Indeed, for most officer cadets it is their Platoon Colour Sergeants who most influence their day-to-day lives on the course. Sandhurst also draws upon the experience of talented young captains and majors for officer training.

The smooth working of the Academy depends upon the extensive supporting departments. The wider Sandhurst 'family' includes the Gurkha soldiers from Sittang Company,

44 Support Squadron Royal Logistic Corps, staff officers in the Headquarters, hundreds of civilian support staff and numerous volunteers. Some of these have served the Academy for several decades and their dedication helps maintain the magnificent surroundings that are so important in subtly shaping those who commission from the RMAS.

Throughout the one-year commisioning course the cadets 'family' is their company and platoon, to which they display a fierce loyalty. Of course friendly competition is intense and in every intake the outstanding platoon is designated the Sovereign's Platoon – a mark of considerable achievement albeit with an extra burden of drill! These companies are named after some of the great battle honours of the British Army, a list which includes Blenheim, Normandy, and Waterloo. However it is a foolish army that studies only its victories so there are also companies named after the Somme, Arnhem and Salerno. Though these names rotate with each new intake of officer cadets it seems certain that whatever victories or defeats the British Army will encounter in the future, RMA Sandhurst will continue to adapt to provide new officers with the best possible set of skills to face the conflicts of tomorrow.

chapter nine:

Town and Gown

TIM BEAN

The purchasing of a site for the Royal Military College on the edge of Bagshot Heath in the parish of Sandhurst in 1802 had a profound and lasting impact upon local communities. What had once been barren heathland, renowned for highwaymen and described by Daniel Defoe as 'frightful to look at, not only good for little, but good for nothing', was gradually transformed into a vibrant locality.

The need for staff and servants, demands for goods and services, and the fashionable status conferred by the presence of the College were a major stimulus to growth in the local area. York Town and College Town were created to supply the demands for goods and services. The building of the Army Staff College nearby saw a similar pattern of development, with the founding of Cambridge Town by Major Spring and Captain Knight in 1856. By 1867 over 200 buildings were clustered around the Staff College gates where only a single farm house (today a Premier Inn which sadly replaced the 'The Staff' pub) had originally stood. Many inhabitants, such as shoemaker John Stallwood, moved with the College from Marlow in 1812. Others found employment as servants and staff. In the 1840s girls working at the College laundry received three pence a day for ironing ninety shirts: the drying shirts blanketed the embankments of the London Road each day. Such was the number of people employed that they were able to hold their own sports events in the College.

In the latter part of the nineteenth century retired officers and civil servants, alongside a rising professional middle class, were tempted by the rural tranquillity, and relative ease of access to London. The result of such a concentration of former officers was a distinctive society, with the town receiving the nickname 'Colonel's Town'. Indian Army and civil officials were the most notable group, attracted by advertisements in the Indian military magazine. Their Indian servants were a regular sight in Camberley High Street, whilst their houses bore Indian names, such as 'Kashmir Cottage' in Claremont

York Town in 1849 showing the junction of Frimley Road with Duke of York Posting House (near right) and St Michael's Church under construction on the left. Sketched and drawn by Gentleman Cadet J.N. Colthurst and published by William de la Motte, Drawing Master at RMC.

Avenue. The increasing number of ladies of leisure attracted tradesmen such as Mr Wellard's hairdressing salon from London. Wellard's shop was mentioned in *The Seven Pillars of Wisdom* by T.E. Lawrence, who visited regularly to chat with attractive young ladies. The presence of the College drew other famous people: King Alfonso XIII of Spain bought a house in anticipation of his abdication in the 1930s and the late King Hussein of Jordan – a former cadet – maintained a residence in the area and was a regular visitor to the Academy and the town.

The wider local population and the College proved of benefit to each other. In 1832 Captain Stow bequeathed a fund to assist retired servants and widows. The building of the Royal Memorial Chapel in the 1920s was supported by local money donated in a series of fundraising events; the most notable was a two-day pageant in May 1921 involving a charity match between Tottenham Hotspur and Fulham that raised over £5,000. A similar event in 1930 saw the Commandant donate a share of the money to Yateley Cottage Hospital. In the present day the Commandant adopts a local charity each year, whilst others receive aid from the endeavours of staff and cadets.

Ma Hart of York Town, who died in 1931, pawnbroker to generations of gentlemen cadets.

MRS. HART.

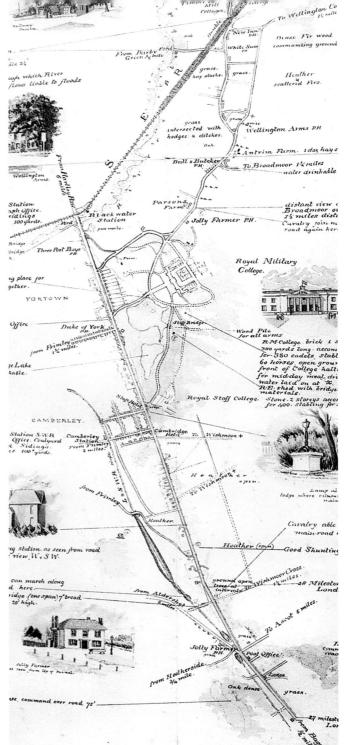

A route reconnaissance report of 1899 by Gentleman Cadet Crispin, showing watercolour sketches of all the public houses between the Golden Farmer and Sandhurst village. Crispin graduated into the Northumberland Fusiliers and was Adjutant of RMC 1910–12. He was killed in 1914 commanding the Royal Sussex Regiment. His name is recorded in the regimental panel in the Royal Memorial Chapel.

Until 1973 the grounds were open to the public, who enjoyed walks, picnicking, and boating and ice skating on the lakes. Others benefited from poaching from the trout lakes. Barossa Common exercise area proved a rich source of income to local children, who scavenged empty brass shell cases to sell in town, the pickings from a used machine gun position being the most lucrative source of cash. The closure of the estate boundaries as a result of the arrival of Princess Anne as a wife on the patch and terrorist threats ended this intimate relationship. Today the grounds open only once a year for a Heritage Day.

The cadets' relationship with the surrounding area has traditionally been less intimate. From the outset access to the local settlements was restricted to purchasing essential goods and hiring horses. Socialising was strictly controlled. Cadets were forbidden to drink within the area from Bagshot to the Hartford Bridge Flats. Prior to the First World War there was a slight relaxation of the rules; tea could be taken at Betty Brown's and Mandarin's, whilst lunch with parents was acceptable at the Cambridge and Duke of York (today flats), both enjoying the more respectable sobriquet of 'hotel'. The underlying purpose of these controls was presumably to preserve discipline and morals, and avoid conflict with locals. In reality it proved problematic to curb the exuberance generated by the concentration of a large number of institutionalised young men. In the 1820s staff sergeants were to report any cadet seen smoking or emerging from a public house. This did not prevent Gentleman Cadet Samuel Dalgety being severely punished after drunkenly letting off fireworks at a local fair. Such unruly behaviour towards locals was not uncommon. A favourite ritual in October was the ransacking of Blackwater Fair. Despite one senior officer's

defence, that this resulted from the stallholder's encouragement of licentiousness amongst the cadets, in 1831 the Christmas term was moved in order to avoid this source of conflict.

Yet if all is fair in love and war, then the former has also been a hallmark of the relations between the cadets and the local population. The noted suffragette and composer, Dame Ethel Smyth, wrote that one of the joys of growing up in Frimley as a young girl was the unfailing supply of young men, adding, in hasty justification, that she was speaking for her father, who had six daughters to marry off. Of course relations were not always of a high moral tone. Colonel Butler in the 1820s acknowledged that cadets consorted with prostitutes, but argued that the problem was not as widespread as at other similar all-male institutions. The cadets summed up their relationship with local girls in song:

Oh what will the Girls of Camberley say
If the RMC was to march away
And leave them all in the family way
With the hell of a doctor's bill to pay.

Today relations are less vexatious, but the restrictions on socialising remain – and so do the infringements.

The intimate economic and social connections between the Academy and surrounding area have gradually diminished as Sandhurst has withdrawn behind its gates. The closing of the Academy to public access in the 1970s was the most obvious sign of this change; no longer can locals cut through Academy grounds after a night's reverie in Camberley. Equally, the distance between town and gown is indicative of socio-economic change. Local towns are no longer dependent on the Academy in a manner once comparable to Oxbridge Colleges and their localities. The growth of industry, commerce and influence of London have all eroded Sandhurst's economic pre-eminence, and with it the

links between the civilian and military worlds. Serving and former officers no longer feature in local social life as did figures such as Captain Reginald Cheeseman who ran a livery shop outside the York Town gate serving the Academy's needs (in the days when all Gentelmen Cadets were required to ride). He also served as Chairman of the Camberley and District Club for local gentlemen and businessmen (still situated off the London Road opposite the Academy) whose military members proved a vital source of whisky during wartime rationing. One of the earliest Presidents of the Camberley Working Man's Club was a retired Colonel – no doubt out of that earnest Victorian concern for the moral rectitude of the working man. In the 1960s Major General A.L.F. 'Alf' Snelling, Field Marshal Slim's chief logistician with 14th Army in Burma during 1943–45, resided at Tamia Ridge just above the Staff College. The trend of serving and retired officers settling near the Academy has died out in recent decades, and in conjunction with economic changes, the result has been an end to the once intimate links between the local community and Academy. Even so, it still remains the case, as a Victorian historian commented: 'The parish of Sandhurst is chiefly notable as containing the Royal Military College', now RMAS.

LIFE ON THE PATCH

Chapel Square and Tea Caddy Row were built for officer and academic staff in 1810 and 1812. Other ranks married quarters were limited to the rooms in the basement of what is now Old College or if you were lucky enough to be a gatekeeper, you could cram the family into the small cottages at the entrance gates. Families lived in the basement rooms of Old College until the 1920s. A Mrs Newman and the two Misses McLaughlin, who were in charge of linen, were the last persons to occupy one of the original 'married quarters' in the basement until the McLaughlins retired in 1925 and Mrs Newman left her quarters in 1926–27.

A number of married quarters for other ranks were built in the 1870s, and in 1886 fifteen double detached cottages each holding two families were built in Church Lane below where the Academy Sergeant Major's house, built in 1910, now stands. These were demolished in the 1970s. A number of quarters were built in the 1920s, with the major expansion of other ranks married quarters in the late 1950s.

Annabel Elliott has lived at Sandhurst three times. She cried when she first saw her house in Epsom Close, 'One in a circle of 1960s terraced houses, completely uninteresting and functional with flat roofs.' But its situation saved the day. On the edge of Barossa Common, it was a perfect place for dogs and children. There were three sorts of house on that estate – the 'wedge-shaped' like Annabel Elliott's, the 'railway carriages' and the 'squash courts' so named because of the shape of the sitting room. 'The ceiling went right up to the roof ensuring all the heat went up there too.' Her second home was 15 Staff Quarters (now know as Slim Road), 'rather more grandly known as Hillwood House, a redbrick, four-bedroomed house in a large garden, edged thickly with rhododendron bushes, wonderful for hide-and-seek. It was the first time we had lived in

Far left: Enjoying the lawns in front of Old College.

Far right: The climax of the Music by Fire Festival, 2004.

Right: No. 1 Chapel Square.

Below: No. 7 Chapel Square.

a detached house, separate and hidden from any other house. The children were at boarding school, my husband was away and our dog was in quarantine. I felt I could die and no one would find me.' The feeling soon vanished. Like other families living on the patch, she had the support of a wide circle of friends. Her third house was 9 The Terrace, or Tea Caddy Row, 'a tall, very attractive, listed Georgian house shielded from the busy and dirty A30 to the east by tall trees and bushes, but not from its noise'. Its best point was the proximity of the lake where Annabel would 'watch with fascination as a diver in a wet suit would harvest the overstocks of water lilies or a pair of swans would set a wonderful example of parenthood'.

Margaret McQuoid also lived in Tea Caddy Row. 'They were lovely houses. Three rooms had open fireplaces and the houses were so big, we were allotted a part-time cleaner.' Soon after they moved in, a death in the family necessitated leaving their children briefly with the family at No. 1. On the McQuoids' return their mother asked them how they had enjoyed their stay and the daughter told her that, 'A lovely lady had come to read to her in the middle of the night. When I thanked their hostess and asked her to pass on my thanks to their nanny, I was told it was the resident ghost! Apparently there is still a resident ghost at No. 1.'

An earlier resident of No. 1 was Major (later Lieutenant General Sir) Douglas Brownrigg in 1921: 'This row of little Georgian houses originally consisted of thirteen pairs of semi-detached residences, but in the course of time each pair had been converted into one self-contained detached house. Such conversions always result in quaint insides and No. 1 was no exception. On each floor rooms ran into one another in an almost embarrassing way. Being the end house in the row we had the largest garden, but being the nearest to the Blackwater Gasworks we also got the strongest smell.'

Elizabeth Hill was surprised by how quiet Chapel Square was when she first moved in, but 'was warned by the stream of welcoming neighbours that this would change on the first day of the new term. It did. The new intake seemed to hold all their muster parades outside the house; they were not, but it seemed that way. The bark of the Colour Sergeants marching

their new charges to and from other places in the Academy soon became part of the atmosphere. After a couple of days we, the children and I, could recognise the individual instructors from their tone, loudness and their idiosyncrasies. It was about the same time that the dog stopped barking every time another platoon marched, shuffled or doubled past the house. We never imagined that we could get used to the early starts and the constant calling out of the time by the cadets, as they have to do in the first five weeks, but like the dog, we hardly noticed it until it stopped in the next recess.

'At times the maternal instinct makes me want to tell the cadets that it all gets better in a few short weeks, or to assist the blistered limpers as they struggle to catch up with their platoons. Just watching from the windows I can plot the progress of the drill, see the effect of the first exercise and finally, towards the end of term see the difference in the confidence of both staff and cadet as they realise they are almost a third of the way to their goal. It is rather a good place to live, but I wonder if our 260 neighbours think the same. Probably, but long after they have left, I suspect.'

Sandhurst has always been something of a wonderland for children. Apart from the all the advantages of space, trees and water where they could play, Mary Heathcote writes of 'holiday sporting activities where children were coached in tennis, cricket, canoeing and more exotic sports like fencing, if someone on the staff was expert in it.' Until relatively recently there was a thriving Sunday School and a Brownie pack. The Academy also had its own nursery school for three- to five-year-olds, the Oakgrove Play School, open to children who had a parent living or working in the RMAS or Staff College. It started in 1952 in a Nissen hut near the College Town Gate. The premises leaked and parents became used to coming to collect their children and finding the corridor and main room littered with buckets catching the drips from the roof. The Commandant, Major General Sir Philip Ward, arranged for the old Dental Centre to be refurbished and converted into new premises for the school, and the children moved in to their new building (behind the Hospital) in 1979. The school and Brownie pack closed in 1996, when Staff College moved.

chapter ten:

Chapels, Memorials and Memories

Revd Mike Parker, CF

*T*he command is given to 'fall out' and immediately hundreds *of officer cadets stream through the arches of the red-brick colossus that is the Royal Memorial Chapel. As you enter you are struck by the sheer volume of names which cover almost every inch of wall; it gives you a sense of the heritage which we have as officer cadets and the immense responsibility which comes with that.*
Officer Cadet Martin, 2004

Officer Cadet Martin captures the reaction that most cadets, staff and visitors to the Royal Memorial Chapel experience when first passing through the west doors and into the nave of this fine building. It is a reaction that spans the generations who have gone before. A fitting response to the physical manifestation of the Academy's motto – *Serve to Lead*. The grandeur of the interior is not universally replicated in the utilitarian red brick exterior, as observed by a gentleman cadet in 1938:

To many the chapel was an eyesore; to me it was rather lovely. It was more than a chapel; it was a memorial to the Sandhurst men who had died fighting. The interior was large and white and rhythmic. The roof was supported by square marble columns, and on each of these were tablets

recording the dead of a different regiment. Every fitting commemorated some past member of the college.
Anon, 1938, *Infantry Officer: A Personal Record*

From the beginning, chapel was a central theme in College life. In 1902 the future Lord Carnock wrote:

Church parade at the RMC, for instance, was in my day a very splendid sight. The battalion in scarlet, the Instructors, both Officers and NCOs, in the gorgeous panoply of old time full dress – Highland bonnets, bearskin caps, busbies, etc., scarlet and blue and gold tunics, the dark green and scarlet plume of the KRR, the shako of the HLI Lancers, Dragoons and Hussars, a mass of waving plumes, and a kaleidoscope of colour. Furthermore, the Staff College in India had not been started, and students from the Indian Army went to [the British Army Staff College] Camberley, and attended the parade in their handsome uniforms, which added a note of Oriental magnificence to the scene. No wonder church parade at the RMC attracted people from all over the country. The post-war soldier has no idea what the Army has lost in colour and picturesqueness by the adoption of drab khaki; useful no doubt, but certainly not ornamental.

Cadets marching to Church.

Sketch by Gentleman Cadet Arthur William Donnelly Harrington from his Sepia Sketches of Life at the Royal Military College Sandhurst, *1890–91.*

The Royal Memorial Chapel.

It may not be as colourful today, but it still has the capacity to move one's spirit. As to the service itself, cadets of every generation can be unforgiving and, in the past, pageantry was not enough to allow the padre to stray outside acceptable time bounds in his sermon:

Revd Murphy, the Chaplain, reads the service and preaches a sermon, for which the cadets give him exactly ten minutes; when this has expired and he is still preaching a clattering of bayonet scabbards on the pews remind him of the fact and he hastens to the end. One Saturday evening the cadets saw to their astonishment in Orders that there would be voluntary church the following Sunday. This was done at the Chaplain's suggestion as he wished to see how many cadets were of a religious disposition. However as only two cadets turned up this plan had to be abandoned and Church Parade has been compulsory ever since.

Gentleman Cadet Arthur William Donnelly Harrington, 1890–91, *Sepia Sketches of Life at the Royal Military College Sandhurst*

Below: The Royal Memorial Chapel main entrance.

Below right: Colours to Chapel Sunday. The eye is always drawn to the memorials of those who died fighting.

Cadets of the contemporary era get off relatively lightly in comparison to their forebears when it comes to compulsory chapel attendance. Academy Sunday marks the beginning of term, closely followed by Juniors to Chapel Sunday for those new to the Academy; Old College Sunday welcomes friends and relatives of the junior intake to a chapel service and the term closes with Colours to Chapel and the Commissioning Service of the senior division.

THE COLLEGE CHAPEL 1812–79

At the opening of the Royal Military College in 1812 the room off the main entrance became the College Chapel and continued in that function for the next sixty-seven years. One of the first purchases was for an organ and provision was made for an organist at £20 a year. An organ and choir loft was built; this was dismantled in the 1950s. A photo of the chapel in the 1860s shows a plain room; the apse window was not yet decorated with the stained-glass memorial windows to Gentleman Cadet George Ascough Booth, who died in 1868 while at RMC. His image appears in the lower-left corner of the window, wearing a scarlet jacket, depicted in his room with a view of the Grand Entrance of Old College through his window. The chapel walls were inset with memorials to officers and their families, and these were moved to the porches inside the two entrances into Christ Church when it was completed in 1879.

CHRIST CHURCH 1879–1922

The expansion of the College with the opening of the Staff College in 1862 and the completion of the two trident accommodation blocks in January 1863 and 1877 saw the need for a larger chapel, which was completed in 1879.

The Christ Church of 1879 was a long narrow building standing on a north–south axis in Chapel Square. It was a curious building, unlike what one would expect for a church in a military establishment. Colonel R.H. Williams, RE, responsible for the building, modelled it after a Romanesque church in Florence and the interior, with its patterned brickwork, was copied in the fashion of Siena Cathedral. In 1883 a fund was established to set up 'War Panels' inscribed with the names of graduates who had lost their lives on active service. Circular marble tablets commemorating past governors were also erected down each

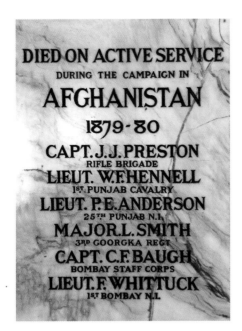

Memorial to the dead from an earlier Afghan campaign.

The carved wooden reredos in the Chapel of Remembrance, which hides the plaster frieze of the original altar.

Part of The Boer War Memorial.

wall of the chapel. By the time of the Boer War ten panels had been erected bearing the names of those who had died in the campaigns from 1855 to 1898, and it was hoped to fund the commemoration of earlier campaigns including the Peninsula and Waterloo campaigns.

The number of casualties during the Boer War frustrated that intention and the need to accommodate the 262 names of former cadets who died in that campaign led to the redesign of the chapel based on the recommendations of Mr G.F. Bodley, RA. This included a new altar, the oak reredos, the oak seats and desk in the chancel and the repainting of the figures in the dome above the altar. The words *Dulce et decorum est pro patria mori* were also inscribed into the arch above the altar. It was this text that formed the basis of the Chaplain's sermon on the last Sunday of the term in July 1914, shortly after many of those listening joined their regiments and went to war never to return.

THE ROYAL MEMORIAL CHAPEL, 1922 ONWARDS

An enlarged chapel was discussed after the completion of New College in 1913. This was given urgency by the size of the post-war intakes and the need to commemorate the 3,274 graduates who lost their lives during the First World War. The chapel enlargement programme to commemorate this loss of RMC graduates was devised in 1917 by a plan to double the size of the existing chapel by expanding it on an east–west axis. This was the design of Captain Arthur Campbell Martin, FRIBA, who was on the staff at RMC during the war. The names of the fallen were to be grouped into regiments on white marble panels with the regimental crests and badges emblazoned on the top. Public funds were not available, and the existing Memorial Fund became the basis of a national appeal to raise the estimated cost of £50,000. Every regiment responded to the appeal and presented its own panel. In 1919 the chapel was closed and handed over to the builders for reconstruction. One of the driving forces was the Chaplain, the Reverend H.W.

'Harry' Blackburne, who devoted the rest of his life to raising the funds to see his church completed.

The old chapel, now the Indian Army Memorial Room, which at that time was No. 3 Lecture Hall, was temporarily reconverted to a chapel and used for all services, except that permission was granted for the cadets to use St Michael's Church for Sunday morning service. The Archbishop of Canterbury consecrated the east end on 5 May 1921. The original Christ Church Chapel was then altered and the memorial panels installed: the Bishop of Oxford dedicated these on 5 November 1922. It was a further sixteen years before funding allowed the completion of the structure of the chapel as we see it today. However, the architect's dream of a central tower was never realised: only the plans in the RMAS Archive show his

One of the memorials to past Governors and Commandants.

intentions. The Archbishop of Canterbury consecrated it on 2 July 1937 in the presence of King George VI, Queen Elizabeth, Queen Mary and Princess Elizabeth, with representatives of every regiment and corps.

ONE NAME AMONG MANY WHO SERVED

Julian Royds Gribble was born in London on 5 January 1897. He entered Sandhurst in late 1914 and was commissioned into the Royal Warwickshire Regiment the following year. He won his Victoria Cross in France on 23 March 1918 during the German Spring offensive.

The citation says: 'The 10th Battalion had orders to hold on in face of heavy German attacks. On the 23rd the Germans broke through on a wide front but Captain Gribble and his Company would not yield. When last seen he was still fighting, surrounded by the enemy. By his courage and determination the enemy were unable to obtain mastery of the ridge for some hours and the rest of his Brigade was able to be withdrawn.'

Gribble was wounded and taken prisoner and held in a camp at Mainz. On the news of winning the Victoria Cross, his fellow prisoners celebrated by carrying him around the camp on their shoulders.

Sadly, he never saw his medal. Whilst waiting to be repatriated at the end of the war he caught pneumonia and died on 24 November 1918.

Above: Captain J.R. Gribble VC.

Right: Memorial to officers of the Royal Warwickshire Regiment who lost their lives in the Great War.

Below: Each pew is inscribed with a regimental or corps crest.

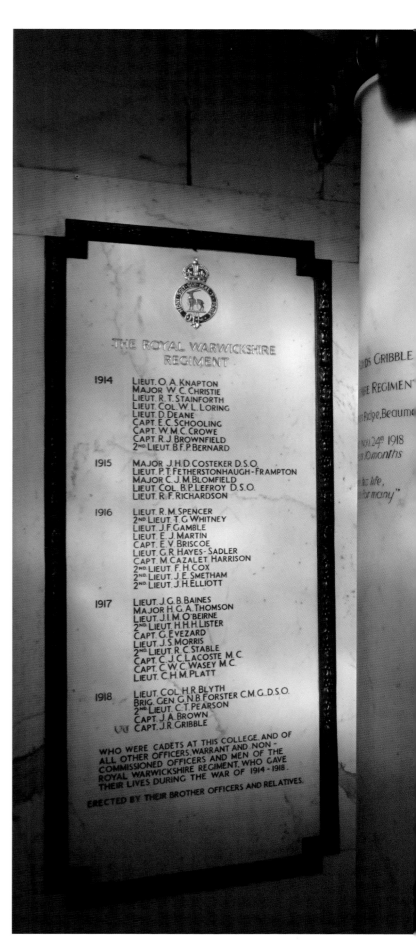

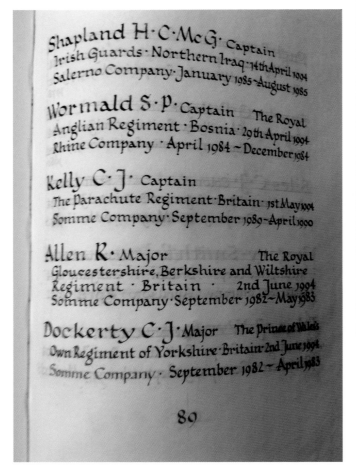

Far left: Page 89 of The Book of Remembrance graphically illustrates that the RMC is not just about remembering major conflicts.

Left: A page of the Roll of Honour is turned while the procession waits.

Captain Harry Shapland – Killed when the helicopter he was flying in was shot down by a US aircraft in a 'friendly fire' incident over Iraq.

Captain Stephen Wormald – Killed when his vehicle ran over a mine while on UN peacekeeping operations in Bosnia.

Captain Chris Kelly – Accidentally shot during a night shooting exercise in Kenya.

Major Richard Allen and *Major Chris Dockerty* killed in the Mull of Kintyre Chinook helicopter crash.

A reflective visit to the Royal Memorial Chapel is one of endless surprises: every artefact, every bench, every lamp, every window generates an act of commemoration to those who have died in service. There is the Woolwich Memorial with a roll of honour to those who died in the First World War. The Friends of the Chapel from the wider community are also recognised. It is a living memorial that reflects more than any other building at Sandhurst the integral links between RMAS, the Army and the nation it serves. It is rightly considered the spiritual home of the officer corps.

Memorial to Captain Andrew Griffiths.

THE SECOND WORLD WAR MEMORIALS

The Second World War memorials in the chapel commemorate all officers of the British Commonwealth who gave their lives in the Second World War regardless of where they were trained or the nature of their commission. The Roll of Honour of Officers of the Armies of the Commonwealth 1939–45 records the names of 19,781 officers. Roger Powell, who was tutor of bookbinding at the Royal College of Art, designed the binding. The roll is the work of Elizabeth Friedlander, one of the outstanding calligraphers of the period, who worked on it from 1951 to 1956 in a script based on the Humanistic writings of the Italian Renaissance. Oak pews bearing the crests or badges of corps and regiments of the British and Commonwealth Armies were commissioned to furnish the nave and to complete the seating in the chancel. A new organ was constructed over the original main doors above a screen and twin columns bearing the badges of the regiments of the former Indian Army designed by Sir Hugh Casson.

THE CHAPEL OF REMEMBRANCE

The original sanctuary of the 1879 chapel became the South Africa Chapel. On 13 October 1957 this was renamed the Chapel of Remembrance, containing the Book of Remembrance. This book contains the names of all officers of the Royal Military Academy who died on active service as well as the names of those officers who died while serving in the forces.

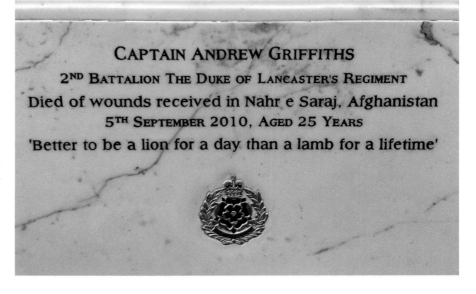

Not surprisingly, and in common with other similar institutions, the organisation and format of the chapel choir changed over the past century. Like many cathedrals and parish churches, maintaining an all-male treble line proved a tough task from the late 1960s. It became clear that women should be admitted to the choir, and this occurred in the late 1970s. The boys remained for a few years but slowly they disappeared from the choir stalls. The choir and the music of the chapel suffered a degree of neglect over many years and subsequently, on the appointment of the present writer, his mandate directed that the music must be improved and made worthy of the 'Cathedral of the Army'.

Changes were inevitable and from 2002, the choir underwent a radical restructuring with the introduction of a deputy system, almost unique outside of the cathedral-choir world, and a rolling programme of re-auditions. To date, the reorganisation of the choir has been a success and, as a result, the choir has greatly increased and expanded its repertoire. More significantly, the standard of singing and presentation has greatly improved. As well as being present at all the large services and Sunday morning services, the choir has performed at special services and concerts outside the Academy and has made a number of CD recordings. Many visitors ask about the composition of the choir, where they come from, and perhaps more pertinently, why the success. Firstly, the choir maintains the tradition of encouraging officer cadets to join their number (out of choice I might add) and this is most welcome. The remainder of the choir consists of military and non-military personnel. The success is due to an absolute commitment to excellence so familiar to the military community; it is a unique setting which brings out the very best from those who understand the privilege of contributing to chapel life.

'To sing is to pray twice.'

MUSIC IN THE CHAPELS
Peter Beaven, Organist and Director of Music

Music has always played an important part in the complex fabric of Sandhurst life. That military band music is and always has been an integral part of the Academy is without doubt. The spiritual dimension of Sandhurst life also finds expression and reinforcement through worship and sacred music. The marriage between ceremonial and sacred music is not a combination of opposing forces. The traditional nature of the Royal Memorial Chapel and its history blend easily with its multi-faceted and chameleon-like functions. It is a memorial chapel, a collegiate chapel as in any other seat of learning, and it is home to a worshipping community. As a consequence the music has a kaleidoscopic aspect too. To say that music within the chapel is rigidly traditional is untrue, for both traditional 'cathedral-style' music rubs shoulders happily with grand military and ceremonial music: and it would be true to say that the two complement one another. By the same token, as a collegiate chapel, officer cadets are encouraged to take part in and lead worship, either by the spoken word in scripture or prayer, or by singing. On other occasions the worship is less formal and it is true to say that, in musical terms at least, no one Sunday is exactly the same as another. As St Augustine put it, 'to sing is to pray twice', and many of the most profound spiritual statements are often both expressed and absorbed through the medium of music. This is, perhaps, why music has maintained a prominent part in chapel and Academy life.

THE CHOIR

From the early years of the first chapel right through to the present day, the maintenance of a robed choir has been a feature of life in the Academy. As with every ecclesiastical, musical and even perhaps military organisation, the RMA choir has waxed and waned throughout its history. For many years, as was common elsewhere, the choir consisted largely of boys and officer cadets.

THE ORGANS

The present organ at the chapel is the fifth instrument at the Academy. It marks a radical departure from its predecessors as it is an entirely digital instrument. Such a departure risks the reaction from certain purists that the instrument must be of inferior quality and tone to that which it replaces. A visit to the chapel will soon prove otherwise. The organ was installed in November 2010; a four-manual, custom-built digital instrument by Allen Organs. There are fifty-two speaker cabinets located in four areas of the chapel, one of which breathes continuity

from the pipe organ to its replacement. The majority reside in the main pipe organ case, carefully placed to ensure that none of the speaker cabinets are visible anywhere in the building. This has meant that the Rushworth and Dreaper instrument retains its place in the case designed by Sir Hugh Casson, which, with the carvings, badges and inscriptions beneath, stands as a memorial to the British Indian Army of the Second World War.

THE ORGANISTS

Amongst the notable holders of the title, the first organist who appears in the archives was a Mrs Timme, who served the College for fifty-seven years from 1815 to 1872. In the twentieth century her record was nearly surpassed by Mr Jesse Spyer who spanned both the First and Second World Wars from 1909 until 1964, a total of fifty-five years. Following the retirement of Dr Douglas Hopkins (1971–6), the additional post of sub-organist was created, enabling the Director of Music to marshal his forces more effectively.

CATHOLIC CHAPEL OF CHRIST THE KING

There was, at first, no Catholic Chapel within the Royal Military College, and it was not until 1948 that No. 2 Lecture Room in the upstairs East Wing of Old College was converted into the Catholic Chapel of Christ the King. This was on the initiative of the first Commandant, Major General F.R.G. Matthews, DSO, and under the direction of Colonel Guy Elwes. It was designed in a Regency style in keeping with its setting, and the temple-like canopy above the altar was adapted from the design of the Grand Entrance.

Before the opening of Christ the King, Roman Catholics attended Mass in Camberley. In 1875 the Reverend I.B. McKenna was appointed to officiate to Roman Catholics at Sandhurst on a fixed salary of £20 a year. After difficulties the RMC journal for 1875 relates:

The R.C. Chaplain wrote complaining that the Cadets, when they did come to service, invariably came late and thus disturbing very much his congregation. That the R.C. Cavalry soldiers had not been for some Sundays and that as to the R.C. employees, many of them soldiers, seldom ever came and he suggested that the Cadets should be marched to ensure punctuality, that the soldiers be allowed their overcoats so as to prevent any excuse as to rain and that employees should be marched pointing out that if these servants did not attend to their religious duties they would not attend to their temporal duties properly.

The cadets in turn complained that they were asked to pay one shilling for seating at the R.C. Church for attending Divine Service and some refused. The Chaplain stated that the bench rents were towards the support of the Church but they were not obliged to give it although he expected that they would as 'the sons of Gentlemen'. He also refused to admit that either himself or his church was in any way whatsoever under the Government in spite of being paid a small remuneration.

For forty-two years from 1906, when he arrived in Camberley, the Very Reverend Canon Patrick Twomey held the appointment of Officiating Chaplain to the Royal Military College. This continued through both world wars and then with

the Royal Military Academy in 1947. At first Mass was held in a temporary tin hut, but after the First World War Father Twomey was the driving force in fundraising for the construction of a new Roman Catholic church in Camberley, which was built on the London Road almost immediately opposite the Staff College Gate. Father Twomey was a character in the town and throughout his tenure of visits to the RMC did so on horseback. In 1924 the Church of St Tarcisius was consecrated and is named after the boy martyr who was adopted as patron saint by the Christian soldiers of the Roman Legions. It is a memorial to the officers and men who died in the First World War, and a tablet in the porch commemorates the role of the units who raised funds to build the church.

The opening of the Chapel of Christ the King in 1948 abruptly cut the association with St Tarcisius, and the completeness of the break rankled with the priest who had given so much to RMC and RMAS. Canon Twomey died in 1950 and is buried in the grounds of the church he founded.

The Chapel of Christ the King was redesigned and rebuilt in 2004–5. A dual brick and stone stairway replaced the tortuous iron fire escape, so dangerous in the wet. An amphitheatre of seats surrounding a carved stone altar has replaced the

Pews and altar in the redesigned Chapel of Christ The King.

The official war artist Stella Schmolle, who served with the ATS and Sandhurst during the Second World War, completed the stations of the Cross.

The ship's bell of HMS Sandhurst *stands in the Chapel.*

Regency design of the original chapel. The fourteen Stations of the Cross painted by the official war artist, Stella Schmolle, who was in the ATS and stationed at Sandhurst during the war, remain, as does the bronze cross that she executed which stands over the altar. A fifteenth Station, depicting the resurrection, has been added. The artist Luke Elwes is a nephew of Colonel Elwes and so continues the link with the original 1948 chapel. Stained glass in each window reflects Sandhurst life and the shared histories of RMC Sandhurst, RMA Woolwich, the Army Staff College and RMAS.

THE CEMETERY – 'BURYING GROUND'

The cemetery or 'Burying Ground' appears on the earliest maps of the Royal Military College. Once it was a quiet spot, set apart from the College by the high ground of Flagstaff Battery. It is still an oasis of calm among the bustle of cadets moving from place to place, overshadowed to the east by the swimming pool and gymnasium – only towards Old College is the view as it would have been. The cemetery has been enlarged a number of times and a stroll round the headstones gives one a history of both RMC and RMAS.

There is a plan of the graveyard and a list of names against the numbered plots by the main entrance, and as you pass through the gate you are among the former inhabitants of Tea Caddy Row – the professors and their families who followed the College from Marlow to Sandhurst when it opened and who laboured here for the rest of their lives. Plot 1 is William Steven, for thirty-five years Professor of Military Surveying and Drawing, who died on 30 April 1843. At plot 6 is Frederick Timme, for twenty-eight years Professor of German, who died on 10 January 1839; buried with him is an infant daughter and Eliza, his wife. It was Eliza who was Organist to the Royal Military College for fifty-seven years until she died at the age of eighty-five on 16 March 1872.

Plot 182 is Sergeant Major William Lendrim, VC, late Royal Engineers, late Royal Military and Staff Colleges, who served forty-six years in Her Majesty's Service, born 1 January 1830 and died 28 November 1891. His name is wrongly spelt on the

gravestone but the outline of his medals and the details of his service are set in the distinctive obelisk.

The earliest cadet graves are at the western end: the first plot being Gentleman Cadet George W. Rogers, who died on 30 March 1822 at the age of sixteen, and next to him, Gentleman Cadet W.C. Brookman (plot 19), who died on 1 September 1822 at the age of seventeen. Entries in the College register give no clue to the causes, only 'Died at half past 4 o'clock in the afternoon' in the case of Rogers.

Over in the right-hand corner as you look towards the swimming pool is the soldier servant area. Some died young but the older ones – mostly military pensioners – died of the effects of the grog. This was noted by Alf Hayes, a servant at RMC in 1875, who, commenting on the number of funerals of both officers and servants, blamed alcohol as the primary cause. 'There are a lot of Old Soldiers and it takes a lot of drink to wet their dry throats.'

Two notable interments are those of former Academy Sergeant Majors. At plot 426 is John Clifford Lord, Grenadier Guards, RSM 3rd Battalion The Parachute Regiment and Academy Sergeant Major 1948–63, who died 21 January 1968 aged fifty-nine. Near this at plot 418 is 'Bosom' Brand, Regimental Sergeant Major Arthur John Brand, MVO, MBE, Grenadier Guards, RSM of RMC and of RMAS 1937–48, who died 10 January 1975, aged seventy-eight.

The cemetery contains a number of Commonwealth War Graves Commission headstones, including three of the five officer cadets who died in the German bombing of D Wing of New Building on the evening of 29 January 1941: Officer Cadet T.W. Nutter, Coldstream Guards (plot 471); Officer Cadet G.N. Owen, Coldstream Guards (plot 472); and Officer Cadet J. Morrow, Irish Guards (plot 473). Behind these plots is Colonel W. Capper, CVO, Commandant of RMC 1907–10, who died on 15 January 1934 and whose lasting legacy is the Roll of Honour that he kept so assiduously during the First World War.

Every headstone has a story to tell and the cemetery provides a peaceful place to spend a few moments of reflection before returning to the bustle of Academy life.

Right: The graves of three of the cadets killed in the 1941 bombing.

Far right: Final resting place of Major General Philip Tower, Commandant 1967–72.

BRIDGING & PONTOONING

SURVEYING PARTY

VIEW of COL

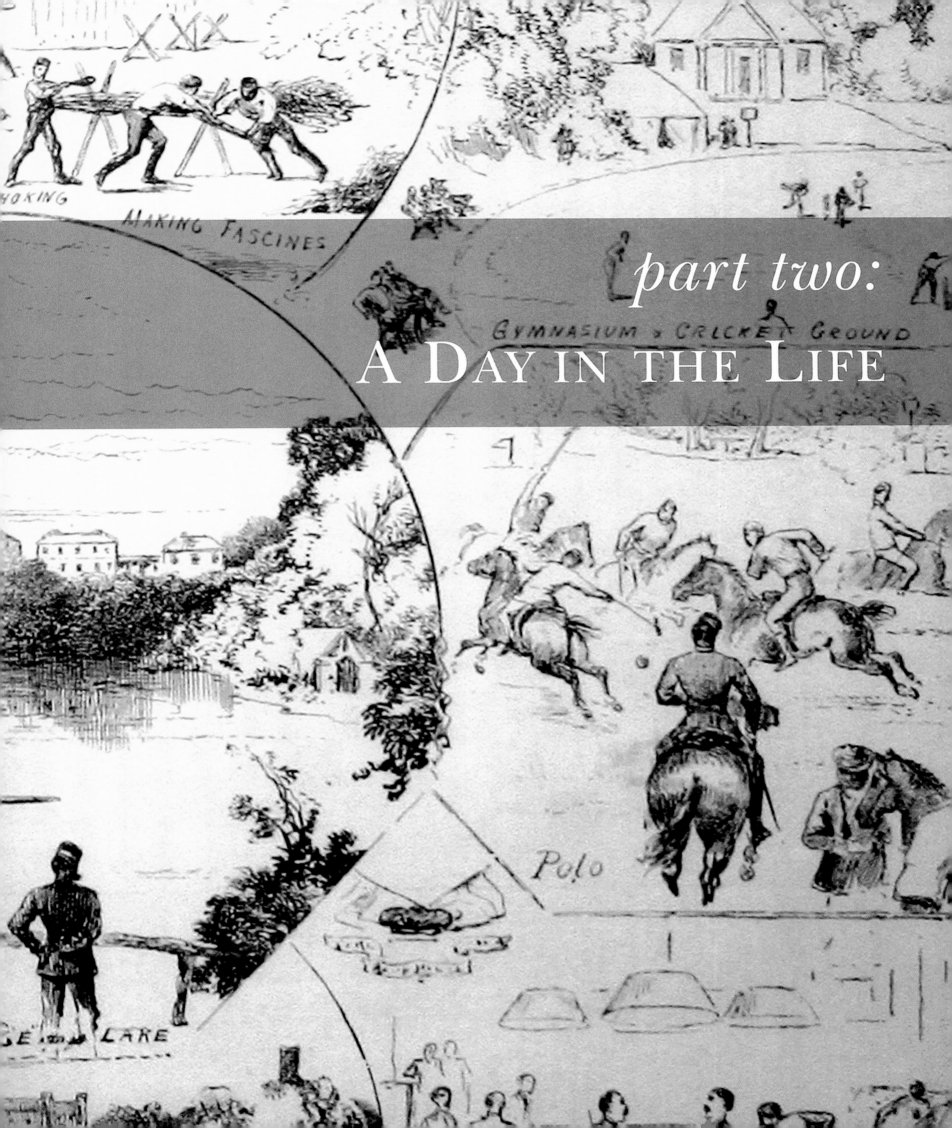

part two:

A Day in the Life

chapter eleven:

A Day in the Life

CAPTAIN RICHARD GRIMSDELL

*I*t's hard to describe the feeling of walking up the Old College steps on your first day at RMAS; an extraordinary mixture of apprehension, excitement and obliviousness. Most indescribable however, was the feeling that I was in the right place, on the right career path for me, and realising my potential, all before I was shouted at for daydreaming and told to do my first twenty press-ups of my Sandhurst journey.
Officer Cadet Rosie Wild, 2016

The course at the Royal Military Academy Sandhurst has gone through many combinations and permutations. These grounds and buildings have been home to generations of cadets whose training was shaped to suit the demands of their era. Looking back over the years it is interesting to see, in the words of those who trained here, how much has changed and how much has remained remarkably the same.

Final adjustments before Sovereign's Parade.

who laid claim to the loudest voice in the British Army. From that moment our feet hardly ever touched the ground.

Officer Cadet K. West, 2016

I remember queuing in the gorgeous sun surrounded by familiar faces from the Pre-Commissioning Course Briefing and being walked over to the accommodation. We threw our items into our rooms and quickly changed into our coveralls. I stood among the fellow 'orphans', a name given to those who had arrived at Sandhurst alone, as we watched everyone say goodbye to their loved ones. The remainder of the day became a blur of issued kit and basic drill movements. I do however remember still rushing around at 0130 to complete some resemblance of a 'week 1–5' bedroom whilst completing various other admin jobs delegated to by the Colour Sergeant, as I was duty cadet.

Officer Cadet Pywell, 2004

My memory of the first day is a six-foot-something Grenadier Guards Colour Sergeant, in immaculate Service Dress, saying: 'Come here … You're mine!'

Left: The First Day, *charcoal sketch by Joan Wanklyn, who was one of the most prolific artists to record Academy life in the 1970s and 1980s.*

The First Day

Officer Cadet E. Caddy, 2016

The shock of capture. I remember driving through the front gates, squeezed between my sister and ironing board, and I could feel my heart in my throat. The rest of the morning whizzed by in a blur of goodbye tears, nervous hellos, and then the yelling started. I was finally at Sandhurst; it had begun.

Officer Cadet Peter Harrington, Intake 2, 1947

Our days of idleness were over. As we got off the troop-carrying vehicle we were assailed by the most almighty bellowing any of us had ever encountered. It was Academy RSM, WO1 Brand,

On parade for the first time.

Orders in the field.

Shooting.

THE FIRST TERM

Officer Cadet B. Foster, 2016

'ON THE LINE!' echoes down the corridors at 0530 as everyone shuffles out in varied states of dress to sing the National Anthem or a pre-determined Disney classic. Everyone then rushes around the lines trying to polish everything in sight whilst mopping and hoovering – all in the mutual effort to get to breakfast before the 200 other cadets get there and form a mile-long queue. The day's activities vary greatly during the commissioning course but no other job would allow you to fire SA80s, endure CS gas, navigate on your own at night and learn how to communicate on radios all within one Monday-Sunday working week. With the day wrapped up you are in the lines with your platoon where you all chat until the early hours whilst ironing your kit for the second time and polishing your boots to mirror-like standards. After all this your twenty-hour working day is over and it's only four hours before you get to do it all again!

Gentleman Cadet John Masters, 1933, *Bugles and a Tiger*

Between parades we had five or ten minutes to change clothes and be on parade again, always spotless, puttees tightly tied. We learned the techniques of frantic hurry. We learned to stand still. Every morning at dawn they held a shaving parade, ostensibly to see whether we were properly dressed and shaved but in reality to order us to have another haircut. I had my hair cut three times in one week.

Gentleman Cadet William Magan, 1927, *Soldier of the Raj*

If you could stand the first six weeks at Sandhurst, you could stand anything. We were chased from morning till night. In particular, we were drilled unendingly into parade ground automatons, with unremitting square-bashing and arms drill. RSM Brittain was a genius. You couldn't like him, and he certainly didn't set out to be liked, but you had to admire his skill. His timing was always 100% perfect. He must have been one of the best drill sergeants the Army has ever had. When he had brought us up to standard, some of us would occasionally take an opportunity to watch the Guards drilling in London – the Changing of the Guard for instance. We thought they were rotten compared to us.

Officer Cadet Iain Powrie, 1967

Term one passed in a blur of drill, weapon training, PT and minor platoon tactics. In the early days the cadet government exercised considerable influence especially when it came to inspections. The daily routine began shortly after the alarm went off at 0630 and the corridors reverberated to the cry, 'Stand to your doors Juniors'. It was time for the first inspection of the day – a 'white glove' room inspection carried out by the JUO or cadet sergeant. This was the first occasion of the day on which one could lose one's name or be given an instant 'Show Parade', which would take place later in the day when the offending item would be re-inspected. Every nook and cranny was checked for dust, and weapons were checked to ensure that they were secured and that the working parts were stored in the small safe. I should point out that each cadet was responsible for his personal weapon throughout the term and it was a very serious offence to have an insecure weapon. If you survived that, the next challenge was Breakfast Roll Call when our personal turnout would be inspected, usually by the Platoon Sergeant.

Anon, Intake 1, 1947, 'First Impressions', RMAS Archive

For the first few days I think everyone lived in a confusion of conducted tours, kit issues, form-filling and such-like, and nothing stood out to mark the passage of time. But after numbers of tests and lectures by various departments, life began to assume a more ordered pattern. We began to know one another, to know who our particular instructors were, where the 'FGS' (Fancy Goods Store) was, and when it opened, and we even began to realise that our particular staff-sergeant was human, and that even the CSM had a sense of humour behind his imposing moustache! Life was never boring. Soon the drill test loomed on the horizon. The thought of a weekend pass brought about many a miracle. Of an evening the corridors upstairs rang with the noise of rifles being hit as practice feverishly occupied every spare moment. This hurdle finally cleared, a welter of tactics, administration, mathematics, science, modern studies and the rest closed about us. But now we are beginning to emerge again, looking to that as yet distant gleam – leave. As we emerge we find that the RMAS has left its mark on us already; its first impressions of traditions and work have changed us.

Officer Cadet S. Nicholls, 2015

My alarm goes off at 0515; my day starts on less than four hours sleep. Water parade, block jobs and breakfast all before 0645. Then it's smocks and webbing on for a morning at the range rifle shooting. A quick lunch followed by a six-mile tab out on the training area, with some hill sprints for a speedy turnaround before heading back to the classroom for a couple of hours of battle preparation lessons before dinner. Following dinner, it's admin, admin, admin until I decide that the punishment for not having something done is a reasonable swap for an extra hour of sleep!

Officer Cadet Sean Lumley, 1998

The 'shock treatment' inflicted on us in the first five weeks seemed to have been very cleverly conducted, but only in hindsight, however. As time progressed, the pseudo-prison term that we had all volunteered for began to ease a little, and not only that, it began to make sense! It seemed that the task of turning a bunch of young men and women into both soldiers and leaders of a reputable standard in just five weeks is just too ambitious, but somehow it was done. Taking a step back and seeing people master drill and the safe handling of a rifle in just over a month, as opposed to three months in an Army Training Regiment, along with all the accompanying leadership pressures and responsibilities, was most impressive. I would be lacking integrity if I did not admit that I have frequently questioned

myself as to why I am here and what the point of putting myself through all of this is, but then there have been other times either on the drill square or in full blues or just bumbling along to sport on a sunny afternoon when I have stopped and realised where I am and how long I have tried and worked to get here. It is at such times that I smile and walk off thinking 'I must be doing something right … '

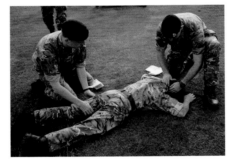

A Typical Day?

Officer Cadet H. Buckley, 2016

Sandhurst seems to be in its own little world, working on its own timeframe. The days flow from one to the next at 100 miles an hour, leaving you unable to remember when you've eaten or slept or what day of the week it is. Until the weekend: that's definitely the weekend.

Officer Cadet John Akehurst, 1948–49, *Generally Speaking*

One of the characteristics of the daily programme was that precious little time was allowed for the frequent changes of dress as we moved from drill to PT, or weapon training to classroom. Not only were fresh clothes required, they had to be clean and smart. Most graduates retain into their dotage the ability to dress quickly and accurately and to be suitably organised for their purpose.

Officer Cadet W. Thacker, 2016

Time at Sandhurst follows its own set of rules, which are hard to find elsewhere. Even when not on exercise, in the relative lull of camp, time moves too fast to catch – always rushing, trying to get one step ahead but never quite managing it. And yet somehow, at the end of the day, you can never remember exactly where the day went. If there is such a thing as a typical day it is best captured by this sense of panic, rush and brief relaxation at the idea of some rest before the cycle starts again.

Gentleman Cadet William Magan, 1927, *Soldier of the Raj*

Our programmes of work were so arranged that we had to change our clothes as often as possible between work periods. Thus drill would be followed by riding which would be followed by PT which would be followed my musketry which would be followed by a classroom lecture. For each we would have to be differently clad. That meant a dash to our rooms, and a very quick change – and we had to be immaculately turned out or we were 'idle' – and back on parade in time. Almost the worst of all offences was to be late for anything. I can still hear the clatter of boots as fifty Gentleman Cadets rushed up the stone steps, their rifles banging on the floor or against the walls in the general stampede.

MEMORIES OF A LIFE, 2016

My first day, standing in boiler suits and waving goodbye to my parents.

Not being able to master the about-turn.

Getting the giggles during room inspection and being given press-ups for it.

Exercise SELF RELIANCE and the coldest and most miserable I have been in my life.

Winning Exercise LONG REACH.

My first command appointment as Platoon Commander – and it all making sense.

Staying awake for fifty-six hours straight and falling asleep stood up.

The disappointment of coming fourth in the Log Race.

Being accepted into the Royal Artillery.

Bayonet training and screaming at my Colour Sergeant.

Feeling like you were in the middle of a fireball while being petrol bombed.

Officer Cadet S. Carew, 2015

Time and time again you get told there is no typical day at Sandhurst. There are indeed exceptional days where you might be in the respirator-testing facility, breathing in CS gas or running around a bayonet range screaming yourself hoarse. There are also ordinary days. An ordinary day might go like this. Breakfast is at 0615, before morning muster with swords. From there we might have a boot run where we run around Barossa training area, ploughing through muddy puddles. After this we have a quick change and we're onto the drill square to practise slow marching. After a rushed lunch we then might head to Faraday Hall, a relative paradise of tranquillity where

Waiting for the enemy.

we listen to sympathetic academics who treat us to extra-long coffee breaks. In the evening we may have been set a task such as writing a set of orders for the next day. A final iron of the kit and polish of the sword ready for inspection tomorrow and then it's finally off to bed.

Officer Cadet Clark, 2005

Everything is a rush! Eating, getting to classes, getting into different orders of dress. You get used to it but still feel you are holding your breath and racing until you get into bed … and then it all starts again. Sandhurst as an institution and a place is absolutely amazing but you lose sight of it whilst actually here. The glamour and kudos of the establishment only catches you for a fleeting moment now and again, or when you are telling your civilian friends about it. It is curious how quickly it has become everyday normality.

Officer Cadet A. Gill, 2016

Before coming to Sandhurst I had been told stories from previous cadets about how hectic your days can be, but I never truly appreciated it until I came here. Never in any other career will you wake up at 0500 for five weeks, drink a litre of water and sing the national anthem at the top of your lungs whilst your CSgt shouts 'LOUDER' in your face. Nonetheless, in no other career will you spend the morning marching back and forth across a historic parade square, followed by an afternoon crawling through a muddy field, firing a rifle and undertaking section attacks.

Officer Cadet G. Thompson, 2016

Juniors was the 'civvie to soldier' term where rucksacks become daysacks, clothes become rig, food becomes scoff, and you become a cretin, lizard or creature! Inters had me saying 'if I pretend to lie here dead, do you think they'll make me do it?' But you do do it, and then order a pizza at the end of it. Seniors had me relieved not to be doing rifle drill and, in amongst the mess dress fittings, looking to the future when I would have the opportunity to truly put into practice everything I had learned. One of the best pieces of advice I received was 'as sure as the sun will set, it will rise again. So just get on with it.' When times get tough I learned to smile or grimace, or take a photo so I could laugh at myself later!

chapter twelve:

The Overseas Connection

CAPTAIN JEREMY SATCHELL

The first overseas cadet was Count Alexander de Souza Holstein, the son of the Portuguese Ambassador, in 1828. In the nineteenth century only members of foreign royalty or nobility came to Sandhurst, young men such as the Duc d'Orléans, Prince Vajiravudh the Crown Prince and future King of Siam (now Thailand) and King Alphonso XII of Spain. When Prince Victor Albert Jay Duleep Singh, son of a maharajah, arrived in 1887 his trustees suggested (and paid for) a special room with 'an arm chair, piano, table, carpet and a bed wide enough to allow him to rest with comfort', as he was apparently broad-shouldered.

It was not until after the First World War that it became policy to encourage overseas cadets to compete for places, with six cadets arriving from India in 1919. Since that time there has been a steady flow from nearly a hundred countries around the world. Many attribute the lessons learned at Sandhurst to their future success, whether they went on to senior positions in the army, or became key players in government or business.

According to the late King Hussein of Jordan his father used to say, 'No man can rule a country without discipline. Nowhere in the world do they teach discipline as they do at Sandhurst.'

Right: The Crown Prince of Siam, 1898.

Below: King Abdullah II of Jordan and three of his brothers, all graduates of Sandhurst, as were two of his sisters.

FROM THE RMC RECORDS

20/8/1878 On the grounds of Public Policy Prince Alamayne of Abyssinia was to be admitted to the RMC without examination … He was given a very high character by the Headmaster of Rugby, the only weak point being 'unwillingness to work at distasteful subjects and an Oriental indifference to time'.

5/7/1879 A letter from Captain King to the Governor discloses that G.Cadet Prince Alamayne was not doing well due to his 'dreadful sensitiveness, his thin-skinnedness to petty teasing, his irregularity and his (natural) dislike to the English'. He was subsequently withdrawn from the Royal Military College at the request of his Guardian, the Chancellor of the Exchequer.

Thus inspired, three generations of the Jordanian royal family came to Sandhurst.

Some remember particular aspects of the training. Mohammad Ayub Khan, later President of Pakistan, found 'it was much harder and much tougher than any of us had suspected'. A cadet in 1926, he soon adjusted and 'began to thrive on the demanding Sandhurst life and even enjoyed the fifteen-mile run'. A Tanzanian cadet, Aidan Ngaraguza, found, 'the best thing was the instruction, especially leadership training in peace and war. We were taught by people with real experience who had been in all sorts of operations. However, the worst thing was the weather.'

The memories below are a small sample from former overseas cadets of different ages and from a variety of countries. They reveal not only lessons learned but the affection they still feel for Sandhurst, an affection reciprocated by many British cadets who, through them, have learned about other cultures and forged long-term international relationships.

THE RMC IN 1926

From the autobiography of General J.N. Chaudhuri:

I found myself in front of my Company Commander, Major the Lord Ailwyn, a slim, soft-spoken man. Obviously fatigued by the whole business on a warm summer afternoon, he barely looked at me. Languidly picking up a piece of paper he said, 'I see you spell your name C-H-A-U-D-H-U-R-I. I don't know how you pronounce it in India, but while you are here at the RMC you will be called Chawdree.' … Even the pronunciation of a name was decided upon by the authorities and not the individual! To my friends in the British Army, Chawdree I remain to this day.

It was interesting to find that the Indian community at the RMC, over a period of years, had evolved an unwritten code of conduct, a break from which would have meant ostracism. The rules were fairly simple. An Indian Gentleman Cadet was to tip his servant 5 shillings weekly, which was double the normal rate. At the cinema, the Indian GCs were to use the more expensive balcony seats and not the cheaper stalls. Visiting 'Ma Hart', the RMC's favourite pawn shop, was taboo. Attendance at the end of term ball, a very colourful affair, was forbidden unless one could bring an Indian girl to it. Finally, cutting in on or filching another Indian GC's girlfriend was the greatest crime of all. I suppose the first three rules were designed to show that Indians were not a poor race. Rule 4 made sense and Rule 5, looking at the shortage of girls who in those days would be seen out with Indians, was a safety device.

THE FIRST CEYLONESE CADETS

Officer Cadet A.J.B. Anghie, 1950, Sri Lanka

In January 1950 the first ten Ceylonese cadets entered Sandhurst in Intake 7. The influence of Sandhurst on the political history of the island in microcosm is reflected in the careers of these officers: two became generals who commanded the Army; two were charged with an attempted coup d'état. Two others became very senior civil servants on retiring from the army. One of the generals became Sri Lankan High Commissioner to Australia and then Chairman of the Ceylon Tobacco Company and another became High Commissioner to Canada. Four have emigrated due to political changes and pressures.

Since then, 123 officers have graduated from the RMAS, thirty-two reaching the rank of general officer; five commanded the army and five were appointed ambassadors or high commissioners. Sandhurst has indeed contributed to the public life of the nation as it has no doubt done in other emerging countries of the Commonwealth.

RECOLLECTIONS

Officer Cadet Amzi Hamid Bidin, 1968, Malaysia

The eighth day of January 1968 at seventeen years and eight months I saw snow for the very first time. I was told it does not snow in London. Deprived of a mac, the English kind not to be mistaken for the American invention, or wind-breaker of any kind, the four of us surely must have looked like a bunch of comedians, each of us involuntarily taking turns slipping and bumping on our behinds courtesy of leather soles on ice. We were soon to be gentleman cadets of the Royal Military Academy Sandhurst, arguably the best military academy in the world, so said the Commandant of the Royal Military College, Sungei Besi, Malaysia, from which we had all just come. He also told us that gentlemen only wear leather sole shoes. He did not mention the ice or compacted snow!

Well I'm glad to say we arrived at Sandhurst. Parade time, apart from the obvious attire, paper and pencil in jacket pocket was a must. You lose your name if you turn up for a parade without it. This habit remains to this day. Many years later, travelling in a car with a minister he asked me why I must always take notes. I quip Sandhurst taught me that. He said our memory was under-utilised. A decade later when he became the Deputy Prime Minister I was pleasantly surprised when he whipped out a notebook.

Come the time for our first defence position exercise. Well-concealed pyrotechnics would be let off from time to time simulating enemy shell rounds and we were expected to take cover in our trenches. Out of nowhere came this rather odd sound, a loud noise of objects hitting trees and metal. I put my helmet on and dived into my trench, weapon at the ready. I looked around to see the British cadets going about their activities nonchalantly. Well did I feel stupid, my first hail storm!

The Colour Sergeant overlooked that I was a Muslim and that pork was out of the question. My fellow British cadets were so worried that I would go hungry that they removed the sausages from the beans. Of course I would not eat the beans either. I was not complaining. After last light a British cadet crawled up to my position and asked for my backpack. He returned in a jiffy.

In the moonlight I read 'Mars'. All of them had surrendered their Mars bar! I was nearly two years younger that the British cadets. They must have taken it upon themselves to ensure that I did not go hungry and just expire in the cold. Thank you guys!

A CROWN PRINCE REMEMBERS

Officer Cadet Sheikh Mohamed bin Zayed al Nahran, 1956, Crown Prince of Abu Dhabi

During my time at the Royal Military Academy Sandhurst, I was struck by the significant differences that I experienced there. Not just the cultural differences between my own home country, the United Arab Emirates, but in particular the contrast between military service and civilian life. My experience at Sandhurst reinforced in my mind the concept of self-discipline and the significance of a military ethos, which promotes the achievement of the task over personal preferences and individual comfort. 'Serve to Lead' is a principle which holds true in all walks of life and countries.

The UK weather was and still is in stark contrast to that of the blue sky and hot sun of the UAE. I have fond memories of the UK in summer, but I am not sure that I wish to sleep overnight in a Sennybridge forestry block in winter again! Language differences created many challenges. Much is said in the English language, but even more is implied.

A LESSON IN LEADERSHIP

Officer Cadet Godfried (Fred) Twum-Achaempong, 1969, Ghana

At the Ghana Military Academy, there was always hot competition among the thirty-something cadets in training each year to be selected for the internationally acclaimed Royal Military Academy Sandhurst. We all knew that getting the opportunity to train at Sandhurst was not only an honour but it also meant getting a superior leadership training with huge prospects for accelerated career advancement. I was naturally delighted to be chosen as one of two candidates from my class of 1969 to train at Sandhurst.

*Above: President Museveni of Uganda
with his son, Muhoozi, 2000.*

Left: Command Task.

Just a few weeks after arriving at the Academy, I received my most practical lesson in true Sandhurst leadership, and my source was none other than the Commandant, Major General Tower. I still recall vividly that evening when he walked into my room unannounced and sat on my bed and began to chat with me. He asked me how I was adjusting to my new environment and he seemed genuinely interested in my welfare and general well-being. He even asked me about my family and friends back home. He also encouraged me to pursue my training with zeal and to enjoy my time at the Academy. Although his visit lasted barely ten minutes, it made a lasting impression on me and taught me a valuable lesson in leadership and in life: that a leader, regardless of his status, must be humble enough to draw close to the people he leads. He must show interest in their well-being, motivate them and, in so doing, win their respect, trust and confidence.

Thirty years later, I still find that the leadership skills I developed at Sandhurst continue to serve me very well in my post-military life. My instructors often challenged me to have an enquiring mind, to pay attention to details, always set realistic goals for myself and to aspire to greater heights.

Another valuable aspect of my Sandhurst experience was the opportunity to meet and exchange ideas with many high-calibre officer cadets from the UK and several foreign countries. These interactions helped me to improve my interpersonal communication skills and broadened my world view. Undoubtedly, Sandhurst leadership training gave me confidence in my abilities to succeed both in my military career and in life in general.

A Lesson in Values
Officer Cadet Narayan Singh Pun, 1970, Nepal
I was just a typical Nepalese village boy who dreamt of becoming a soldier in the British Gurkhas one day. Today I feel happy that I have achieved much more than that not only for myself and my family but for my society and my country and continue to serve my country and the people of Nepal. After my military career, I became successful in business and won a parliamentary election, becoming a senior cabinet minister

within three years of having joined politics. Now I have my own political party. My life has been very much influenced and guided by what I saw, experienced and learnt while in the UK, particularly at Sandhurst. I was taught at Sandhurst to 'Serve to Lead'. Since then this has been my philosophy of life whether I am engaged in business or politics. It is about doing things honestly and sincerely, always setting an example for others. It is about being loyal to friends, your society and your country. It is about integrity, truthfulness and unselfishness and being ethical. It is about caring for others, particularly those below you or in need of help. It is amazing how you can influence other people's lives by doing these things. It makes you feel good too! No matter what profession you choose these values will help you achieve success. Thank you, Sandhurst, for changing my life.

A Saudi Girl Comes to Sandhurst
Officer Cadet Al Sharifa Asma al Ghalib, 2002, Saudi Arabia
Even though it was not my intention to join the army I believe that the time spent at the RMAS helped in building the person that I am today. I learned how to keep calm during stressful situations and realised that anything is possible if you work hard enough to achieve it, giving it 110%. These are valuable lessons that are useful for everyday life. I come from a conservative community in Saudi Arabia, where women's roles in leadership are very limited. The RMAS gave me the chance to prove to myself and to my community that I can do it. Hopefully it will open the door for more Saudi women to take on leadership positions.

A Roller-Coaster
Officer Cadet Iskandar bin Abdullah, 2005, Singapore
I feel that Sandhurst is just like a roller- coaster ride. Different emotions keep twirling around me every day. It is the ride that makes me much stronger as a person and it is the ride that I am relishing thus far. Every overseas cadet will experience the same set of problems. The cold, the loneliness, the culture shock and the homesickness. I do not think that it will ever be an easy task to train here as an overseas cadet.

His Majesty King Abdullah I of Jordan inspecting RMAS, 24 August 1949.

Above: A St Cyr Cadet on the June 2005 Colours Parade.

Right: French liaison staff visit RMC in 1939.

New Skills

Officer Cadet Al-Saud, Saudi Arabia, 2016

Forty-four weeks ago I didn't have any military experience, and I had a very particular perspective towards work etiquette. It was very difficult for me to meet deadlines, be disciplined or punctual. However, having the privilege of attending Sandhurst, I have been able to acquire many skills. I learnt so many skills, from basic skills such as ironing kit properly to commanding a platoon in a very complex and tough environment. Also I've been in situations very tough both physically and mentally and done things I never thought I'd be able to do, but thanks to Sandhurst I've done it and accomplished a lot in forty-four weeks.

I have met some of the most outstanding people in my life, and have learnt an abundance of professional, social and leadership skills which will last me a lifetime. I have also grown as an individual, constantly being pushed to the limit and knowing I am capable of doing many things. Moreover, I have had the opportunity of being in situations and various environments, which realistically I never would have been had it not been for this year.

Also, I have broken many social boundaries by allowing myself to overcome many obstacles, mental as well as physical, which would have been deemed impossible to do beforehand. I am forever grateful for everything this academy has taught me, and I could not be more thankful for the all of my experiences and all of the powerful moments I have witnessed whilst at Sandhurst. These memories will be cherished and everlasting.

Officer Cadet Al Khalifa, Bahrain, 2016

When I first arrived at RMA Sandhurst, I had wrongly assumed that I was completely prepared for everything that it would throw at me, as I had trained and prepped extensively for it in Bahrain. Little did I know that it would require a level of resilience that I never knew I had.

A Shared Experience

Officer Cadets Cynthia Sunnu (Ghana) and Amged George Nasif Gerges (Egypt), 2016

Being an overseas cadet in Royal Military Academy, Sandhurst is a challenge. You have a lot to learn from language to the way of life, the weather, food and most of all military tactics. You meet people who will understand you and some who will misunderstand you. Friends you make here in Sandhurst lasts forever. In all, the key to success as an overseas cadet is to adapt, improvise and never stop learning. Exercises, drill and physical training are some of the times that you need to work most hard. In fact, everything in Sandhurst is hard work. If you are lazy, then know Sandhurst is not for you.

From an overseas perspective, we have acquired so much knowledge ranging from basic soldiering, reaction to stress, being a good leader, understanding situations before making decisions, tactics, combat estimate, personnel management and confidence. Sandhurst is not only about military; you also improve on your social, spiritual and mental life. We will be commissioning as officers from Royal Military Academy, Sandhurst, the best military academy in the world. In summary, as overseas cadets we have learnt to simply Serve to Lead.

Connections With Other Military Academies

Officer Cadet Iain Powrie, 1967

The trip to St Cyr was a highlight of Term 5, memorable for the excellent French hospitality, the fact that the French ration packs included a miniature of brandy and that French cadets were incapable of doing anything quietly.

French was the language of tactical instruction when the Senior Division opened at Marlow in 1799, and languages remained part of the curriculum from then on. After the First World War

MARGARET JONES

Margaret Jones, who died in December 2016 at the age of 90, served at Sandhurst for well over fifty years, giving support to hundreds of overseas officer cadets often acting as a surrogate aunt for those far from home. As one cadet described her – she was 'an institution within an institution'.

ten officers of the French Army joined the RMC staff in 1919 to teach French, but these posts were lost in the financial cuts of the 1920s. Sports teams exchanged visits between RMC and St Cyr in France in the late 1920s. In 1928 the cadets paraded the Sovereign's Banner at St Cyr, and in 1931 the St Cyr cadets presented a colour on behalf of their college.

In addition, a strong tradition has grown with the United States Military Academy, West Point, centred on the Sandhurst Cup, a 'march and shoot' competition that has grown into much more and which is fiercely competed for between the academies. Following its inauguration in 1992 RMAS was a frequent winner of the competition but, in recent years the opposition has become significantly stiffer with West Point winning the 2015 event.

The competition epitomises the spirit that each institution strives for and which General Eisenhower spoke of at an OCTU passing out parade at Sandhurst in April 1944 a few weeks before D-Day:

You young men have this war to win. It is small unit leadership that is going to win the ground battle and that battle must be won before that enemy of ours is finally crushed. It is up to you men to give your units – whether it is a tank crew, platoon, or becomes a company – leadership, every hour of the day, every day of the week. You must know every single one of your men. It is not enough that you are the best soldier in that unit, that you are the strongest, the toughest, the most durable, and the best equipped technically. You must be their leader, their father, their mentor even if you are half their age. You must understand their problems. You must keep them out of trouble. If they get in trouble, you must be the one to go to their rescue. The cultivation of human understanding between you and your men is the one art that you must yet master and you must master it quickly. Then you will be doing your duty and you will be worthy of the traditions of this great school and of your great country.

EXCHANGE OFFICERS

Continuing the line of Australian Regular Army Officers to have served at the Royal Military Academy Sandhurst has been a truly humbling experience. You cannot help but be drawn into the

prestige and history which is embodied in not only the physical grounds, but also the values, customs and traditions which are maintained. My time as an exchange instructor was spent fulfilling numerous roles, the highlight being a Pl Comd within CC161.

At all times I have been viewed as a fully integrated member of the permanent staff therefore the chance to serve alongside some of the very best British Officers was a learning experience, both for me and for them! The opportunity to train and lead extremely talented and impressive young Officer Cadets has proven to be the most rewarding time of my career to date and an experience I will treasure. Hopefully, I have been able to leave the Academy in a better place for my time served here and the tradition of exchanges will continue for many generations to come.

Top left: The West Point window in the Catholic Chapel of Christ the King.

US Exchange Officer at RMAS.

chapter thirteen:

Women at Sandhurst

LIEUTENANT COLONEL LUCY GILES

'The headlines ran variously from "Girls of the right stuff" in *The Sunday Times* and "Petticoat parade breaks 171–year tradition at Sandhurst" in the *Daily Telegraph*, through "Girls of Sandhurst march out and attract atten-shun!" in the *Daily Mail*, remembers Major Diana Langford. 'We'd featured on the newly established breakfast TV and on lunchtime and evening news bulletins on all channels. We'd appeared in TV programmes and newspapers from Germany as well as the Middle and Far East and we'd filled column inches by the score in local newspapers in all parts of the UK.' All this media hype was

to mark the novelty of Diana Langford's commissioning course as the first group of women to pass out from Sandhurst. Apart from the war years, when ATS training was based at Sandhurst, the now familiar sight of female cadets dates back only to 1984, when the WRAC College at Bagshot closed and moved to Sandhurst. Inevitably there were a few teething troubles. The first cadets, for instance, found they could not keep marching pace with the men because of restrictions imposed by the width of their skirts. A solution was found by reducing their stride from the regular 32 inches to between 27 and 28 inches. Within a few years it was clear that integration was the right way forward. In 1990 Major General Tim Toyne-Sewell, then Commandant, recalls deliberately placing a handsome but dim man next to a very pretty and competent woman at one of his breakfasts:

At that stage they were on separate courses and rarely met. He turned to her and asked what speed she did, obviously referring to her typing speed. She replied 'sixteen minutes', referring to the speed at which she covered the Battle Fitness Test. He looked more than a little abashed because he had no idea that the women's course was already an almost exact replica of his.

The Women's Standard Course ran from the mid 1980s to the early 1990s with the last female company passing out at RMAS in August 1992. In September 1992 the Regular Commissioning Course was introduced, which combined graduate and non-graduate officer cadets of both sexes into a single intake, the ladies forming one or two platoons within each intake. In January 2015 the first fully integrated platoons of men and women were formed as part of a revised Regular Commissioning Course; the cadets are accommodated together, train together, study together and are subject to the same physical development. Ladies account for between 12–15% of the Course, dependent on intake, and there are a range of female SNCOs, platoon commanders and company commanders as part of the permanent staff.

The Queen consort inspects the ATS, 1940.

Life before Sandhurst

Officer Cadet Pepita Simpson, 1972 and DS 1983–84

On 4 January 1972, I met Jenny and Julia on the train from Waterloo and, today, not one of us has a clue how we recognised each other as destined for the same place – that erstwhile Ladies Finishing School known as the WRAC College. It was a very civilised establishment where the highest standards of good grooming were instilled in us and the learning was focused on the management and administration of servicewomen. The minority male members of staff were respectably married mature gentlemen, who delivered instruction in Army organisation and map reading. Games were gentle and the practical exercises tested welfare, problem solving and orienteering prowess. No immaculately manicured fingernail was ever broken. However, although flower arranging was considered an essential skill, all was not a bed of roses. In fact, I did not sleep in my own bed for the first four months of training. It had to be 'barracked' for daily inspection and I very soon realised that it was easier to sleep on the highly polished floor of my room rather than disturb the immaculate presentation of my bunk, once it had been passed as being of an acceptable standard. Neither did I use the sink as the taps were stuffed with cotton wool for fear of a stray drop of water sullying its sparkling appearance.

One of our number was put on extra duties for being spotted on a Saturday wearing trousers, and on a visit to the Palace of Westminster we were obliged to wear hat and gloves without smart civilian suits. My father's recollection of our very exclusive commission ceremony (there were just eight UK students on my course) was that it 'was like witnessing your offspring joining a convent'. Not marriage to the Church – marriage to the Army!

In January 1983, I returned to the WRAC College as the instructor to take the first female platoon from that fiercely feminine environment down the road to the Royal Military Academy Sandhurst, where they were to adorn the very first Sovereign's Parade to include women. Some things had not changed. The cadets were a collection of fresh-faced, rising-twenty non-graduates. However, the syllabus they were about to face was definitely different from that I had survived eleven years earlier. An emphasis on military tactics and a rigorous regime of physical fitness training had replaced floral artistry. The young women in my platoon quickly adapted form being the stereotypical ladies who were 'finished' at the WRAC College to the challenge of competing on equal terms with men.

At first, the women were closeted in Old College, and on Sovereign's Parade they were kept on the sidelines and marched as a separate squad. Then, when the Sovereign herself attended the commissioning ceremony she enquired why 'her girls' were not parading. Her Majesty eschewed the excuse that their skirts restricted their pace to less than that of their male counterparts and observed it had never been a problem when she had been in the Army!

In subsequent platoons, lady student officers were two-third graduates mixed with school leavers and, having been exposed to the increasing demands of full assimilation, the end product was a more sophisticated, street-savvy young officer with a much clearer idea about what she wanted in terms of a military career.

The assault course, 1984.

Early Days

Officer Cadet D.E. Langford, 1984

The time I am describing may only be a little over thirty years ago – but it was a different age in virtually every respect. This was just a year after the Falklands conflict and Mrs Thatcher had returned to power on the back of the feelings of pride and patriotism engendered by events in the South Atlantic. At that time, women in the Armed Forces did not have combat roles and did nothing remotely associated with war-fighting operations. They did not go to sea or fly aircraft. Until our course, women didn't wear combat kit or wear boots and if they were lucky enough to go on exercise, they tended to be put up in a hotel rather than live 'in the field' with the men they were there to administer. The jobs they performed were pretty much restricted to teaching or administrative positions and they tended to be patronised by officers and other ranks alike and to be called 'dear' or by their Christian names instead of by their rank and surname, a courtesy which was universally applicable to everyone else in the Army.

Although the women's course was to be 'the same' as the men's, it wasn't – and couldn't be for a variety of reasons. Firstly, and for reasons I do not recall, we formed up for the first time three weeks after the men's courses we were to parallel. Immediately, therefore, we were put at a disadvantage and

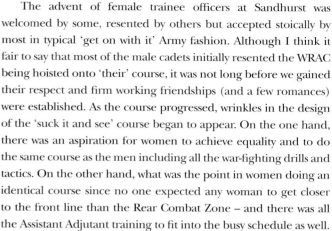

The advent of female trainee officers at Sandhurst was welcomed by some, resented by others but accepted stoically by most in typical 'get on with it' Army fashion. Although I think it fair to say that most of the male cadets initially resented the WRAC being hoisted onto 'their' course, it was not long before we gained their respect and firm working friendships (and a few romances) were established. As the course progressed, wrinkles in the design of the 'suck it and see' course began to appear. On the one hand, there was an aspiration for women to achieve equality and to do the same course as the men including all the war-fighting drills and tactics. On the other hand, what was the point in women doing an identical course since no one expected any woman to get closer to the front line than the Rear Combat Zone – and there was all the Assistant Adjutant training to fit into the busy schedule as well.

I have not described Exercise PASSING CLOUD, one of the most exhausting but exhilarating few days of my life. Nor have I mentioned the sheer joy of marching, even swaggering to the Academy Band playing 'our tune' – the 'St Louis Blues'. These memories and a hundred others jostle for my attention whenever I look back on my commissioning course; the most physically and mentally challenging six months of my life but also the most stimulating, enjoyable, unforgettable and fulfilling experience – and one I wouldn't have missed for the world. It was an honour and a privilege to have been a small part of it.

NOT FOR THE FAINT-HEARTED

Officer Cadet Ann Salter, 1999

For the first five weeks, we lived in an insular and peculiar time warp within which bubbled a constant swirl of furious activity. It was a remarkably androgynous experience: usually dressed in coveralls with gripped-back hair and scrubbed faces, our world was the platoon and the need to share every bit of pain and to pull your weight was intense. The bonding in the women's platoons happened very quickly and was almost stiflingly close. Physically it was more draining for the women: the assault course, apart from one wall, was exactly the same as the men's, the women carried the same equipment on exercise and pound for pound this was proportionately more. Also, fewer of the women had ever attempted anything similar before and so there was less corporate knowledge.

During the first five weeks we weren't really pitted directly against the male platoons so noticed them only to pass in the corridor as other asexual beings having similar peculiar experiences on the edge of our world. This changed partly, I think, when sports afternoons on Sundays allowed us a little more freedom. Quite a few couples paired up, some taking the liberty to make the most of a captive audience. This, however, did not affect the healthy rivalry with the male platoons, so any small victories were a pleasure, for example finishing digging our trenches before them on an exercise universally known as 'Worst Encounter' (instead of 'First'). Happily for us some of their tranches were located over a bedrock of granite.

Life at Sandhurst was ultimately a year of slapstick comedy strewn with blunders, which could have happened in no other

were destined to play 'catch-up'. Secondly, although we were to study the same syllabus and take exactly the same exams as the men, we also had to fit in the entire syllabus of the 'old' WRAC course as well. Thirdly, and in some ways, most significantly, the preparation of the female accommodation at the Academy was way behind. So although most of our training took place with the men at Sandhurst, we were housed and taught the WRAC elements of the course at the old WRAC College several miles away. As a result of the twenty-minute bus journey, we were always, inevitably and embarrassingly, late for everything. We frequently had to change from one order of dress to another on board the bus, providing a spectacle for the startled inhabitants of busy Camberley, and when there were last-minute changes to the course programme we were invariably stranded at the wrong site and in the wrong form of dress for the activity.

We congratulated ourselves if we made it to bed before 0130, and nights of just two to three hours' sleep were not uncommon. We survived by gorging on glucose tablets, by having at least half a dozen Mars bars concealed about our person wherever we went, and by carrying flasks of hot drinks or soup absolutely everywhere.

The Army was aware of the need to extend the role of women but no one really knew how far that could go in one of the most masculine and potentially dangerous of professions. Further, unlike many other traditionally male occupations where women played no role at all, the Army already had well-established roles for women: as unpaid hostesses of dinner parties, as welfare officers, home helps, social secretaries, function organisers, dog walkers and child carers and so on – and all taken for granted. So the challenge was not only to introduce women into the Army, it was also to change the perception that women were little more than decorative camp followers.

Right: Commandant's Stick Orderly.

Below: On patrol.

circumstances. Where else would you enthusiastically wade through a quagmire of cow mess and mud with an enormous log? Where else would you see a petite woman, wearing assault boots, doggy-paddling for her life whilst trying to keep hold of her rifle? Where else would you see women resembling upturned beetles trying to right themselves, having toppled over wearing oversized Bergens (large rucksacks)?

The Royal Military Academy is not an undertaking for the faint-hearted. Completing the course is something of which any woman can be justifiably proud.

Mixing it up

Captain Lucy Mason, 2007 and DS 2014–16

I experienced being part of a large all-female platoon when I commissioned. I then took charge of an all-female platoon seven years later followed by one of the first integrated platoons. There are many similarities and a few differences in commanding an all-female platoon and mixed platoon. Both types of platoons were strengthened by camaraderie and sense of purpose that was forged in the 'shared experience'; they underwent the same hardships and learned to work with the team they got. The integrated platoon was much bigger – a larger platoon with larger personalities! There was a mix of ability; you still had to lead the team over a 12-foot wall whether you were 6'5" or barely 5'. It definitely supported the development of positive leadership behaviours. The platoon also benefitted from a broader mix of cap badges, particularly the Infantry and RAC, which did not occur within the all-female platoon. Diversity becomes the strength. The ladies platoon paid more attention to detail and were generally

better in barracks; the laundry was definitely better organised for instance. Both were equally ambitious and worked hard. It is healthy to mix the platoons up; when I deployed as a Fire Support Team Commander it would take the company commanders I was working with a while to adjust to having a female on the command team, which may not have happened if this had been introduced earlier. It is my observation that the men enjoyed working alongside females within the platoon as they learnt to consider things from a different perspective. They could see women doing the same job and doing it just as well. Integration sets all newly commissioned officers off on the right foot as they go to Phase 2 training and ultimately lead men and women in the Field Army.

Dawn of a New Era

Lieutenant Colonel Lucy Giles, 1992 and New College Commander 2015

Twenty-three years after commissioning with the last female company – Edinburgh Company – in August 1992, it is with great pleasure that I see how far the Army and RMAS have come with regard to the preparation of its future officers. From the viewpoint of a college commander, it is refreshing to see that the changes are completely sensible (why wouldn't you train as you fight?) and also they ensure we maintain a diverse set of people within the platoon, the building block of officer training. The quality of male and female officer cadets remains high and their enthusiasm undiminished. The integrated platoon concept was considered with a healthy amount of trepidation, but the concerns were not realised as the men and women just got on with it; physical training is streamed according to ability,

Ex DYNAMIC VICTORY is over, giving a chance to wear their new berets.

ablutions are really not an issue and the most important by-product is a solid foundation of mutual respect between all.

On watching the first integrated platoons pass out in December 2015 with HRH Prince of Wales, it was very poignant; I had experienced my TA Commissioning with the WRAC including assessment at Bagshot in 1989, had been part of the last all-female company in 1992, had witnessed the last all-female platoon pass out in August 2015 and was now in the privileged position of ensuring the fitness to commission of all officer cadets under my charge as the Commander of New College; the first female College Commander in RMAS history. Very humbling indeed.

On being asked why she had come to Sandhurst, an officer cadet from a recent intake replied, 'I wanted a career that would be challenging, varied, not nine-to-five, physical and involved the outdoors. I couldn't think of any other career that provided such diversity. Above all I wanted to be a leader of men.'

This, I think, holds true for all of us, past, present and future. We are driven by duty and selfless commitment and ultimately the opportunity to Serve to Lead.

LAST WORDS

Staff Sergeant Alicia Jarman, Platoon Instructor, 2016

I actually think the males bring the best out of the females because they want to prove the point that they are just as good. At the same time, the lads don't like to be beaten by the girls so they raise their game too.

Officer Cadet Steph Hislop, 2016

When it comes to soldiering I think it's approached in a personal way and you apply your character, not your gender – this is especially true when it comes to leadership.

Lt Col Lucy Giles – First female College Commander at RMAS.

chapter fourteen:

Drill

CAPTAIN JAMES HOWLIN

Officer Cadet Al-Kharusi, 2016

In the last week of an intense intermediate term, we were doing drill practice for Sovereign's Parade. The temperature was 14 degrees and many cadets appeared to faint on parade because of the apparent heat. I was thinking, what on earth would they do if they had drill in Oman with temperatures of 48 degrees?! They would definitely melt!

Officer Cadet P.W. Hannah, 1992
'Memoirs of a Gentleman Officer Cadet'

'Drill … 1a, to instruct and exercise by repeating. 1b, to train or exercise in military drill. 2, to bore.'

One can only guess at the huge potential for carnage that must have existed when foot drill was employed for its original purpose. If a group of thirty reasonably coordinated and supposedly educated officer cadets can so completely render as unrecognisable the most basic drill moments, God only knows

what would happen if the 92nd of Foot wanted to execute a 'right form from halt in three ranks with a half twist and double somersault' in order to engage the enemy.

Officer Cadet Balfour, 2016

There is a very unique sense of pride that one feels when smartly completing an 'advance in review order' on Old College Parade Square, in an apocalyptic rain storm, with the twenty-eight brand new friends that you have been through countless sleepless nights with. Until, of course, the Colour Sergeant notices that Officer Cadet Jones's face is wet and he erupts in an enormous cacophony of thunderous expletives that make you wish for a spontaneous localised sinkhole, and you have to start all over again. For me, drill is a cornerstone of instilling a sense of discipline, respect, attention to detail and teamwork in a group of civilian strangers, that starts them down the road to Commissioned Officers.

Gentleman Cadet William Magan, 1927, *Soldier of the Raj*

Up and dressed, we would assemble on the company steps facing the parade ground, on which RSM Brittain would be standing with the Colour Sergeant hovering somewhere about. Brittain called out the right marker and placed him, and then yelled at us: 'No. 4 Company juniors, get fell in!' We would rush clattering down the steps in our nailed boots, almost certainly to be halted by a roar of 'Get fell out again. 'Orrible, get a move on!' Back we would go up the steps, and then Brittain again: 'Now! I want to see you move! Wait for it! Now!' Then a further scream: 'Get fell in!' Somebody always caught it. 'Colour Sarn: Mr Y idle. Take his name.' We were always addressed as 'Mister' by the NCO instructors, which in no way softened the strafing we got. (We had a peer of the realm in our Company. He was 'Mister' as well – 'Mr Lord X'.) For our part, we addressed the NCO instructors as 'Staff', though this didn't apply to the most senior NCO, the Regimental Sergeant Major. He addressed us

on parade and said: 'I call you "Sir". You call me "Sir". The only difference is that you mean it and I don't'.

Officer Cadet P. Hartigan, 1964

It was a sunny Saturday morning and the whole Academy was formed up on Old College Square for the normal Adjutant's parade, Old College on the right, then New, with Victory College on the left of the line. Being a large O/Cdt I was on the right of New College in the second rank: four paces to my right was the left hand file of Old College. Prior to the arrival of the Adjutant, the Academy Sergeant Major gave the order: 'The parade will fix bayonet … Fix!' Now I'm sure you have seen this fairly simple manoeuvre involving reaching behind with your right hand whilst praying that you remembered to place the bayonet in its scabbard before going on parade. Having located it, you invert it and withdraw it so that it sits between the thumb and index finger. On the command 'Fix' the right hand comes around to the front where it is married up with the end of the rifle barrel and the bayonet clicked into place. It should be noted that throughout this process it is important that you don't look down (if you do you will 'lose your name' and be charged with the curious offence of being 'idle'). So you are never entirely confident that the bayonet has locked into the lugs on the barrel. The final command is 'Shun' and you cut your right hand away to your side.

Accidents happen, and on this day there was a lonely solitary tinkle, indicating that a bayonet had not been properly 'fixed' and had left the rifle for the gravel of the square. It was just the one bayonet but the noise was heard by all 1,100 or so of us cadets and it was certainly not missed by any of the instructors. A 'hanging offence' had occurred.

There was a pause (possibly to allow the enormity of the crime to register). Visions of a new H.R. Bateman cartoon came to the minds of many, possibly entitled 'The Officer Cadet who dropped his bayonet at Sandhurst'. The awful silence was broken by the sound of a pair of boots marching in my direction. I should point out here that although I was uncomfortable at the attention directed towards my little bit of space, I was not suicidal. I was fairly confident that it was not my bayonet that had fallen (I couldn't check because of the 'not looking down' rule); also I was sure that the marching boots were not those of my College RSM (RSM Tommy Taylor, Grenadier Guards) but belonged to Old College RSM Victor Sullivan of the Irish Guards. He was heading purposefully towards the (Old College) O/Cdt standing four paces to my right – a good mate of mine named Dick Simmonds.

The boots crashed to a halt and that fearsome brogue was heard: 'Mr Simmonds, Sir, there's a fecking eejit at the end of this pace stick.' The reply from Dick was both instant and stunning: 'Not at this end, Sir.' RSM Sullivan was taken aback

– for all of two nano-seconds. We, his neighbours, now hugely relieved that we were not the centres of attention – did not know whether to laugh or cry. The Academy Sergeant Major, Mr Phillips, called out: 'Is everything all right over there Mr Sullivan?' 'It is, Sir', he replied and then muttered to Dick, 'If I do nothing else Sir, I'll fecking have you for that!'

Officer Cadet Styles, 2004
I remember a Saturday morning – introduction to rifle drill. We were programmed to have a standard two-hour period, however, with two hours of College disposal after; the session ran for four-and-a-half hours. It was the hardest period of my life and all I wanted to do was quit. In fact, I spent most of the time ignoring the rantings of the Colour Sergeant and mentally drafting my letter of resignation.

Officer Cadet Peter Harrington, 1947
A great deal of time was spent in 'square bashing'. We paraded as a company under CSM Ritchie, who had a number of pet sayings. He worked with a sergeant, a 'wooden top', who would note any misdemeanours. Without fail, after a few minutes, Ritchie would bark out 'Mr Harrington idle', this being the all-embracing sin. This happened one day as usual, and the 'wooden top' was about to scribe when he noticed my absence. 'Mr Harrington's not here sir', he said. 'I don't care where he is', said Ritchie, 'I know he is idle!' With fifteen hundred cadets in the Academy it could take a long time getting on parade and the various Sergeant-Majors would quip with one another *sotto voce*, to keep our interest. In his rich Irish brogue, Ritchie would come out with, 'Stop looking around Mr Mostyn, don't worry about your brain, it won't get very far on its own.' His all-time favourite involved Chris Head. He would call out, 'Would you hold your head up Mr Head, would you hold it up, your head Mr Head, would you hold it up?'

Gentleman Cadet John Masters, 1933, *Bugles and a Tiger*
I had been at the Officers' Training Corps at Wellington and had reached the rank of sergeant. Wellington was a military-minded school, and we had prided ourselves on our drill. But this that they were expecting us to do at the RMC was quite different. The sergeant shouted the opening or introductory parts of each command in a loud but fairly clear voice; on the executive word his voice broke into a meaningless screech. At the screech we were supposed to react as though a bomb had gone off under us. *Crash*, we hauled the rifles up our sides, simultaneously bawling '*One!*'. Then we shouted, '*Two, three,*' in cadence, but stood motionless. '*One!*' we smashed the rifles into our left shoulders and smote the butts with the heels of our left hands. '*Two, three*' – motionless. '*One!*' The right hands cut away to the sides and the movement was completed. We were sweating like young bulls. The drill step increased from 120 to 150, 160, 170 paces a minute – anything, just as fast as our legs would carry us. Faster: The sergeants twinkled along beside us like demented sheepdogs, their pace sticks twirling, their mouths baying and yapping an endless stream of commands, threats and objurgations.

'Rightturnleftturnaboutturnleftturnforgodssakegetamoveont heresquadhaltleftturnaboutturnorderarmsslopearmsquickmar chhurryupforchrissakelef'righ'lef'righ' … ' The sweat streamed salt into my eyes and soaked through my flannel shirt into my new heavy serge tunic.

Gentleman Cadet Bernard Ferguson, 1930
The Trumpet in the Hall, 1930–1958

The drill I positively enjoyed. It was good to be one of a squad of 50, or a company of 150, or (when we had graduated to that honour) of the complete Battalion of 600, taking part in arms drill, or marching past in quick or slow time. I revelled with others in the music of the Military Band, playing such classic quick marches as 'Old Panama' or slow ones like 'The Colours'.

Officer Cadet Donner (Germany) Borneo Coy, 2016

Drill is an essential part of Sandhurst life and accompanies every Officer Cadet throughout the Commissioning Course. Apart from the daily marching around in Camp, there are some special drill events such as 'Passing off the Square' in Junior Term, the Drill Competition in the Intermediate Term or the Sovereign's Parades at the end of each term. The way to a good standard is a long and hard one, accompanied by lots of 'encouragement' from the Platoon Colour Sergeant to keep motivation high.

Officer Cadet Alderton, 1952

RSM J.C. Lord MBE: *'No 3 of the front rank of Inkerman Company. Get his name Sergeant Major!'* (The offending cadet had not cut his hand to his side fast enough.)
CSM of Inkerman Company: *'Got 'im Sir – Mr King Hussein.'*
RSM J.C. Lord: *'Mr King Hussein sir – you are an idle king, Sir – what are you?'*
King Hussein: *'I am an idle king. Sir!'*

Officer Cadet Drummond Moray, 2016

'Arms shoulder high and fully to the rear!' bellowed a striking 6'10" Coldstream Colour Sergeant as he marched us off in our infamous green overalls on day one. A truly fond and unforgettable memory that has stuck with me ever since Juniors. In fact, I didn't quite realise what I got myself into until I remembered I was joining the foot guards! Without drill at Sandhurst, I feel it wouldn't complete the excitement and anxiety of a life as an officer cadet at the prestigious academy. Indeed, a sense of immense pride and camaraderie is felt when one is ready to march onto a parade square, especially amongst friends.

Left: RMAS form up to parade on New College Square, 1961.

Below: The RMC cadet battalion parades with its colours in Le Marchant Square, 1883.

chapter fifteen:

Physical Training

MAJOR BOB WHITAKER

Right: PT in the gym in the 1950s.

Officer Cadet Roberts, 2015

What I remember from my first day is a profound sense of confusion and stress. I was a twenty-four-year-old man but I felt like it was my first day at school. I didn't enjoy it. I was very tired; however, it felt amazing to have started my training and I took comfort in seeing other worried faces around the lines.

Officer Cadet Smith, 2015

I had a constant fear of what was around the corner. You find yourself being never quite sure what is right and what is wrong. However, the situation you find yourself in leads to you bonding with those around you almost immediately. Although it feels like a high-pressure workplace, it soon pays off as a strong team grows out of it.

Officer Cadet Morley, 2015

On my first day, I remember lining up to sing the national anthem at 0530, worrying about getting into trouble for not knowing all of the verses and then marching around the Academy grounds, arms chafing in my uncomfortable green coveralls. However, I remember taking comfort in the fact that looking around, many of the others in the platoon were clearly feeling the same way.

Major A.F. Mockler-Ferryman,
Annals of Sandhurst

In 1825 a Swiss officer (Captain Clias) used to instruct the cadets twice a week in the rudiments of gymnastics and poles and ropes were fastened to the fir trees for the purpose. Tree climbing was also taught, but the whole instruction was considered a foreign craze, and, after a two-year trial, was abandoned, the reason given being that gymnastics tended to make the cadets 'too active and nimble, and not stiff enough for the ranks'!

Gentleman Cadet Bernard Ferguson, 1930,
The Trumpet in the Hall, 1930–1958

As for PT, that was hell too. We would fall in outside our company building in our pink-and-white-striped blazers, white trousers, vests and cravats, socks and shoes below, funny little round pill box hats on top, and blue shorts and towels tucked under our arms. Once in the gym, we had to change in the twinkling of an eye and fall in again in three squads and two ranks for fifty minutes of torture. The greatest joy of Sandhurst was when the squat little Warrant Officer in charge blew his whistle and we all froze in our places. He would then scream: 'Towels: GO!' This was the signal for us to strip mother-naked to scamper off to the showers – in and out, no time to linger or relax – dress again at Sandhurst pace, fall in and march back to the company; aching in every limb, but thanking the Almighty that PT was over for another forty-eight hours at least.

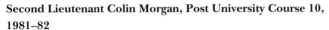

Second Lieutenant Colin Morgan, Post University Course 10, 1981–82

I remember having no time to change after PT, then having to be in Faraday Hall moments later. Fighting the weight of ten men sitting on my eyelids.

Officer Cadet Braithwaite, 2015

The obstacle course at Sandhurst inspires both fear and excitement. Fear, because of the looming threat of the inevitable 'beasting' – being made to run, jump, climb, crawl and fall until your body screams at you to stop and lie down, but still you do more. Excitement, because of the thrill of throwing your body over a high wall and plunging down the unseen side, because of your friends behind you working together to get you through, and the sense of relief and achievement after sliding down the final rope and jogging to the finish. The obstacle course epitomises the purpose of the Academy; physical exertion and ultimate excellence, facilitated by teamwork and leadership in the face of adversity (the adversity in this instance being the excitable PTI, the obstacles lying in the way of your success, and the platoon you are racing against).

The high wall requires teamwork, and over two terms we've become adept at flinging the individuals of our platoon over the wall to continue with the course. Following that, the crawl under barbed wire demands exertion and aggression from each individual, in order to drive themselves to the end and not hold up their team behind them. In only the first two obstacles it can be seen that it is necessary to work as a team at some points, and to push yourself as an individual at others in order for the entire team to succeed, thus representing the spirit and ethos of RMAS – *Serve to Lead.*

'up aloft!'

our confidence. Where there will always be individuals who are confident at height, the tasks at hand genuinely tested us all and helped some to overcome their fears. This unique situation enables cadets to directly support one another in an intimate fashion which leads to boosting confidence on a colossal scale. Whether it's the trainasium, high wires or zip line, all the challenges at RMAS force the cadet to face their fears and overcome them with confidence.

Top left: PT in the gym in the 1950s.

Top: Marching into PT in 1932.

Above left: The high wall requires teamwork.

Officer Cadet Mills, 2015

The commissioning course was introduced relatively early on to the confidence course element. A variety of height-related challenges placed us in an environment which tested and built

Officer Cadet Keith, 2015

I found the trainasium an immensely exciting activity. As an individual who has always been wary of heights, the trainasium was a great way to reassure my confidence and dispel any fears.

The obstacles are designed to test multiple techniques.

Right: The obstacle course makes best use of the Wish Stream.

Left: The gruelling three-mile log race – part of the inter-platoon competition.

The obstacles are challenging, especially when taken at speed and as you progress through the difficulty increases. Perhaps the most rewarding obstacle was the high ropes; these test both balance and composure. The sense of achievement after completing them was immense and this is true of the entire complex.

Officer Cadet John Gilmour, 1950

A compulsory test for the junior ranks was a boxing match of one round of three minutes' duration against an opponent from a different company. For some peculiar reason boxing matches were the occasion for spectators to dress up. They would take place after dinner in grand arena. Perhaps it is the savagery of the most brutish of sports that demands of its spectators the armour of plumage, tails or dinner jacket in the case of civilians and mess kit in the case of the officers. I was relieved that my bout would take place in the afternoon but the few hours before were nerve-wracking. We went hammer and tongs at each other without either of us being hurt and, like everybody, got a round of applause.

Officer Cadet Polly Noyce, 2015

Boxing within the Academy means waking up an hour before the rest of your platoon to get a few extra sessions of physical training in, be that circuits, cardio, drills or sparring. The majority of Officer Cadets are complete beginners and must learn the basics before being allowed to punch their fellow boxers. Some attend to improve fitness but most show the utmost commitment for a chance to represent their college on the Academy fight night, a night where the gym fills with all ranks to enjoy an evening of both skill and aggression and a few bruises.

Returning to Old College from PT in the 1920s. (Note how the wall looked before it was hit by a German parachute mine during the Second World War.)

Below left: Two evenly matched opponents.

Below: A good head for heights is a must.

chapter sixteen:

Dismounted Close Combat

MAJOR ELLIS HARVERSON

Gentleman Cadet Arnaud Foster, 1901

There was a rifle range at Sandhurst, but there was no obligation on the cadet to fire a single shot from rifle or revolver during the whole course of his instruction. Some cadets did go to the range when they could get time off, and I had a better opportunity than most as I was forbidden to ride for my first term. At the range was an excellent sergeant instructor, who taught us all he knew, both as regards mechanism and actual shooting, and this was, of course, of great value to us after joining our regiments. At the revolver range there was also an NCO who wished to be helpful, and he made me into quite a fair shot with the 'blunderbuss' then in vogue.

Below: A page from H.C. Potter's notebook on fortifications.

Below right: On the range in 1886.

Officer Cadet J. Landers, 2015

The DCC Wing trainers have an amazing ability to turn a relatively dull subject into something a bunch of sleep-deprived zombies looked forward to.

Officer Cadet J.L. Tancrel, 1997

I am looking forward to becoming qualified to run a range because that is the first time your soldiers look closely at you as a commander. As I remember, you look at their mannerisms, style, their smartness, their authoritativeness and the big one (for some strange reason), the shape of their beret. This is not just about learning how to safely run a range but about forming impressions (and often first impressions) upon the platoon or company. So I will be concentrating on developing the way I project myself on the range here at Sandhurst.

Officer Cadet A-M. Nicholls, 2005

Nothing is more terrifying and incredible than your first live fire shoot down a street with another Officer Cadet you barely know and dropping three targets at once.

Officer Cadet Robinson, 2005

When carrying out the Annual Personal Weapons Test in the Intermediate Term I managed to pass with a high score and gain Marksman. Unfortunately, during New College Sunday,

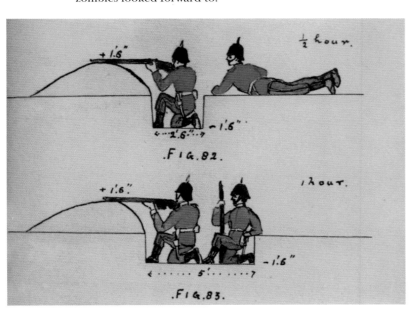

the New College Sergeant Major was announcing the recipients of the award and called out Mr Robinson rather than Miss Robinson. I didn't move at first, but when I did, seconds later, the whole crowd laughed, including all the other officer cadets, parents and staff. I was the only female in my intake to gain Marksman and I have never seen the New College Sergeant Major look so embarrassed. It was very funny and also the first time that I heard him apologise!

Officer Cadet J. Nice, 2015
The hardest physical day at Sandhurst was when we did bayonet fighting. At first feeling a bit ridiculous until you ran, crawled and screamed into a tunnel-visioned frenzy. Running, hill sprints, trying to be the first up to run the final part of the bayonet course. A true rite of passage for commissioning.

Officer Cadet D. Boyles, 2015
Exercise DYNAMIC VICTORY was a fantastic opportunity to push well beyond anything we had done on this course so far. The close quarter battle lane was a combination of a grenade range, bayonet range and automatic firing; and going over the top after the grenade had exploded was a huge rush.

Learning the firing drills.

Coaching on the 25m range.

Rifle Lesson 1 in the DCC Wing.

Right: The moving target range.

Below right: Tactical grenade throwing.

Below: Bayonet fighting assault course.

Bottom: Field firing exercise.

chapter seventeen:

Fitness, Sport and Adventure

Richard Anderson

About the year 1813 the Royal Military College at Sandhurst inaugurated modern athletic sports, but the example was not followed till about 1840, when Rugby School, Eton College, Shrewsbury Royal School and the Royal Military Academy, Woolwich, came to the front. Fifteen years later college meetings had become pretty general, both at Oxford and Cambridge.
'Athletic Sports', *Encyclopaedia Britannica,*
quoted in *RMC Record,* **Vol. 2, July 1913**

Sport and its importance waxed and waned at both the RMC and RMA. The fixture lists in the annals of Sandhurst show the importance of the annual engagements in all sports between the two. Today the revised Commissioning Course places pressure on the cadet's availability to play all the sports on offer. Sports periods that once featured on Monday afternoons have gone and now cadets occasionally enjoy Wednesday afternoon sports,

dependant on the demand of exercises, training and everything else that has to be shoehorned in. Saturday afternoon sports too are not the feature that they once were. Today's cadets would be unlikely to suffer the misery remembered by Gentleman Cadet Arthur Coke Burnell on losing a game in 1912:

'There has been no footer to speak of this week, except our Company was knocked out in the first round of the Company Cup which they ought to have won easily. They lost by 1 to 0. Horan kept goal, and was so miserable after the game that I was glad I was not playing, and Anderson was in my room that evening wanting to commit suicide'.
Gentleman Cadet Arthur Coke Burnell, 1912,
The Making of an Officer

THE CHANGING FACE OF SPORT

The 1960s, shortly before the end of the two-year Commissioning Course, was typical of that period in the history of Sandhurst. Monday, Wednesday and Saturday afternoons were then designated sports afternoons, an integral and compulsory part of the leadership and training process.

In the vicinity of Old and New Colleges, before the advent of Victory College, in winter there were two rugby, three grass hockey and three soccer pitches (one at the athletics stadium inside the running track), with a further occasional soccer and rugby pitch on the lawn in front of the Grand Entrance, Sovereign's Parade permitting. In addition, along the forest track beyond Hospital Hill towards Dawnay Road, Barossa Playing Fields boasted their own central pavilion and changing rooms serving yet another rugby pitch and three soccer pitches.

In summer, within the confines of the Academy were five grass cricket squares; the 1st XI, Round Ground (by the Library), two in front of New College and a fifth by Lake House. Barossa provided a sixth cricket pitch, together with five tarmac

Left: RMC tennis representatives in 1935.

tennis courts. Inside the Academy, too, were four red-shale tennis courts, two tarmac courts (next to the Guard Room) and seven grass courts (five near Oak Grove House and two on the approach to Government House). The dusty shale Oak Grove running track was available for athletics meetings.

Sport at this time was structured through company, college and Academy fixture lists, the culmination of the winter season being a hockey/soccer six-a-side and rugby sevens knock-out tournament.

Officer Cadet Mike Owen, Intake 20, 1957

I was in Intake 20 in Somme Company from January 1956 to December 1957. I was a very tall, desperately thin cadet and not at all taken by the idea of participating in Junior Boxing. The idea was to match cadet roughly by weight and boxing skill and then allow them to beat the daylights out of each other in three bouts of three three-minute rounds. I survived the first two bouts albeit losing both on points. In the third bout I was matched against a very short, very muscular Malayan cadet who proceeded to thrash me. I stayed on my feet until the final bell but had to be carried out of the ring. My nose was distinctly shorter with a positive tilt to the right, I had lost a tooth, my upper gums were badly split and swollen and one eye was virtually closed. I was told that the result was very good for my 'Charlie George', CG, Character Grading!

Sixty years on, the scene has been transformed. Closure of the WRAC College and ultimately integration of male and female courses in the Academy has also contributed to change: for example, with the appearance of mixed hockey teams and separate fixtures for female officer cadets.

The prestigious stadium soccer pitch has been replaced by an all-weather hockey pitch, grass tennis courts have been reduced to three, the four shale courts tarmacked and those on Barossa

abandoned. The entire Barossa complex is now a shell of its former glory, the pavilion and sports pitches have disappeared, though for a time a rusting, bent metal goal post remained a ghostly reminder of the bustling yesteryear. Sports facilities are now concentrated within the Academy perimeter. The grass hockey pitches alongside the 1st XI grass square have gone and the area in front of Old College is no longer used for soccer and rugby. The number of cricket pitches now total one hard composition strip on Round Ground and the grass 1st XI pitch. The New College pitches alternate between rugby and soccer in the winter with polo in the summer and there are further pitches near the athletics ground. The closure of the Staff College also resulted in the transfer of a further winter sports pitch to RMAS.

Elsewhere, there have been significant enhancements. The athletics track is now all-weather and with a covered stadium to replace the concrete terraces of yore and the three squash courts have been renovated. A martial arts centre has been added with facilities for both judo and boxing and the King Hamad Hall, with running machines, cycling trainers and weights on separate floors, has cleared the gymnasium of much of the clutter of fitness machines and associated paraphernalia. Sandhurst also boasts one of the very few Real Tennis courts in the UK and a clay pigeon range with ten stands. Finally, the three pavilions, Round Ground, Qaboos at the 1st XI ground and King Hussain at the athletics stadium, are all modern facilities providing dedicated changing rooms and en suite facilities for winter and summer sports.

The primeval wooden construction by the grass tennis courts in the shadow of Oak Grove House has given way to an attractive summer house and the adjacent straggling foliage has been removed. Behind those flowering shrubs, members of the constabulary assigned to guard Princess Anne, when she resided close by, were wont to snatch a surreptitious fix of nicotine, relying on white-clad players to sound the alarm should a visiting Inspector appear. The musty pavilion lacked any provision for the performance of natural functions and it is thus miraculous that the shrubs survived the constant assault of human acid rain.

The scale and variety of sporting activity in 1969–70 was indeed vast. That winter, the 1st XV's twenty-seven fixtures included games against the second teams of Oxford and Cambridge universities, the Fleet Air Arm, several corps, Hampshire and Surrey A sides, the traditional annual clashes with Dartmouth and Cranwell. The 2nd XV played nineteen fixtures. The soccer 1st XI completed twenty-eight games against a similar range of clubs, universities and institutions as well as a fixture with the FA Colts. The 2nd XI took on thirty-three opponents including many schools. Overall, three hockey teams played a total of forty-nine matches, among their opponents being the Civil Service and an Army XI. There were five boxing matches, twenty-four squash and seven badminton fixtures. The cross-country hare and hounds, gliding, cruising, mountaineering and exploration, basketball, fencing, ski, clay pigeon, shooting and motor sports clubs were all active. Officer cadets were also involved in meetings of the Staff College and RMA Drag Hunt and Sandhurst Beagles. The report of the Modern Pentathlon Club is particularly noteworthy: 'Mr R. Holmes, of War Studies, has managed to pass on something of his professionalism and expertise in handling weapons as well as prompting non-stop entertainment with his lively banter and snappy wit.' Any reader who experienced one of his hilarious, absorbing and authoritative lectures or informative TV series will readily identify the late distinguished military historian Professor Richard Holmes.

During the summer of 1970, the cricket 1st XI played eighteen games against corps sides, the MCC Young Professionals and Metropolitan Police, while the 2nd XI completed eleven

fixtures versus, among others, The Law Society, Staff College Owls and the local Cove CC. The highlight of the athletics season was the Western European Military Cadets Athletics Meetings (WEMCAM), involving Dutch, Belgian and French teams. (This rather uninspiring acronym was retired a few years later when the event was re-branded the Inter Military Academy Games Exercise.)

A team of us travelled to Brussels to stay at the Belgian Military Academy for IMAGE. I was the Sandhurst 200 metres champion and thought I was pretty swift. However, I finished almost three seconds behind an officer cadet from Luxembourg who had been a semi-finalist in the Montreal Olympics. It was quite a sobering experience.
Officer Cadet Vaughan Kent-Payne, 1978

Apart from the triangular occasion with Cranwell and Dartmouth, there were meetings with London AC, the Metropolitan Police and Oxford University as a second team took on Wellington and Lancing Colleges. The boat, dinghy sailing, off-shore sailing, trout fishing, sub-aqua, swimming, polo and saddle clubs all had a full programme.

During the mid-1970s, a dramatic reduction in the basic syllabus and introduction of several short courses created a veritable hiatus on the sports scene. Until some sort of

respect. By its close, only two of the team that commenced the season remained in the First XV. None the less, that XV fulfilled thirty (including the annual Dartmouth and Cranwell contests), the 2nd XV played nineteen fixtures. Similarly, the soccer first and second teams played a total of thirty-three matches, including traditional fixtures against Lloyds Bank, Corinthian Casuals, Chartered Surveyors, Lloyds Insurance and several schools. The Hockey 1st XI had twenty-three games. Although reduced, boxing, cross-country, badminton and squash fixtures also took place.

The summer season witnessed twenty-two cricket fixtures, the athletics track hosted a number of separate meetings between RMAS, Dartmouth and Cranwell, and civilian clubs. The Lawn Tennis Club played sixteen matches, the rowing, swimming and water polo, golf and dinghy sailing clubs were well supported.

In 2004 a report in *Wish Stream Journal* elaborated Major Starmer-Smith's dilemma almost twenty-five years previously: 'Surrounded by loaded marches, circuit training, combat fitness, swimming, assault courses and a general feeling of being run down, rugby could be considered a rather odd choice of sport to play voluntarily at Sandhurst.' The writer went on to complain that, due to exercise commitments, 'the 1st XV is rarely seen … it is often a team comprising only two intakes and, occasionally, only one.'

This *cri de coeur* demonstrates how the face of sport has changed at Sandhurst over the last fifty years. The number and quality of opposing sides have perforce been reduced with no guarantee in advance of RMAS player availability. Distinct college fixture lists have evaporated, although company sports continue to flourish. Perhaps the most striking acknowledgement of change is that choice is central to participation in the Academy rugby team, something reflected in all other sports. Nevertheless, sport in general remains an acknowledged component of leadership training as illustrated here:

equilibrium could be achieved, members of the directing staff, the academic staff and permanent staff were called upon to join officer cadets and junior officers attending short courses to complete fixture lists which, inevitably, in time, had to be severely pruned. Many long-standing opponents could no longer be accommodated.

In 1980, Major J.N.G. Starmer-Smith illustrated the new scenario. Warned that 'you will find it terribly frustrating running rugby at Sandhurst; you will never be able to field the same team twice', he admitted to a 'challenging' season in this

Above: Rowing at Henley in 1963.

Left: Rugby vs Dartmouth.

Right: 'The Cadets' Races; Royal Military College Sandhurst,' lithograph of a sketch by Lieutenant Petley, Drawing Master RMC, 1845–69.

Officer Cadet Alex Wilson, 2016

The day after the Sovereign's Parade, the RMAS Rugby Squad and coaching staff departed for New Zealand. The first two days were ideal, putting the squad into the correct frame of mind for two games that we knew would be highly competitive. After all, the final fortnight of term at RMAS does not feature a lot of time for much beyond foot drill and kit preparation!

In the first match our intense preparations paid off, earning us a solid victory against a youthful but physical NZ Army Academy side. The following day, nursing a host of aches, niggles and knocks, we visited the NZ Army Museum, a fascinating experience that brought home the reality of our employment, when we aren't enjoying the perks of military life. The powerful exhibitions, especially on joint operations such as those at Gallipoli and Crete highlighted the close bond of our two nations.

Such was our preparation for the showpiece game, that against the Officer Cadet School. While there were some attempts to keep us in the bar for a great length of time the night before, it had little effect on our performance as we showcased our talent. After another inspiring *haka*, the teams went to it. As with the previous match, RMAS came out of the blocks quickly, one of the benefits of such a tight schedule. With scrums uncontested, the tight five were able to roam about the field with impunity, with Officer Cadet Butler again putting in some good yardage and setting up Officer Cadet Raleigh for a try which he finished in no uncertain terms by running through the opposing fullback.

The RMAS tour to New Zealand proved a resounding success. We played very competitive matches, and won both convincingly. We were able to experience New Zealand's rich culture, and gained experiences that will stay with us: I doubt anyone will watch an All Black *haka* without remembering fondly our own welcome. We made friends from the NZ Army who I have no doubt we will meet again, either on courses or conducting operations. Finally, we saw and experienced how to run an exceptionally enjoyable international sports tour, and look forward to taking this experience to our Regiments, where we will hopefully be able to undertake our own in the future.

It is highly unlikely, however, that in 2016 an officer cadet would receive official permission to miss training, as one did in 1970, for 'a very pleasant day's shooting' at Barton Stacey, where the 'bag' consisted of twenty-five pheasants, a partridge and a woodcock between the eight guns.

ADVENTURE TRAINING AT RMAS
Colonel John Blashford-Snell

It was 1963 and I had just arrived at RMAS as an instructor when I was summonsed to the Commandant's office. 'You are to be Adventure Training Officer', General Mogg growled. 'Do you know what that entails?' 'No Sir', I replied. 'Well, I want you to get as many as possible of the officer cadets overseas on worthwhile projects for the benefit of their character and the least possible detriment to the Empire.'

with other tasks and in one year, twenty-seven teams set out to improve their self-reliance and leadership skills while carrying out non-military objectives. Soon the world map was filled with coloured pins.

Some expeditions were ambitious and His Imperial Majesty Haile Selassie, Emperor of Ethiopia, hosted several zoological quests. En route to Addis Ababa a group of cadets spent a few days in Aden. The resident brigadier decided it would be beneficial for them to see some real action and despatched the lot to the Radfan. A cadet was on sentry with the machine gun when some rebels decided to test the fort's defences. With a few well-aimed bursts he scattered the enemy. Later, I was confronted by an embarrassed brigade major and asked if I could persuade the cadet in question to forget the incident. He was a Kenyan! However, years later when he himself was a brigadier in the Kenyan Army he enjoyed relating the time he had driven of the Imperialist's enemies.

There were many challenging moments on the expeditions. A couple of intrepid specimen hunters mistakenly peppered an enormous warthog with Number 6 bird shot instead of much heavier shot and spent the night up a tree beneath which a very angry pig waited. One cadet attempting to bring home a couple of live cobra from India greatly upset a testy movements officer, and the carcass of a thirteen-foot Nile crocodile caused an RAF aircraft to make an emergency landing at Malta when the stench overcame the crew.

Iran's Valley of the Assassins and the Libyan Sahara were favourite archaeological sites, whilst Angel Falls in Venezuela provided some exciting rock clambering. Expeditioners had to give a presentation on their return. A couple of wags sent to study a rare grass *arena sterelis* in Greece, showed photographs of them cavorting on a beach with scantily clad girls. They

Walking back to Old College, I was still pondering my new appointment when the College Sergeant Major met me and asked what job I had been given. 'Very good for your career, if I may say so – you'll need an office – this way sir – I've just the place.' With that, he led me to the Old College boot room. 'Pay no attention to the mess, within a couple of hours it will be so clean you'll be happy to eat your lunch off the floor.' The College clerk had now appeared, millboard in hand. As I mentioned my humble furnishing requirements the Sergeant Major snapped out a list. 'Table six foot – officers for the use of, blankets grey … one, chairs desk officers … one, chairs folding flat, 'ard for cadets' use. All officers have bumf to file away so we better get you cabinet, filing, metal, grey … one. And what area will you be dealing with?' 'I seem to have a global brief', I answered. 'One world map' ordered the Sergeant Major. 'How about a 'phone?' I asked. There was a sharp intake of breath. 'Phone is difficult … but I will see what can be done.' So saying he bid me to return at 1400 hours when my office would be ready.

Indeed it was: tables, chairs, filing cabinet and on the wall, a large world map labelled 'Training Area'. Cadets soon began to appear at my door. Some admitted that their College Commander had recommended a spot of adventure training to improve their OQ (Officer Quality) rating. Others came for the fun and the chance to get as far away from Britain as possible during their six-week summer vacation.

The Natural History Museum was delighted by the prospect of cadets collecting butterflies, bugs, beetles and creepy crawlies and offered countless tasks. Kew Gardens came up

explained that *arena sterelis* was Latin for wild oats! Fortunately the Commandant had a sense of humour.

By 1966 General Mogg's ideas were a firm part of Sandhurst life and adopted by the three services. Today our adventure training is envied by armed forces worldwide. The boot room office expanded and, at the General's suggestion, a joint military/civilian charity was founded. Titled the Scientific Exploration Society, it went on to launch the youth character-development programmes, Operations Drake and Raleigh, that have given so many young people a great start in life. It all began at Sandhurst.

Colonel Blashford-Snell's reminiscences echo a bygone era when expeditions could safely travel to Iran, Libya and Venezuela, the slaughter of sundry wildlife was not frowned upon and the RAF still had bases in Aden and Malta. The long summer break meant that cadets could travel across the globe, often by sea, and still have time to conduct scientific research before returning for a spot of well-earned leave. The crowded programme of today's one-year course has cut the time available for exercise planning and preparation and the shorter breaks between terms limit the scope of expeditions.

Today's officer cadets attend an adventure-training course during the break following their Junior term. This gives them a qualification to use when planning subsequent expeditions at RMAS but, perhaps more importantly, they arrive at their units upon commissioning with the ability to conduct adventurous training with their soldiers. During the break following Intermediate term, the cadets embark on a one-week adventurous training expedition. The planning familiarises the cadets with the administration required as well as the process for gaining funding and sponsorship, invaluable skills when they are commissioned. Modern air travel has shrunk the globe meaning that many of today's expeditions are just as exotic as those of the 1960s – if a little kinder to the local wildlife! Nevertheless, as a selection of recent expedition reports show – the spirit of 'Blashers' is alive and well.

Officer Cadet Jones, 2016
The Valbona region, just like much of Albania, is a rich gem waiting to be unearthed. We were greeted upon our arrival at Tirana airport by balmy weather and swaying palm trees. The people were all helpful and friendly and we quickly learned that traffic laws in Albania were treated more like guidelines as we made our way across the country from the southern capital. The roads (and our rental cars) made the six-hour journey to Valbona a perilous one, with numerous memorials along the way marking locations where cars had plunged off the cliffs. We trekked up to gorgeous waterfalls and swam in pristine mountain lakes for a week. We also met numerous local personalities including Ardenis, a young local man who, along with his faithful pony, patrolled the Valbona mountains as a mountain rescue volunteer.

On our last day in Valbona we were reminded of the dangers present in our adventure training when a woman died following a fall off one of the cliff faces in the valley.

Back in Tirana, we met with members of the Albanian Army to go on a trek to the location of a World War II Halifax Bomber crash site. To get there, we had to first travel a couple hours in off-road vehicles and then trek a couple of hours to a very secluded mountain top. Here, on a slope down the side of the mountain, we saw the remarkably well-preserved crash site and spent a solemn moment among the debris.

In summary, this expedition enabled a group of officer cadets to travel to the mountainous heart of a country steeped in Ottoman, Communist and war-torn history. We learned much, not only physically from trekking, but also from the harsh realities of the dictatorship faced by a struggling Albanian populace in the 1980s, to the tactical difficulties of supplying guerrilla fighting during World War II that led to the Halifax crash that we visited. This in particular was a defining moment of the trip and we hope to locate relatives of those involved in the crash to pass on fragments of the plane itself, along with rocks from the mountain that claimed it.

Officer Cadet Aitken, 2016

The expedition saw us attempt to follow the 1958–59 SAS assault route through Oman's Jebel Akhdar mountains. We followed Lt Col Deane-Drummond's route as precisely as the terrain would allow. It's been close to sixty years since the assault route was walked and the footfall thereafter has been minimal. The battlefield is preserved in almost every detail. We located platoon forming-up points, mortar positions and shrapnel from RAF munitions, as well as enemy defensive positions and firing points. The detail was mesmerising, down to the '1958' dates printed on the brass casings and the discarded grenade pins used to clear the enemy cave systems. The entire assault was brought to life and we could visualise it with great satisfaction.

By the end of our expedition our troop of nine had grown to thirteen as we accrued faithful companions, all of whom had families and livelihoods far more important than our wellbeing. Nevertheless they went above and beyond to ensure our safety and enjoyment and we cannot thank them enough. Along the way we were introduced to our guides' families, shared their food, were taught about their custom, their land and their lives generally.

Officer Cadet Kemp, 2015

The trip started with promise as we escaped from Sandhurst quickly after Sovereign's Parade; this was crucial to our plan as we booked an early flight in order to arrive in Namibia early the next morning, allowing us a full day of administration and acclimatisation. The days of canoeing were fun as well as challenging and proved to be very memorable. Immersed in breathtaking scenery, the river was an oasis in the middle of a desert. Many of our party hit the river with no experience; the learning curve was steep but incredibly rewarding. Each day we managed some expeditions in the arid mountain terrain; the most interesting trek was into an abandoned fluoride mine atop Witch's Hat Mountain, to collect the rare green crystal. The crystals proved to be excellent entertainment after the cooking was done as they exploded in the fires creating showers of green sparks.

The day of safari in Etosha National Park was well worth the fifteen-hour drive from the Orange River via Windhoek. We saw an adolescent male lion metres from a rare black rhino and ticked off three of the big five! That evening, after we cooked a gigantic meal at the campsite, we saw sixteen elephants and nine rhinos at the watering hole.

Officer Cadet Bowen, 2015

Nine officer cadets from Rhine and Burma Companies departed for the Torres del Paine National Park in the Patagonian region of Chile. The route took us through all four seasons – sometimes in one day – and across a variety of terrain, from Andean desert to mountainous pass. We saw incredible glacial views as well as some of the local wildlife in the form of condors and a puma.

Patagonia proved a magnificent place to visit, visually, as well as practically, proving excellent ground upon which we could practice our skills and earn our Summer Mountain Foundation (SMF) qualification.

Officer Cadet Cooper, 2015

Nine officer cadets headed out to Lake Elsinore, California to do something that most of us had never tried before: skydiving. Five days isn't long to achieve your A licence, so from Day 1 there was a sense of urgency from everyone as we tried to get as many jumps in as possible.

One of the best things about learning to skydive is the post-jump video debrief. This involves laughing unashamedly at the ridiculous faces pulled by the terrified students as they fall at 130mph towards the ground. Officer Cadet Houston provided us all with the most entertainment over the whole of the trip; his first jump involved 6′ 4″ of dangerously violent kicking legs and flailing arms, while his facial expressions were priceless, most notably the inability to keep his tongue in his mouth as the wind rushed past his flapping cheeks.

To everyone's amazement, by Day 3 it was beginning to look like we would get everyone qualified. Achieving on average eight jumps a day we were able to get through each stage of the Advanced Free Fall course.

Officer Cadet Gould, 2015

Five cadets went on a scuba diving expedition to Hurghada, Egypt, during which they qualified as BSAC (British Sub-Aqua Club) Sports Divers. One of the highlights of our diving trip included getting to dive on an Egyptian minesweeper called the *El Mina*, which lay at 30m, our deepest dive. This was a good test of our skills as well as our mettle with the chance to swim within the hull and explore the corridors – an exhilarating but nerve-wracking experience, knowing that we had to work in a confined space over 100 feet down. Alongside this, we also got the chance to swim on a variety of reefs, allowing us to see a vast array of wildlife: turtles, stingrays, moray eels and the plethora of different fish species that inhabit the waters.

The Edward Bear Club
Officer Cadet Mike Lanyon, Intake 33, 1962–64

'Volunteers are sought' began the notice in January to advertise the Easter 1963 course. After a fitness test and a brief interview, some thirty hopefuls set out to No. 1 Parachute Training School run by the RAF at Weston-on-the-Green airfield.

Our first aircraft jump was to be from a Hastings aircraft – quite different from the silence of the balloon. There was some nervousness as we filed into the aircraft for a ten-minute flight to 800 feet. We stood and checked each other's equipment, comprising the back parachute and a reserve parachute on one's chest. The Dispatchers – one on each door – lined us up to wait for the pilot's light signal above the noisy, windy open doors. 'One green, two green GO! GO! GO!' Out into the slipstream was extraordinary as one rode down the airstream until the static line pulled out the chute. Then we were in two descending lines of troops as the ground approached – fast. We manoeuvred into a side landing position, bent the knees, hit the ground and rolled as trained to disperse the energy of the jump. Afterwards stand up, gather parachute and return to dispersal – there were no injuries but much adrenaline following!

Three more jumps in increasing wind speeds were made and the last was watched by President Mobutu and The Duke of Edinburgh (hosting the state visit). The wind was about twenty-five knots and we were restricted to twenty knots but were sent off anyway. As it was an important jump for the VIPs. We went up in an Argosy aircraft which was just coming into service. Most of us were OK but two of our number were blown off the airfield, narrowly missing a double-decker bus on the main road. The rest of us were spread far and wide across the airfield. The two blown off the airfield were charged with leaving the course without permission.

After ten days on the course, we were to be tested by jumping into Thetford Parachute Training Area to exercise with the French Military Academy at St Cyr. They flew over from France and we flew around the Wash to simulate a two-hour flight into Europe. Exercise LA MADELON was twenty-four hours of hard slog after a great entrance by air. The enemy was the RMAS Demonstration Company of Argyll and Sutherland Highlanders. No one told us who won but all enjoyed the Anglo–French experience.

The finale to Edward Bear was the jump into Hankley Common for dinner at a hotel called 'The Pride of the Valley'. Academy Sergeant Major 'Jackie' Lord jumped with us and he carried Edward Bear himself and launched it at 200 feet.

An Interview with Senior Under Officer Edward Bear
Richard Anderson

Having been the backbone of parachuting at Sandhurst for over twenty years I have now retired and reside in the Academy museum where I often meet old friends.

In September 1950 I was snatched from oblivion by Dick Worsley (later General Sir Richard) and two fellow officer cadets from intake VI on their way to RAF Abingdon to attend the first parachuting course for Sandhurst. I did my first jump inside the smock of one of the cadets and was passed around during the next week until I had ten jumps to my name! Those early jumps were firstly from a balloon and then a Beverley aircraft and we were amongst the first to jump from the door rather than a hole in the floor.

I had a real scare on my first balloon jump whilst tucked into one of the officer cadet's smock. Sergeant Card ordered him into the door of the basket and gave the instruction that on the command 'green light' he was to jump. The order came loud and clear but no reaction. 'Sir, step back, you have one more chance, do not get it wrong again'. I was very nervous at this stage! The order came again but still no reaction so the officer cadet was instructed to step back again, only to find that

we had fallen through a raised trapdoor and were gliding gently down to the ground. Sergeant Card shouted that nobody fails his courses!

I was fortunate to then be awarded my own Denison smock, a specially made parachute and given my own log book. From then on I attended every course and did my own descents. Unfortunately, my parachute was not always reliable and I did sustain a number of serious injuries over the years. In the early 1960s I was most grateful to Moss Bros of Camberley for carrying out some vital repairs to both myself and my equipment.

In the early days there was no such thing as an emergency parachute, so it was very nerve-racking. Also, being quite small and much lighter than the average office cadet, I would drift much further than the others, which necessitated an evening search to find me.

During Exercise TIPPERARY we would jump with the officer cadets from St Cyr and it was during one of these exercises that I was kidnapped and taken to France. I had to remain there for a whole year until I was recovered and returned to normal operational duty. I was kindly awarded the French Parachuting badge after my ordeal. Over the years I have jumped with many nations and been generously awarded their parachuting honours.

My Club awarded every cadet who completed the course the privilege of wearing a small badge of me parachuting on their uniform. This became known as the 'light bulb' for obvious reasons. Members also wore a tie with the same motif.

I have included some photographs which many of my friends have sent me of our parachuting over the years. Sadly, due to so many injuries, I was forced to retire in the early 1970s with over 2,000 jumps to my name and this coincided with the end of the RMAS parachuting courses. In my retirement I have again been 'restored' by Messrs Harrods of London and now, living at Sandhurst, enjoy meeting up with many friends who attend reunions at the Academy.

chapter eighteen:

Field Training and Exercises

LIEUTENANT COLONEL PAUL L'ESTRANGE

Being thrown in as the Platoon Commander for the public order phase on Exercise TEMPLER'S TRIUMPH was by far the most daunting of my appointments at RMAS. Yet after we had formed ranks, lowered visors and began to push the rioters back, it rapidly became the most exhilarating day of the course. Petrol bombs, projectiles and bags of aggression from the crowd; this was the kind of challenge I had joined the Army for.

Officer Cadet Benn, 2015

Field training and exercises today are light years away from RMAS's beginnings in 1947, when petrol rationing limited training to within easy reach of the issued bicycle.

In the nineteenth century there was little need for field camps as every drill period on Old College or Le Marchant Square practised the tactical drills of the day, the climax of which was the march past in slow and quick time on Inspection Day at the end of each term. The one aspect that equated to fieldwork was the study of fortification that was practised in the semi-permanent redoubts such as Fort Narrien and Fort Royal or by digging fieldworks where New College now stands.

Field exercises as recognised today evolved at the beginning of the twentieth century in response to the lessons of the Boer War,

and the First World War accelerated this trend. A disenchanted cadet of 1917 wrote of the days spent training on Hartford Bridge Flat on the road to Hartley Wintney: 'More Company training. All day affair. Advanced Guards etc. Absolute rot! What a loathsome hold the RMC is! No leave, dull work and ham sandwiches to eat. If I don't pass out I shall shoot myself. Miserere nobis.' (Anon, 'Diary From The Great War', RMAS Collection.) In the event, the cadet did pass out, did not shoot himself, and got his wish of being seconded to the Royal Flying Corps.

Today field training is the means by which cadets gain invaluable insights into the art of command, leadership and what the Academy terms officership. Field training covers the spectrum of possible operational scenarios from the basic skills demanded on Exercise SELF RELIANCE to the demands of Exercise DYNAMIC VICTORY, which tests cadets in an urban and rural environment as well as allowing them to act as the

Below left: Exercise LONG REACH in the snow.

Below: A demonstration for the Duke of Cambridge, Inspection Day, 1881.

insurgent and civilian population. These exercises allow cadets to gain practical experience in testing and demanding scenarios that play out depending what the cadet commander at the time does or does not do. Exhaustion and pressure are always present, but the challenges are evident.

Officer Cadet Beresford-Webb, 2015

When I was one of the exercising troops for the public order phase I was the Platoon Sergeant near the back. I still got set on fire numerous times and I was pelted with missiles including one that broke my visor and left it dangling from my helmet. As civilian population I broke the base line and was rewarded with a baton strike to the back of my hand breaking my finger and bending it backwards. My adrenalin was pumping so much it took me a few moments to notice that I had a broken bone.

Officer Cadet Iain Powrie, 1967

Another significant part of junior training was an introduction to minor platoon tactics. The first field exercise took place on Barossa, the back-door training area. This was our first experience of trench living for the exercise was based on a company defensive position. This was occupied mid-morning, with the remainder of the day spent digging, wiring and laying trip-flares. Standing patrols were established, recce patrols dispatched, and we awaited the arrival of the enemy. Tradition requires that all attacks begin at dawn – we were not to be disappointed. As we stood-to after a rather uncomfortable night we peered through the early morning mist in an attempt to spot the enemy, the Gurkha Demonstration Company. Our first warning was the distant drone of a lone piper, Sergeant Flynn of the Gordon Highlanders – quite an eerie sound in the early

Training continues day … and night.

Orders in the field.

dawn and, being a Scot, it sent a tingle down my spine. It was like a sight from the Flanders trenches as the company slowly appeared through the gloom moving at a steady walk, well spaced-out, as thunder-flashes, simulating attacking artillery, exploded around us. That was the first of many such exercises over the next two years that took us through the gamut of defence, attack, withdrawal, patrolling, ambushes, etc.

Officer Cadet Punyawat Takerngkeat, 2004
The most vivid memory for me was the time when I was walking painfully in the Black Mountains; Exercise LONG REACH was my toughest exercise, but at the same time I learned the meaning of friends. My team was the very best, we encouraged each other and fought to the last.

Officer Cadet Mike Whelan, 1995
On the second night of Exercise FIRST ENCOUNTER I was given the command appointment of Platoon Commander. My main aim was to ensure that everyone continued digging

throughout the night. Easier said than done. There was a route that took in the six trenches being dug, the sentry position and the Platoon Sergeant's trench. This took approximately fifteen minutes to cover. However, I could guarantee that once I had left the trench, people would be asleep – some on their knees with the shovel in the ground, others on their feet with a pick thrown over their shoulder and even those who had fallen asleep against each other in the bottom of a trench. It was an uphill battle which I feel I did not handle too well at all. At about 0001 on the Tuesday morning, I moved to my trench to get fifteen minutes' sleep as I was dead on my feet. I had already walked into a trench by accident, fallen asleep walking between

Cadets are given the support they will have on operations.

two trenches and walked into the wire fence fifty metres to the left of our position and had become totally disorientated on a number of occasions. I was exhausted. Unfortunately, the Company Commander found me in the trench with my Radio Op asleep. He informed me that the entire platoon was asleep. At the time, I felt like correcting him by telling him that was not strictly true as he had just woken me up. Quick-fire humour at that hour of the morning is not a viable option.

Officer Cadet D. Young, 2015
The public order phase of Exercise TEMPLER'S TRIUMPH was not only an exciting experience but one that provoked the most camaraderie. The challenge for me as the Team Commander was to maintain the troop's composure and the formations. The opportunity to 'fight' against our sister company was a well-deserved bonus.

Officer Cadet Barker, 2004
I think my most vivid memory is lying in mud, cold and wet, waiting for H-Hour during our company attack. It was a strange sensation, because although I was absolutely freezing and shaking like a leaf, I had a huge sense of excitement as I realised what I was part of. At times like those you really understand what an achievement it is to be at RMAS and how lucky we are.

At the end of the final exercise – and with the end in sight – there is chance to celebrate … and wear their regimental headdress for the first time.

chapter nineteen:

Time Out

MAJOR OLLIE STEAD

Gentleman Cadet D.L.M. Robbins, 1937

There was much rivalry between the Old College (2 and 4 Companies) and the New College (1 and 3 Companies), which often led to physical roughhouses. The attractive RMC lake played a part in one's life. I recall that anyone unpopular or disliked was thrown unceremoniously into the lake. On one occasion dozens of chamber pots with lighted candles were found floating about … . After dinner nights in New College someone inevitably climbed the tall tower of the building to put a chamber pot on the flagpole – a dangerous exploit. The pot was shot down the next morning by an instructor, always cheered by onlooking cadets.

Gentleman Cadet Arthur Coke Burnell, 1912,
The Making of an Officer

The numerous gramophones here (in the Barracks) are absolutely deafening. It is rather hard to describe the effect of 'The Chocolate Soldier', 'The Dollar Princess', 'Quaker Girl' etc., all on at once! A friend of mine has just won a £4 one for two shillings in a lottery at the Fancy Goods Stors, but after two and a half hours of it I have had to hide the needles.

Officer Cadet Robin McNish, 1947

Later in the course Old College 1 and 1A put on a mock Sovereign's Parade, watched by most of the Academy and many of the Camberley public. Space does not permit a full description of this hilarious event, but companies on parade included 'The Gas, Light and Coke Company', the 'Genuine Bedouin Arab Company' (us) and a company mounted on bicycles.

Officer Cadet Iain Powrie, 1967

'Band Nights', or formal dinner nights, were also an opportunity to let off steam. During one of the earlier terms there was one

*Every platoon wants that
unique platoon photograph.*

particular evening of note when, immediately after dinner, Normandy 42 was ordered by the seniors to change into PT kit and be prepared to defend the company anteroom against attacks by all-comers, but particularly Rhine Company. The evenings ensued with running battles in the corridors resulting in some minor casualties – one being Cadet Chabandi, who fell from a first-floor window, and another who had a close shave with a fire extinguisher. The climax was the drenching of Rhine Company anteroom using the fire hoses. I am pleased to record that our defence was successful and that Normandy Company anteroom remained untouched. The Rhine Company cadets occupied the drill shed for some days after to dry out. As far as I recall there were no significant repercussions although there was a collective barrack damage charge deducted from our bank accounts. (It is worth recording that the latter were run by the Paymaster through the Academy Bank as a means of ensuring fiscal prudence and supervision!) No doubt in today's politically correct environment such outrageous behaviour would result in litigation, damages and disciplinary action of a draconian nature inflicted on the participants!

Gentleman Cadet Brian Horrocks, 1912, *A Full Life*

In October, 1912, I passed into the Royal Military College Sandhurst, bottom but one. It was a most undistinguished start to a military career. Apart from the games side I achieved nothing at all and remained a Gentleman Cadet (the equivalent of a private soldier) throughout my time at the College. Let me be quite honest about it: I was idle, careless about my turnout – in army parlance, scruffy – and, due to the fact that I am inclined to roll when I walk, vey unsmart on parade. Throughout my military career I have always been allocated a position on ceremonial parades where I was least likely to be

seen. To make matters worse I got into trouble with the railway officials during a return journey from Gatwick races. We had gone there with such an absolute certainty for the third race that I refrained from buying a return ticket in order to have more to invest on the horse. I did not even buy a race card so certain was I of a lavish win. As might be expected the certainty did not materialise and the railway company took strong exception to my return journey ticketless and penniless. The result was three months' restrictions which meant that I was unable to leave the premises during my last term and spent the time doing additional fatigues and parades. I was lucky not to be rusticated. *(Note: After this inauspicious start, Horrocks rose to become a Lieutenant General and subsequently Gentleman Usher of The Black Rod.)*

Top right: The RMAS coach to Ascot in 1950.

Right: Cadet R. Bonner's RMAS bank account slip, 1947.

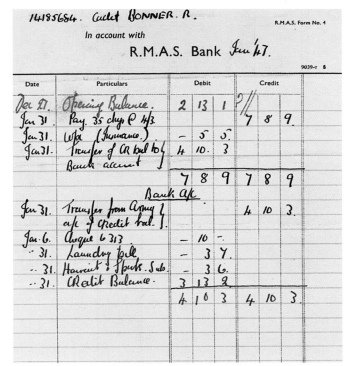

Officer Cadet Philip Erskine, 1952

I treasure the many skills I learnt at Sandhurst, not least how to defeat the system. For example at 7.15 every morning was BRC (Breakfast Roll Call). Every cadet was on parade and inspected by one of the under-officers. As a junior it was inevitable that frequently one was caught, and minor punishments followed. There were occasions when I got asked to parties in London, the last train out of Waterloo to Camberley was soon after midnight and then nothing till the next morning. The so-called milk train which arrived in Camberley a few minutes before seven was a very tight fit to get a taxi back to Sandhurst, get changed and be in time for BRC. You either lost your name for being late or your kit was not up to standard. The way to beat the system was to put your name down for Holy Communion in the Chapel and as long as you were there by the end of the service you were in the clear. Apart from the advantage of not being subjected to inspection the extra half hour made the milk train the easy option.

Officer Cadet John Akehurst, 1947, *Generally Speaking*

Bounds were carefully defined and it was forbidden to enter any public house within three miles of the Academy. A small

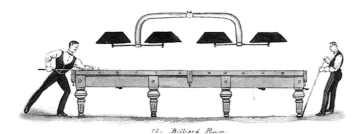

The Billiard Room.

The R.M.C. Lake in Winter.

group of us in my company prevailed upon the landlord and his pretty daughter at The Queen in Blackwater to allow us the use of a back room whenever we rang ahead to book it. We always approached warily through their back garden, and left, perhaps more noisily, at some later time bearing little relationship to licencing hours. Cadets had to wear hats when going out, which was claimed to be the gentlemanly way to dress, but was actually to make anyone breaking bounds more readily identifiable. Given the haircuts inflicted upon us, identification of a cadet was probably easier when hatless. At weekends we had to book out and report in on our return, when a duty under-officer (a cadet in his senior term) would record the time and the letters 'SPD' or Sober and Properly Dressed. Some latitude in the condition required to match this description was often allowed to the more senior cadets, but never to juniors.

Anon, 1938, *Infantry Officer: A Personal Record*

The grounds of Sandhurst are very beautiful, and are dominated by the lake. On Sundays, Harry, my best friend, and I would often spend the afternoon on it in a dinghy hired from 'Mrs Admiral', the boat-keeper, from whom, at the right time of the year, you could buy strawberries and cream. The lake also played its part in the dances which occurred about once a month; it was considered the thing to row around it for an hour or so with your partner, whatever the temperature. The dances were great fun. The chief occasion of the year was the June Ball, for which large marquees were erected and a dance-floor laid down among the trees, which were festooned with coloured lights; and the islands of the lake were softly illuminated.

Officer Cadet John Gilmour, 1950

Only those in the senior term were allowed to keep a car or motorcycle; none but the senior under-officers were permitted to keep their cars in the grounds. In our Intermediate Term one of my closest friends kept his Triumph 500c motorcycle in a lock-up garage in Little Sandhurst village. We frequently went out at the weekends, John driving and me riding pillion. Bogey time to cover the distance from the Staff College gates to Hyde Park Corner was thirty minutes. The A30 was the main road into London and was busy by the standards of the day. There was no by-pass at Staines and for much of the route the road was a single carriageway. We only succeeded in covering the distance in under thirty minutes and that was in the early hours of the morning.

Officer Cadet Richard Avens, Intake 20, 1957

On one occasion, we arrived at the dining room after Breakfast Roll Call to find that ALL the cutlery was missing. During the night some cadets had removed everything, rowed out on the lake and dumped them all on the island. Those involved were interviewed by the Commandant and gated, which we all felt was a bit hard. However, I remember us all being rather annoyed at missing breakfast and having to spend money in the tuck shop later on!

For reasons that are hard to explain, all the cadets at RMAS ran riot one evening and rolled the cannon on Old College square out onto the A30 in Camberley. Thunderflashes were exploded from the barrels, much to the horror of the poor

Above left and above: Lighter moments in 1890–1.

The 2nd Battalion Cameronians (Scottish Rifles) centrepiece given to RMAS for safekeeping on the disbanding of the regiment in 1968.

Right: A proud mother is escorted into the Intermediate Term Parents' Guest Night.

Far right and below: Applying the finishing touches before a Company Dinner Night.

wretched motorists and all the traffic was diverted up onto Old College square. The chaos that ensued had to be seen to be believed and that is the reason why the cannon are now padlocked and chained! We all moved swiftly back to our rooms when the local police appeared with dogs! Nowadays such behaviour would cause a Parliamentary enquiry.

Cadets who were old Wellingtonians attended the Wellington Summer Ball and caused chaos by igniting smoke bombs in the marquee. Several dresses were ruined and those involved were banned from Wellington, some for life. Irate mothers and the Master bombarded the poor Commandant with complaints and the problems continued for several weeks!

An Officer Cadet destined for the Household Cavalry challenged another to a race from RMAS to Hyde Park Corner, one on horseback and the other in his sports car. The horseman was allowed to start from Staines and reached the finish first! An amazing feat even in those days and nowadays impossible.

Officer Cadet Allaway, 2004

In the last week of term, we were woken up by the fire alarm about half an hour before reveille and all piled outside in various orders of dress. Whilst the roll was being taken, there was a strange noise round the corner and the band marched onto the parade square playing at full blast. As they got closer the mutter went round the assembled ranks, 'They're wearing Santa hats!' They halted and RSM Duggan yelled, 'Old College'. The thought went through our minds that we were in serious trouble for something when, after a dramatic pause, he continued with, 'Merry Christmas. Follow the band!' The band started up again and marched up the steps with 270 Officer Cadets streaming behind them. In the hall, we were given Santa hats and ordered to attend breakfast, exactly as we were. The dining room was laid out with crackers and the band were playing carols as the DS served us orange juice and tea laced with rum. It was one of the random factors about the Army that I love so much.

Gentleman Cadet Bernard Fergusson, 1930,
The Trumpet in the Hall, 1930–1958

On Band Nights the programme always ended, before God Save the King, with a regimental march. The Band worked its way religiously through the whole Army list, and in those days there were many more Regiments than there are today, you were lucky if you heard your own during your mere eighteen months at Sandhurst. I am sure I was not the only one by a long chalk who felt moved when we stood to drink the loyal toast: 300 dedicated young men, half the College, aged eighteen or nineteen; all in uniform, all with aspirations to go into this Regiment or that, all committed to a career in the honourable profession of arms. All of us were of that brotherhood by choice.

Reverend Mike Parker, Company Dinner Night, 2016

God bless our Company gathered to dine,
on sumptuous food and plenteous wine,
and keep us safe from all that harms
like five-ways runs and Wish-stream baths.

Reverend Bob Mitchell, Burma Company Dining In,
June 2005

For time to stop and be at leisure
For food & wine in ample measure
For cooks & service we applaud
For music, friends in fine accord
We give you thanks Our loving Lord

Top left: The silver model of Old College displayed in the Officers' Mess.

Top right: Central briefing in The Churchill Hall before the Intermediate Term Parents' Guest Night.

Above: The Father's Guest Night of yore has been replaced with a Parents' Event.

chapter twenty:

Long Days, Short Courses

LIEUTENANT COLONEL GEOFF WEIGHELL

S ituated in prominent positions at both entry gates to the Royal Military Academy are signs proclaiming Sandhurst to be 'The Home of The British Army Officer'. Although the public may associate Sandhurst with the Regular Commissioning Course and the high-profile Sovereign's Parade there are many other officer training courses running at the Academy.

THE RESERVE COMMISSIONING COURSE

As a Reservist Officer the impact of attending RMAS has been immeasurable; all the tenets of leadership I have learnt, developed and applied throughout my military service have defined how I work and engage with family, friends and colleagues in all areas of my life.
Officer Cadet Roger Harrison, 1989

The Reserve Commissioning Course (Res CC), has a pedigree dating back to the Territorial Army Commissioning Course (TACC) of the 1930s. In its current form it consists of four modules

(Mods A to D) which must be successfully completed prior to commissioning. The modular nature of the course is designed to accommodate potential reserve officers with limited annual availability and could be completed over several years. The Res CC at RMAS is eight weeks long, enabling those with the time (usually university undergraduates) to complete the whole commissioning course in one go with those with more limited availability dipping in and out to complete one or more of the modules.

Much has changed since the days when the two-week TACC was a very separate entity to the regular course. Cadets attending today's Res CC are integrated male and female and complete many of the, albeit truncated, modules of the forty-week course. They are issued with No. 1 Dress uniform and drill boots, attend a regimental guest night and take part in a commissioning parade identical to their regular counterparts, including the College Adjutant riding the horse up the steps of Old College. Indeed, only the fact that the course is so concentrated prevents the reserve cadets from learning sword drill. Following the parade their proud friends and relatives attend an identical commissioning lunch. In short, the gap between the 'part-time' and professional officers has narrowed to almost nothing as befits a force that heavily depends on its reservists and has fully embraced the 'one Army' concept.

I was the youngest on my Reserve Commissioning Course and I was amazed at the diversity. We had a teacher, a solicitor, a postman and a research assistant at the House of Commons. One cadet had a daughter who was older than me and another cadet had been a film extra working on Captain America *and* Fury. *He'd already been thrown off a building by Chris Evans and shot by Brad Pitt – and I was still only eighteen!*
Officer Cadet Connor Kent-Payne, 2015

PROFESSIONALLY QUALIFIED OFFICERS COMMISSIONING COURSE

The British Army requires the service of a broad array of professionals to enable it to deliver operational effectiveness.

*Only a lack of swords betray this as
a Reserve Commissioning Parade.*

This includes doctors, nurses, physiotherapists, vets, lawyers, dentists, padres and cyber specialists. The Professionally Qualified Officer (PQO) Course aims to instil the ethos, values and standards of the British Army. The course ensures that PQOs commission with an understanding of the structure and doctrine of the British Army, an understanding of their role within the Army and on operations and the necessary command, leadership and management skills required of a commissioned officer. The nature of the contemporary operating environment routinely sees these individuals deployed on the frontline and this requires them to be trained to a high military standard and so there is a strong emphasis on military skills and fieldcraft.

To meet these training requirements, the course has been expanded and now runs for eleven weeks. This includes an initial three-week period which acclimatises the PQOs to military life and begins to inculcate them with the ethos of the British Army. They are exposed to key military skills including fitness, navigation, weapon handling, communication and drill. The course then branches out to introduce them to the orders and estimate process, leadership skills and basic military tactics. Finally, there is a strong academic component delivered by the three core RMAS academic departments. This prepares the PQOs to deploy on a series of field exercises which increase in intensity and complexity throughout the course.

The course itself is designed to be progressive and the instructors aim to make extensive use of the experience and skills that will invariably be found within the cadre of cadets. For many

this is a second career begun in their later thirties or even forties, for others in their twenties this is the first job after completing their professional qualifications. Irrespective of their journey to RMAS, all PQOs leave the PQO Commissioning Course trained to the standard required to lead soldiers both on and off operations.

*Above: The Wish Stream is just as
gruelling for regulars and reserves.*

*Right: A variety of capbadges are on
display as the Professionally Qualified
Officers march past.*

The Tactical Recognition Flashes of the RAMC and QARANC are the only indications that these are not cadets on the Regular Careers Course.

RESERVE PROFESSIONALLY QUALIFIED OFFICERS COURSE

Like the PQO Commissioning Course, the Reserve PQO Commissioning Course brings together professionals heading for many branches of the Army. Like other members of the Army Reserve, these individuals have chosen to commit a significant amount of time to serving their country, in addition to extremely demanding civilian careers – an impressive and commendable commitment. Like their regular PQO counterparts, PQO reservists will be required to lead soldiers and deploy on operations around the world, and the course is designed to rapidly bring them up to the required standard.

The four-week course is broken down into two modules, each module lasting two weeks. The first module focuses on developing basic military skills. This includes lessons on navigation, field craft, drill and battlefield casualty drills. The second module seeks to develop the command, leadership and management skills required of commissioned officers. This is assessed through command tasks, an introduction to the orders and estimate process, and a wider look at Army doctrine. Throughout the course, the Officer Cadets are tested physically, so that they are aware of the standards they must maintain when they leave the RMAS as Commissioned Officers.

At the end of the four weeks, the Officer Cadets have the privilege of passing off Old College Parade Ground and marching up the steps of Old College in front of their family and friends, the traditional finale to any commissioning parade.

THE LATE ENTRY OFFICERS COURSE

The following are three quotes from students on the LEOC in 2016. In the greatest tradition of the long-serving British soldier – they wished to remain anonymous:

It was a thoroughly enjoyable course and far better than the myth of expectation. It does stretch your imagination and expose areas I have never thought of or considered.

This has been the best Army course that I have attended in twenty-two years. The entire programme has improved me in a good way.

Overall it was a really good course. I'm glad I attended within months of commissioning as it has given me a solid platform from where I can develop my knowledge, skills and experience to progress in my career.

In addition to the Regular Commissioning Course, each year Sandhurst trains some 250 Late Entry (LE) Officers. These 'LEs' as they are colloquially known, are highly experienced former Warrant Officers and Senior Non-Commissioned Officers, selected by their cap badges to fill roles at regimental duty, and now increasingly, are employed more widely across the Army.

The purpose of the Late Entry Officers' Course, or LEOC, as it is universally known, is simple – to deliver a Late Entry Officer who is, 'current, competent and credible.' This is achieved through exercises, assessments and presentations around four main subject areas: defence writing, military estimate planning, defence and international affairs and war studies.

Far left: Several hundred years of experience as the LEOC attend a central presentation …

Left: … and in the Syndicate Room.

LE officers will have become deep specialists in their own cap badge or specialisation over a period of many years. The course aim is not to undermine this, but is about breadth – ensuring that the LE cohort is exposed at the strategic level. In addition to the classroom and field elements, visits and briefings are undertaken to the Houses of Parliament, MOD Main Building and at Army Headquarters in Andover. Defence policy and procurement decisions, for example, can only really be understood when some of the underlying pressures are exposed.

AFGHAN NATIONAL ARMY OFFICERS' ACADEMY (ANAOA) MENTORS COURSE

The Afghan National Army Officers' Academy (ANAOA) Mentors Course runs twice a year and is the final stage of training for Officers and Senior NCOs who are deploying to the ANAOA in Kabul Afghanistan. Mentors are from all four partner nations, Australia, Denmark, New Zealand and the UK, often meeting for the first time, so the training programme not only develops the individuals skills but also enables the teambuilding to begin prior to deployment. The course comprises of a number of pillars and is underpinned by serving ANAOA staff who deliver the role-specific training and in-theatre experience. The RMAS Coaching and Advisory Team (CAT) teach a module on interacting with students and the delivery of training and RMAS staff explains the key facets that make RMA Sandhurst so special.

MEMORIES OF ROWALLAN

I began my time on Rowallan Cadre, and the grandeur of the grounds and the buildings were very much secondary to the intensity of the physical training, the non-stop and secretive training programme, the high standards expected of cadets, and the calibre of the directing staff. Rowallan Cadre and all that it entails – being completely knackered, having feet cut to ribbons with blisters and the camaraderie of training with people seeking a common goal – are my first impressions of RMAS.
Officer Cadet Snell, 2004

Rowallan Company was formed in 1977 because the Army was not then getting enough young officers. It was felt that too many candidates were leaving the Regular Commissions Board at Westbury disappointed, having failed entry to the Academy and been advised to get some character-forming experience then

ANNEX H TO
EX BRECON BRENDA

CLASSIFIED INFORMATION

TO: OPERATIVE No...... R ....

FROM: OPERATIONS OFFICER BLUE BOAR BUNCH

INFO: MOVE AWAY FROM THIS AREA INTO COVER.

        YOU MAY NOT RETURN TO YOUR LINES OR BASE LOCATION.

        YOU MUST REPORT TO THE FOLLOWING GRID AT 1900 HRS
        SUNDAY 20 MAR 83.

        SHEET 160 (Brecon Beacons) GR ~~006170~~ 025 249

        A FRIENDLY AGENT WILL MEET YOU

        YOU MUST NOT IMPART THIS INFO TO ANYONE EXCEPT IN AN EMERGENCY

        IT IS IMPERATIVE YOU MAKE THE RV

        GOOD LUCK AND GOD'S SPEED.

DTG:

reapply in a year's time – which they generally did not do. Why not tell those young men that they could come to Sandhurst, spend twelve weeks on a strenuous course which would exercise their bodies and minds, and above all unlock their leadership potential, after which they would be reassessed? It worked.

A typically vague Exercise Instruction from 1983.

It was a tough course, based to some extent on the principles established at the Highland Field Training Centre by Lord Rowallan in the Second World War. It was full of challenges and surprises: not for nothing did the company tie feature a row of mushrooms – kept in the dark and fed a load of excrement. The military content was minimal, just enough for the youngster to pass muster at RMAS and find their way around on exercise. There were endurance runs, swimming and obstacle work, even squirming through storm drains half filled with water. There was interrupted sleep and red alerts to react to and a sixth sense to be developed. There were inspections and weekend initiative tests: forty-eight hours in which to get the autograph of an Admiral, travel to Malta and other such outlandish tasks.

Some outsiders and even non-military were involved: a colourful Hell's Angel came down from London to tell how he had rowed the Atlantic single-handed. One of the early academics attached to the Company was Bill Jenkins, who, in 1944, was the youngest to win the DSO. Another would recount how he had escaped an erupting volcano in Ecuador while the military staff observed which cadets offered the most intelligent questions. These sessions led to an analysis of what a leader should be, what he should know and what he should do.

Rowallan Company was reduced to a cadre in 2002 and then placed in suspended animation two years later. The reason was in part financial, but the buoyant pass rate at Westbury made Rowallan largely redundant. Some 3,050 cadets went through Roco (as it was affectionetely known), two thirds going on to the Commissioning Course. Many went on to achieve senior rank and even those who did not last the distance acknowledged how beneficial the time spent at Rowallan had been. It was a huge success.

In 2016 a falling pass rate at the renamed Army Officer Selection Board (AOSB) resulted in a reappraisal of the Rowallan model. The original model was very much of its time with more than a passing nod to the initiative tests devised in wartime. The problem was still the same – how to give those who had failed to meet the standard at AOSB a realistic chance of passing while keeping them in a military environment and away from the temptation to embark on a different career. So, in September 2016 Slim's Company formed up with forty-eight young men and women.

SANDHURST LEADER DEVELOPMENT COURSE – SLIM'S COMPANY

Slim's Company delivers the RMAS Leader Development Course (LDC), to improve those candidates who have been selected by the AOSB for further development before they retake AOSB Main Board. The first LDC started in September 2016 and lasts for twelve weeks based in Victory Building. The forty-eight students on the pilot course hold the military rank of Private; however they hold the appointment of Potential Officer and are addressed as such. They wear the cap badge of the General Service Corps.

A conscious effort is made not to specifically train the potential officers for the assessments they will face on the AOSB Main Board, rather to develop character over the course through a breadth of topics in both military and non-military spheres. During the course, they develop their physical fitness and agility, as well as taking part in regular but varied sporting opportunities. They undertake theoretical and practical map reading by day and night, which often forms part of a wider planning exercise. Regular rounds of command tasks which vary from the 'traditional' to the obscure create opportunities for individuals to lead and to learn whether they succeed or fail.

There is a week of Adventure Training (including kayaking, mountain biking and climbing) allowing the potential officers to experience new challenges, lead groups in new situations and gain accredited qualification which they can build on during the Regular Commissioning Course. Minds are broadened through daily current affairs discussions, guest speakers and external visits to historical sites, galleries and policy institutes. Academic staff within the Academy also teach a range of subjects which culminate in periods of sustained research and considered presentations. Several short field exercises build to a final endurance event on Dartmoor which sees a culmination in the use of the skills and experiences they have gained throughout the LDC

The Directing Staff within Slim's Company have all instructed on the Regular Commissioning Course and, using this experience, create an environment that allows for coaching, mentoring and learning through self-assessment. That said, this environment is bounded with appropriate military grip, adversity and challenge that will test and develop their character, preparing them for a second attempt at the rigours of AOSB Main Board, the Regular Commissioning Course and command on first appointment.

Above: Rigorous Adventurous Training is a common thread with the Old Rowallan Company.

Left: Slim's Company spend their first night in the field.

part three:

SERVE TO LEAD

chapter twenty-one:

The NCO Instructional Staff

WO1 MARIE OVENSTONE

A *fter vacillating when told to select one of the platoon for a particularly nasty duty my Colour Sergeant bellowed: 'Get on with it Sir; just pick the best first; if you are picking a high jump team you want one man that can jump seven feet not seven men that can jump one foot!'*

Officer Cadet Bryan Johnston, SMC 20, 1980

You have to be very good at what you do to become an NCO Instructor at RMAS. Only the crème de la crème are chosen in a process that parallels the Regular Commissioning Board procedures for the officer cadets. All the NCO instructors have to pass the Cadre Course. This is a highly intensive four-week course that puts every one of the sixty who attend through all aspects of instructional technique. Before that, they have been pre-selected by their parent units, sifted through by formation headquarters, and those selected have attended many weeks of courses before even starting the Cadre Course. Competition on the course is extremely high and the benchmark is set accordingly – between 50% and 60% are selected of the sixty who attend. All are highly capable and selection is based on those who are the most suited to teach today's officer cadets, most of whom are mature graduates. Those selected for a posting to RMAS return for a further two weeks' continuation training – many of those who are not become instructors in training units throughout the Army.

Being an NCO instructor at RMAS is a totally involving commitment that is as demanding for the Colour Sergeants and their families as it is for the cadets. From day one they are the first on the scene in the morning and last to bed. The constant changes in timetabling that afflict most days at the Academy affect platoon staff to the same degree as the cadets. This has always been the case.

The hardest thing is the work – six days a week, with Chapel on Sunday. You've never really finished a day's work, things still happen at six or seven o'clock in the evening. If there's a long period of time before a change I would probably receive six letters from everybody and his dog telling about it. But I could be told on the telephone at twenty minutes' notice. If I was a cadet I'd think 'What a stupid bloody system, why couldn't they have told us that before?' but I find out only ten minutes before they find out. That's the Sandhurst system.

Michael Yardley, *Sandhurst: A Documentary,* **1987**

This comment, from a CSM at RMAS is mirrored today with emails instead of letters. Sandhurst, to the NCO instructors, is a 'make it happen' world – a change occurs and somehow or other the programme has to be achieved. Each of the three terms presents its own demands – the first term in Old College until Week 5 is particularly demanding, but every aspect of the

Right: The Warrant Officers and Sergeants, RMC, 1879.

Commissioning Course and the other short courses conducted at RMAS presents equal challenges, with each instructor being individually measured and assessed by every student looking for clues into the role he or she will be asked to play in their commissioned service. It is also easy to forget the demands that are being made of the support staff in the Q-store to make it happen and to ensure that be it bagged lunches or rifle oil, it is there when it is needed.

The appointment to RMAS is highly sought after, because getting there is not easy and it marks an NCO out within their parent unit. For families, the summer break makes it worthwhile because it is a family break written in stone, and that is rare in today's busy Army.

All this is a far cry from the role of NCOs in the nineteenth century when RMC was first established, when their job was to report on cadets, with staff being rewarded accordingly. It was a climate of 'don't get caught', with the sergeants on the watch to report any transgression. 'Of course, the Sergeant has no power to touch or arrest you. He could chase you if he chose to do so, in order to see the number on your cap, and otherwise identify you; but these sergeants were mostly old soldiers and did not

care much about running; besides, we could hide the number by a sprig of heather.' (Gentleman Cadet John F. Mann, 1835, *RMC Magazine*, No. 56, Autumn 1938). This led to a staff of specially selected swift runners being appointed to RMC:

Of these the best known was a Sergeant Crook (generally called 'Porter'), who in cunning and speed could get the better of most gentleman cadets. Sergeant John Davies was also a brilliant sprinter, and so well did he perform his duties that he was eventually given a commission and became adjutant and quartermaster of the College. Another noteworthy personage of those old days was McLaughlin, the cell-sergeant, of whom every cadet had a wholesome dread. 'Cells' carried with it a bread and water diet, consequently when a prisoner was out of confinement for study or parade he took the opportunity of procuring a piece of cheese or other luxury to eat with his bread, but McLaughlin was generally ready for this, feeling the prisoner all over and making him take off his boots before he locked the cell door.

Major A.F. Mockler-Ferryman, *Annals of Sandhurst*

Those days have long gone, and now at RMAS the role of the staff is that time-honoured process of moulding individuals into a group, who feel themselves very much under siege in those first exhausting five weeks, and from that point instructing them in a range of skills from fieldcraft and tactics to first aid and encouraging them to express themselves with growing confidence. For the cadets, the first impressions are of 'tall

Top left: The NCO staff are always there to offer advice during field training.

Far left: The medals show the immense depth of operational experience of today's Senior NCOs.

Teamwork: the platoon Commander and the Colour Sergeant are the two most influential people in the cadet's time at Sandhurst.

we returned to RMAS, slightly gloomy, following the weekend leave after the first six weeks of training. McKay was waiting for us in the platoon lines as we drifted back in, and realising that morale needed a boost, he invited us all back to his married quarter where, in a friendly and informal setting, we drank a lot of his Glenfiddich malt in the course of the next couple of hours. Not only did this serve to bond us together as a unit and raise our spirits about the rest of the course, it also gave me a lifelong liking for that particular whisky.

The second occasion was on exercise (Thetford, I think), at the dawn stand-to. I was in a sorry state in my trench (which was of course knee-deep in water after a night of inevitable rain), cold, dirty and tired, peering through the dawn mist over my rifle sights at a non-existent enemy. I felt a sharp tap on my tin hat and looked up to see Colour Sergeant McKay standing behind me, pace stick in hand, immaculately turned out, not a speck of mud anywhere, combats pressed, boots shining. What he said as he disappeared into the mist was such an intense lesson in personal admin that it serves me to this day. 'Any fool can be uncomfortable, Sir.'

Eddie McKay was the best senior NCO I ever met. He was a superb leader who understood soldiers and knew how to get the best out of them.

Most platoons had their Eddie McKay, who worked in close partnership with the CSM and company officers to inculcate standards. Even if cadets cannot remember their company commanders, they never forget their colour sergeants.

THE COMPANY SERGEANT MAJOR
Officer Cadet S. Brooks, 1999

To talk of my Sandhurst Sergeant Major's physical attributes would lend this record artistic licence; he was big and tall and impressive in all aspects and immaculate, as one would imagine, powerful in every sense of the word. I could address the officer instructors with relative ease, safe in the thought that one day I might hold a Queen's Commission – but he had something I did not possess and that made me feel as if he was a man to be humble in front of, and that I should be apologetic for cluttering his beloved parade ground with my awkward movements.

In retrospect two aspects struck me most about him. The first was his sharp humour, which could never be relied upon and would only be released at his timely discretion; if his anger was a storm to shelter from, then his rare release of wit was a sunny spell and a moment to bask in the warmth and glory of it all – it was almost intoxicating. Second, and more importantly, at the end of our course was his sharing with us of his own experiences of war. As a young soldier he had been aboard *Sir Galahad* and the only indication of the matter was the fading scar tissue upon his arms and neck. We had received a number of informal talks with the great and the good of the Academy, each with the individual's experience and character reflected in the tales told. I had an overwhelming feeling that the instructors knew that the majority of us would soon pass out of the gates to command the mythical beast that was the British Army soldier,

uniformed Colour Sergeants who stalked the corridors like sharks as we carried our bags in'. Officer Cadet Tancred's reflections on his platoon sergeant in 1992 applies to every intake: 'As the weeks wore on, our penal reputation surfaced less frequently and more people came to recognise that Colour Sergeant Bannon may after all have had a traceable parentage.'

It has been ever so and now, in the tightly focused course of three busy terms, it is the NCO instructors who provide the continuity and sense of tradition once provided in the two-year course by the cadet hierarchy. The NCOs provide the officer cadets with an introduction to the professionalism and skills of the British soldier – the cadets see and are taught by the best, and assess from this the standards they have to achieve to be worthy of command. The best NCOs stamp a hallmark of excellence that remains with those taught for the rest of their careers.

MEMORIES OF EDDIE MCKAY
Officer Cadet George Owen, 1978–79

I was an undistinguished cadet in 7 Platoon, Burma Company on SMC 19. We were lucky enough to have the unparelleled Colour Sergeant Eddie McKay SG as our platoon Colour Sergeant; his excellent leadership guided me through the syllabus and into a short but happy commission with the Royal Engineers.

Colour Sergeant McKay exhibited leadership skills at all levels, but two particular incidents stand out. The first was when

NCO advice is an integral part of the development of the cadet.

and that we now needed tempering, perhaps even reassurance, before we met the coal-face workers.

The Sergeant Major was the last to talk, being the only non-commissioned staff member to do so, and he walked before us deep in contemplation. He began to tell us about the South Atlantic campaign and what life was like on *Sir Galahad*, the usual cheery recollections he told when talking of his battalion. Then he told us of the wall of fire that had engulfed him below decks that fateful day. He spoke simply of the movement above deck, forming ranks to load the casualties and remaining so as to evacuate the burning ship. He broke each statement with a pause, allowing the reality of the situation to sink into us, and it was then that I looked at him and saw the look in his eyes. I realised that the pauses were not for dramatic effect, nor the look one of contemplation, but that he was reliving the experience as a young guardsman who was trapped below in a little piece of hell, and how this had felt.

He moved on to talk about the casualties and it struck me how he knew all the names of those who had perished, their homes, their family details and how they fared in the years to follow. We all sat silent, watching this mountain-like figure telling us of the worst day in his life. It was a strange feeling to hear of such a tragedy by a victim and feel no pity, only pride in having known him. He concluded by saying that he, and now we, had all been trained for war but 'you'll never be prepared …'

It struck me that this was the man's strength; that having suffered such an ordeal he had built upon the experience and had soldiered on. He knew the worst that could happen and

carried that burden with him, and now used it as a tool to show us the courage that may be asked of us, one day. The unanswered question sat prominent in my thoughts, was I as strong as he?

Years later I met the now commissioned Sergeant Major again when his battle group relieved my own in Southern Iraq. I saw him approach, and as he drew near I thought of slinking away to avoid his gaze – but he had seen me, and it was to see me that he had come. He shook my hand and congratulated me on what my men and I had achieved. I felt almost a form of closure:

that I had gone some way to justify his time and effort when I was a cadet. I then grew conscious that a great number of the men were looking interestedly at us and I felt a little awkward. He spun me around and boomed to them all, but no one in particular, that I was one of his 'boys', as if this was the answer to all their curiosity. I took the opportunity to thank him and reminded him of his final words to us all those years before, which I never forgot. Perhaps he too received some closure from this – although I never dared to ask.

THE GURKHA COMPANY (SITTANG) RMAS

The Gurkha Company (Sittang) RMAS is, first and foremost, a Gurkha rifle company, manned by fully trained professional soldiers. The company must be able to deliver infantry skills at every level to a high professional standard. Generations of cadets who have 'fought' against this Gurkha 'enemy' will attest that this is indeed the case.

Apart from a short-notice nine-month operational deployment to Cyprus in 1974 and a six-month tour in the Falkland Islands in 1982–83, Gurkhas have provided continuous support to RMAS since 1971. The first Gurkhas known to have supported Sandhurst were a platoon from Support Company 10th Princess Mary's Own Gurkha Rifles, which was the UK resident Gurkha battalion at the time. By 1972 this modest platoon had increased to full rifle company strength which was provided by the resident UK Gurkha battalion rotating one of its four rifle companies. This became known as the Gurkha Demonstration Company. In those days it was a bold step to send a Gurkha company away from its own regiment to work closely with British officers and senior NCOs. English was not widely spoken below officer/senior NCO level, but for the next ten years, nearly all of the regular Gurkha rifle companies were rotated through Sandhurst on a six-month temporary tour of duty.

This led to the Gurkha Demonstration Company RMAS being formally established in April 1981. Because of the incentives offered by a posting to the United Kingdom, this

Seremban Troop.

became a highly sought-after appointment. The move of the Brigade of Gurkhas to the United Kingdom after the 1997 withdrawal from Hong Kong has meant that the company has had to change with the times and reflect the changes imposed within the Royal Gurkha Rifles by it being largely UK based and the opportunities available in each battalion with operational deployments to Bosnia, Kosovo, Sierra Leone, Afghanistan and Iraq.

In response to this the company has focused on presenting itself as an organisation that not only continues to meet the existing high standards expected at Sandhurst, but is also able to give something of value back to the Brigade of Gurkhas in the development of young soldiers, junior and senior NCOs awaiting promotion. A carefully organised and rigorous training programme is matched by the experience of being put through their paces in the Sandhurst training exercises under the close supervision of the experienced platoon commanders in the company.

44 SUPPORT SQUADRON ROYAL LOGISTIC CORPS

With a mission 'To provide transport and tactical mobile communications support to RMAS' The Squadron can be traced back as far as 1900. Originally known as 44 Company Royal Army Service Corps, it served at Loos, The Somme, Ypres and Monte Casino.

Today, forty-four Support Squadron supports over nineteen exercises each fourteen-week term as well as day-to-day activities within the Academy. The Squadron has the ability to remain self-sufficient holding most of the facilities that would routinely be found in a Royal Logistic Corps Regiment. These include a Centralised Service and Inspections Bay, Light Aid Detachment Workshop and a military fuel station. The Squadron currently holds approximately 181 vehicles, ranging from DROPS, MAN SV and specialist Land Rovers that are fitted for radio (FFR).

A Troop is by far the largest troop, working alongside a small civilian team (B Troop) moving Officer Cadets to and from Exercise areas all over the UK and supporting the Cadets final three-week Exercise in Germany, Ex DYNAMIC VICTORY.

Last but not least is Seremban Troop. Established on 8 May 2015 the troop is named after the town of Seremban in Malaysia where the Queen's Gurkha Signals were formed on 23 September 1954. This is a sixteen-strong team of Queens Gurkha Signallers who deploy with the Officer Cadets on exercise, providing communications expertise.

chapter twenty-two:

Regimental and Academy Sergeant Majors

WO1 (ACADEMY SERGEANT MAJOR) DAVID MACPHEE

*O*n Saturday mornings the cadet battalion paraded under the command of the Regimental Sergeant Major, one Crooke. Crooke had originally enlisted in the cavalry, but being apparently totally unable to learn to ride, had been transferred to the Grenadiers. He was quite the smartest soldier I have ever seen, and his power of command of a battalion on parade was amazing. Standing far away, not a move escaped him – 'Number 2 of the rear rank of "E" Company (my humble self) moved 'is 'ead. Tike is nime and give 'im an extra drill.' But somehow or other the name was never taken and the extra drill never materialised. Crooke was an excellent fellow, as indeed were the majority of the NCOs at Sandhurst.

Gentleman Cadet Arnaud Foster, 1910

In 1991 General 'Monkey' Blacker wrote: 'Senior officers at Sandhurst come and go, but the personality which the cadets usually remember best is the Academy Sergeant Major, a Guardsman, and invariably a man of outstanding qualities and charisma.'

WO1 D.S. Macphee took over the appointment in 2015:
Having first worked at the RMA Sandhurst in 2004 as a Colour Sergeant instructor you could not fail to be impressed with the ethos of the place and the officer cadets in everything that they do. Returning again in 2008 as a Company Sergeant Major gave me a second opportunity to serve here and contribute to the education of officer cadets once again.

The enthusiasm of all the directing staff at RMA Sandhurst and their ability to get the best out of all the cadets is something to be admired. They demonstrated the highest standards of the British soldier both in barracks and in the field.

Having now had the pleasure of being selected as the Academy Sergeant Major I find myself in the unique position of serving at the Academy longer than most officers. In doing so I can assure all that the high traditions and standards that you expect from a place like Sandhurst are still alive and kicking today in the officer cadets and directing staff alike.

ACADEMY SERJEANT MAJORS
REDESIGNATED 1960

Dec	1960	J.C.LORD. MVO,MBE.	Gren Gds.
Aug	1963	C.H.PHILLIPS. MBE.	WG.
Dec	1970	R.P.HUGGINS.MBE.	Gren Gds.
Feb	1980	D.P.CLEARY. MBE.	IG.
Sep	1987	M.NESBITT.	Gren Gds.
Aug	1993	D.L.COX.	Gren Gds.
Jul	1994	R.D.McCORMACK.	COLDM GDS
Apr	1997	A.J.CRAWFORD, MBE.	Scots Gds.
Apr	2000	R.CONVERY,	Scots Gds.
Dec	2002	M.GAUNT, OBE,	Gren Gds.
Aug	2005	S.NICHOLS, MBE,	IG.
Aug	2007	P.J.CARR,	COLDM GDS
Apr	2010	R.A.MARTIN,	IG.
Dec	2011	A.J.STOKES,	COLDM GDS
Dec	2013	G.J.HAUGHTON,	Gren Gds.
Apr	2015	D.S.MACPHEE,	Scots Gds

'An honour to have my name on the same board as J.C. Lord'.

The first RSM of the Academy was WO1 'Bosom' Brand, who had been RSM of RMC since 1937 and held that position during its OCTU war years. He was a figure of legend. Major General Sir Desmond Rice was an officer cadet in 1944: 'I remember one foggy morning when we were all paraded on the road by the Lake. The RSM, WO1 Brand, Grenadier Guards, was standing on the steps of the Old Building, some 150 yards away. Out of the fog came his voice "Press on your rifle butt, Number 2 of the front rank 4th Troop A Squadron", and three instructor NCOs descended on the poor cadet.'

Brand came out of retirement to take the appointment of RSM of the Academy. As Peter Harrington of the 1947 class remembers: 'He wore an old fashioned 1914–18 uniform with

The Academy Sergeant Major is in.

RSM WO1 'Bosom' Brand.

MEMORIES OF J.C. LORD

Officer Cadet Stuart Money, 1954

Academy Sergeant Major J.C. Lord needs no introduction (did his parents bestow those initials out of ambition for their son, or did he take them on by deed poll for much the same reason?). Even then he was a legendary figure and held in awe by cadets under his authority.

Most cadets would have little or no direct contact with the Academy RSM. A typical scenario might have been on one of his drill parades, when a cadet would be a victim of his eagle eye at a distance. The 'monologue' would be along the lines: 'Inkerman Company, centre rank, third cadet from the left … no from the LEFT I said, sergeant, not the right! … yes that's the man; he's being IDLE! Get a grip on him sergeant.' One never knew what was the euphemism for 'idle', but the concerned would, no doubt, suffer the close attentions of the rebuked sergeant.

Apart from parades the Academy RSM was responsible for a lesson on boot cleaning. In the best practice of 'methods of instruction' Lord started the lecture by demonstrating how not to clean boots and shoes – applying the polish with one brush and taking it off with another, just as I had always done. With absolute logic, he questioned the idea of putting polish on and then taking it off again: whereupon he discarded one of the brushes. The other, he said, served both to apply polish and then to brush it *in*. I have observed that structure to this day, recalling RSM Lord each time I clean my shoes!

Lord, who would reign over RMAS from 1948 to 1963, was the first to assume the appointment title of Academy Sergeant Major when it was re-designated in 1960. No one has since matched Lord's time in the post but in those years incumbents were given time in appointment to make an impact. Phillips served for seven years 1963–70, Huggins for ten, 1970–80, Clearly for seven, 1980–87, and Nesbitt for six, 1987–93. Only recently have Academy sergeant majors had two- and three-year postings as do mere mortals.

Officer Cadet Paul Arnison-Newgass, 1955–57

Perhaps the Academy's most enduring achievement was its impeccable drill – parades orchestrated by the Brigade of Guards finest whose wit, intolerance and precision was a unique art form if at times terrifying. The Academy Sergeant Major then was the renowned RSM J.C. Lord, MVO, MBE, Grenadier Guards, whose demonstration of slow marching was little short of ballet – and I can see it today.

Officer Cadet Richard Avens, 1956–57

Looking at TV programmes recently I appreciate how times have changed and how relevant training now is, but I have happy memories of my days when we were treated like officers from the outset, we had batmen. The language of other rank instructors was not coarse (J.C. Lord would not have allowed it) and had time to enjoy life, play sport to a high standard and make lifelong friends.

puttees up to his knees: as though he had come off a Kiwi shoe polish tin. He once gave a demonstration of sentry drill on a six-foot table, only to forget the parameters of the table as he stepped backwards smartly into his "Sentry box" and vanished from sight. The parade hurriedly ended.' Brand retired in 1948 and was succeeded by the legendary J.C. Lord.

Officer Cadet Charles Shea-Simonds, 1961

I was in Ypres Company, Intake 30 whilst the legendary John Lord was Academy Sergeant Major. Lord had been the first RSM of the 3rd Battalion The Parachute Regiment and had been wounded and captured during the epic battle of Arnhem in September 1944. Early in our second year Lord approached our platoon formed up on the square. He commanded us to come to attention in turn as he reached us and to give him our number, rank, name and regiment of first choice. I shouted out as firmly as I could: '23855166 Officer Cadet Shea-Simonds, Sir, The Parachute Regiment.' He did a perfect 'double-take', came back a pace to me and said: 'Which battalion, Sir?' 'The Third Battalion, Sir', I replied. 'Not if I can help it, Sir!' he said, and strode off!

My great-uncle won the Anson memorial sword (later known as the Sword of Honour) in 1900 and was commissioned into the Munster Fusiliers. As Second Lieutenant Geoffrey Norman Shea he was sadly killed in South Africa during the final days of the Boer War. I was fortunate enough to have inherited his sword and, as a junior under-officer, was keen to carry it on my own passing out parade. I was told that only the Academy Sergeant Major could grant such permission – gulp! At the end of a parade a couple of weeks later I plucked up courage and marched across to the great man. I came to a halt in front of him and said with as much confidence as I could muster:

'Sir!'

'Yes, Sir', he replied, 'what is it?'

'Sir, I request your permission to carry this sword on my passing out parade.'

'What is its significance, Sir?' I told him.

'Allow me to have a look at it, Sir.' I passed him the sword and he read the inscription on the blade before handing it back to me.

'Carry it with pride, Sir!'

And I did.

About six months after I had joined 3 PARA, the great man retired from the British Army and we dined him out of the Officers' Mess. As a very insignificant second lieutenant I was standing just inside the front door of the mess with my colleagues to welcome him. As he came through the door with the Commanding Officer he spotted me and said: 'Mr Shea-Simonds, Sir, how nice to see you – how's it going?'

There were 960 officer cadets when I was at Sandhurst and I'd only spoken to him twice while I was there. What a man and never to be forgotten!

MEMORIES OF RAYMOND HUGGINS

Officer Cadet Dick Crombie 1973

In the early 1970s, the Commissioning Course was a lot less frenetic than it is today, and during that period, clubs and societies flourished in the officer cadets' spare time. One such society was the Sandhurst Amateur Dramatic Society, who put on various entertainments on a termly basis. As there were no

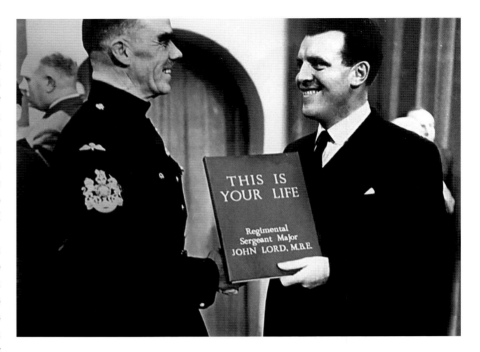

John Lord appears on This is Your Life.

female cadets at RMAS then, and although the WRAC College was not far away, the females for the cast and crew, particularly make-up and costumes, tended to be family members of the Permanent Staff. Amongst these were the two lovely daughters of the Academy Sergeant Major. Not infrequently after a rehearsal or a show, the cast and crew would go and have a meal and a couple of drinks in a local hostelry, and one Friday evening, as we departed quite late from the pub, one of the Academy Sergeant Major's daughters invited us back to Oak Grove View for coffee. 'Don't worry about the parents,' she said. 'They won't mind … and they'll probably be in bed by the time we get back anyway … '

With some trepidation, a group of us entered the lair of the great man, were ushered into the living room and the door closed, whilst the girls made coffee in the kitchen. We all then sat chatting, oblivious of time, until the door suddenly opened very slightly, and a well-known voice said 'It's time for bed, gentlemen'; and the door closed. We cadets didn't need a further hint, and so said our farewells and returned quickly and quietly to our respective Company Lines.

Saturday morning – Barrack Dress order with brown shoes. A well-organised cadet, I'd had everything pressed and shoes bulled up prior to the rehearsal the evening before, and so there was no need to rush to get ready for Muster Parade. All was going well and a few minutes to spare. One shoe on, second shoe on and … SNAP! A moment of doubt; then a dreadful realisation that I didn't have a spare pair of brown shoelaces. With not long to go, I swiftly readjusted the broken lace and tied the shoe. Out on parade the Colour Sergeant went by and said nothing … phew. Then, from behind the squad, a well-known voice said 'I think I'll inspect Blenheim Company this morning, Company Sergeant Major.' Moments later, standing before me with that mischievous twinkle in his eye stood the man with that well-known voice. Game up! 'Tell me Sir, are

Still an imposing figure – Raymond Huggins, In-Pensioner at the Royal Hospital Chelsea.

an imposing figure on the battlefield. And so it is with Academy Sergeant Major Ronnie Convery. Here is a man who has devoted his life to the service of his country, his Regiment and now future Officers. As Academy Sergeant Major I remember him drilling us hard, encouraging us on exercise and saluting us once we had commissioned. Such professionalism and dedication are admirable qualities. We all utterly respected him and trusted him to ready us for the biggest and proudest day of our lives – the Sovereign's Parade.

MEMORIES OF A.J. STOKES
Officer Cadet Peter Ward, 2012

In 2012 the Academy Sergeant Major of the Royal Military Academy Sandhurst was the most senior serving soldier in the Army. However, when I was lucky enough to walk through the gates of Sandhurst in 2012, I knew none of this. I didn't even know his name.

As an officer cadet on the very first day of the course, and many more times in the first couple of weeks, I probably hurried past him without even realising. He was just another rather large bloke with a rather large badge, who walked very calmly carrying a rather large stick. It was only over the first five weeks when I had to memorise all the names of the various permanent staff at the Academy did I start to appreciate his almost godlike status in the Academy and wider army.

In day-to-day life as an officer cadet there was not much interaction with the Academy Sergeant Major. It was only at the end of the term at the Sovereign's Parade did it all start to make sense. We got up and readied ourselves for the day with our Colour Sergeant who gave us some words of encouragement. After this we formed up as a company on New College parade square where the Company Sergeant Major had a go at us and promised that if we didn't strike the weapon hard enough he would do unmentionable things to us with his pace stick. It was then the turn of the College Sergeant Major who told the whole college a story about how he impressed the Queen on a previous parade, his supreme confidence infecting all of us. Finally, after Old College had joined us, it was the turn of the Academy Sergeant Major to give us a final pep talk. After calling in the two College Sergeant Majors, who sprang quickly to attention in front of him, he commanded the whole academy through a few final practice movements before reminding the senior division of the significance of the day and how they would never forget it.

His other big appearance to us when at the Academy was his final leadership lecture. This gave him the opportunity to tell us what he expected from junior officers who he served with in his battalion. As opposed to his barks on the parade square he calmly went through the do's and don'ts of battalion life and imparted his considerable wealth of experience. It was unfortunate that for most of the lecture we stared in disbelief at his highly polished shoes wondering if we would ever be able to achieve the same standard in the short time before the parade at the end of term!

you really so impecunious as to not to be able to afford a set of shoelaces?' Before I had a chance to try and respond, the well-known voice bellowed 'Idle on Parade, Company Sergeant Major!' And with that it was exit Square left, at 'the rift' to the Academy Guardroom.

I now always have a spare set of shoelaces available.

REFLECTIONS OF RONNIE CONVERY
Officer Cadet Peter Middlemiss, 2000

The Academy Sergeant Major was what I imagined a Guardsman to be when I joined the Army – immaculate on parade but also

chapter twenty-three:

Officer Staff

LIEUTENANT COLONEL ANDREW SPEED

The two terrors of the place are the Battalion Sergeant Major and the Adjutant, a very formidable combination!
Gentleman Cadet Michael Carver, 1933, *Out of Step*

Example at Sandhurst has always been driven by officer and NCO staff working in combination at every level from the formidable duo that Carver remembered, to the close working relationship within the platoons between the platoon commanders and colour sergeants that is central to the development of potential officers at RMAS today.
Officer Cadet Maurice Taylor, from a letter to his younger brother, 1947

Our instructors are the best. Every one seems to have a DSO or an MC. Some of the best ones are Captain Hunter DSO, OBE, MC and 2 bars – he is from the King's African Rifles. Another Captain from the 3rd Hussars has a DSO, an MC and 3 bars. However, one of our Sergeants in the Shropshire Light Infantry has the VC which beats them all. In our PT Staff we have a Scottish international, a Welsh international, a champion heavyweight boxer, Arsenal's left back plus many more famous sportsmen.

In a reminiscence in early 2016, Taylor's memory was crystal clear:

I moved from Somme Company into Gaza when it was first formed on the arrival of Intake 1A. My Company Commander then was Major G.W. Goschen, DSO, MC, RA and the 2i/c was Major M.E.M. MacWilliam who got his MC when he was twenty and then picked up three DSOs before he was twenty-four. He was in The Queens Royal Regiment. Not only did he command his battalion fighting up through Italy, he also had a brief command of his brigade for a time. What a man! Looking back he was only a 'boy' aged twenty-seven after the war in 1947 when he was one of our instructors.

It is the same today. I graduated from RMAS in August 1993 and am currently Commander of Old College. I completed the first combined commissioning course (CC923) when the graduates and

non-graduates were trained on the same course for the first time. I have also been a platoon commander and the Academy Adjutant.

The officer cadet today is a very focused and determined individual – much more so than when I joined. They have been brought up on a diet of twenty-four-hour news coverage. So the realities of Afghanistan and Iraq are very much in the forefront of their minds. Certainly during my time as Academy Adjutant in 2010 they were very clear on the dangers that faced them on first posting. They are, therefore, inquisitive and enthusiastic to learn. The staff have to be on their toes more than ever – 85% of them are graduates so they come with age and a degree of maturity. The staff at RMAS remain a very talented and experienced bunch. When I was an OCdt, even the most senior officers would have only two or three medals. These days most officers from Major onwards have at least five medals. It reflects the pace of operations over the last decade. So in terms of being a role model the staff are on the front foot. They have lived and breathed the operations that the officer cadets have been hearing about.

The support to the instructor has changed considerably since my days as a platoon commander in 1999 and 2000. Then, you went to the Faraday Hall and signed out a box of view foils (inevitably incomplete) and you then magically became an instructor. Today the staff attend an Army instructor's course at Pirbright and at RMAS they are supported by a dedicated team of professional trainers. There is a virtual learning environment where staff and officer cadets can access learning material. To make sure that we are getting it right we are inspected not only by the Army but also Ofsted. All of this contributes to a training environment that is always seeking to improve.

But the principle of an RMAS instructor being the role model for the future has not changed since I was an officer cadet. The example that the staff set is everything. Not only are we shaping their behaviours in the Army we are shaping their futures for the rest of their lives. The Army's values and standards and the Army's leadership code will, I believe, set them up for success no matter where their lives take them.

Ollie Campbell commissioned in December 2000 as a member of CC001, and is currently a Company Commander:
Collectively and individually, today's OCdts are impressive – they arrive at Sandhurst having climbed mountains, sailed oceans and travelled far more extensively than most OCdts of yesteryear. As a result, they bring with them a breadth of experience and cultural awareness. They are also very focused; they have grown up against a backdrop of enduring operations – the average OCdt was about ten years old during the invasion of Iraq – and although they will not necessarily face those same challenges, the OCdts appreciate that the uncertainty of today's climate and the challenge of contingency operations will inevitably present them with their own unique set of leadership challenges. Linked to this focus is a desire for continuous improvement, both from themselves and from the permanent staff. The permanent staff have responded by adapting their approach; there is much more given by way of feedback and as a result the OCdts are perhaps more self-aware than previously.

What has not changed, however, is the fabric and ethos of the Academy, and a graduate of the Academy from previous eras would recognise instantly the nature of training being undertaken by today's OCdt, even if the exercise names have changed! While the content of the course may have changed, the requirement for leaders to set the example and demonstrate selfless commitment has not. The observer from yesteryear might also note that in many respects the Commissioning Course is probably more demanding now; certainly there is greater intellectual pressure placed on the OCdts, and they have to deal with increased complexity. What is perhaps most striking, and humbling, is the fierce desire that OCdts possess to lead soldiers. Untainted by cynicism or world-weariness, all they want to do is get out into the Field Army and command men and women, preferably on operations, and make a difference. That makes the Academy an incredibly refreshing place in which to instruct.

David Hill graduated from RMAS in 1978 and was Old College Commander 2004–05:
The example that the staff set is everything. Indeed, everything an officer does is a lesson to someone. If you are a platoon commander at Sandhurst, you are the man that every one of your cadets wants to be

and so everything that you do is important. In that sense, staff at RMAS are never off duty.

Captain Paul Goodall, who was a member of CC083 graduating in 2009, sees the platoon commander's role growing in importance with each consecutive term.

All the permanent staff at the Academy have a part to play in setting an example to officer cadets, but platoon commanders should personify the role of an officer for the cadets on a day-to-day basis. In the first term this is in support of a hardworking Colour Sergeant or Staff Sergeant, who is then the key point of contact, instructing OCdts on basic soldiering skills. Getting the balance right between you and your Colour Sergeant and establishing a strong working relationship is central in the successful development of your platoon. His or her significance steadily decreases in terms two and three once the platoon is able to administrate themselves. As the course progresses it is the platoon commander who increasingly leads and mentors OCdts through a greater number of moral and conceptual challenges designed to prepare them for an uncertain world on first appointment.

Major Peter Harty, Chief Instructor Old College:

Having commissioned with CC991, I returned to RMAS with happy memories and I continue to enjoy a busy, but immensely rewarding posting. I was initially Officer Commanding Alamein Company

P.C. TRIAL SKETCH . THE START .

Map reading in 1893.

(CC143) and latterly Chief Instructor Old College. Some endure and others enjoy Sandhurst; I believe it presents opportunity. RMAS in 2017 reflects how the British Army has evolved through Iraq and beyond our learning in Afghanistan. Whilst 'new basics' have emerged, the core elements of Old College training reflect the best of our traditions, core values and contemporary operational learning.

Old College encapsulates many aspects of Sandhurst life, learning and culture. Our training focuses on a foundation in military skills, initial leadership development and an introduction to tactical command. Beyond the basics, we set the individual OCdt's development on a pathway of life-long learning and progression; we influence their military DNA at an impressionable stage. In Old College we consciously and carefully shape their perceptions and individual standards that will echo throughout their military careers.

Today, the Junior Term of the Regular Commission Course has been thoroughly revised, following the introduction of Project McNAMARA in 2015. As an organisation, Old College is an Ofsted-endorsed learning environment. We now better understand the outcomes required as a College and the processes/resources that enable those outcomes. For example, Exercise LONG REACH is more than just an epic walk over the Welsh Black Mountains, with a big pack and lots of command tasks. From the outside this exercise appears to have changed little; as Chief Instructor I have flashbacks to my experiences as an OCdt in 1999. However, we now recognise the value gained from each phase and their relationships with subsequent aspects of training. Exercise LONG REACH remains a challenging physical and moral experience, one which expands each individual OCdt's conceptual comfort zone. For some it bursts their bubble and resets a new understanding of

Left: Orders in the field.

Below left: Words of guidance on Exercise DYNAMIC VICTORY.

Below: Platoon Commander and Colour Sergeant – 'a strong working relationship'.

Major Peter Harty with three 1 R IRISH-bound cadets, wearing their Caubeens for the first time at the end of the final exercise.

what they can achieve, deliver and endure. The sustaining aspect of the exercise focuses hard on structured periods of reflection, essential in consolidating valuable experiential learning. Our deliberate approach to reflective learning seeks to generate a life-long attitude of honest self-awareness and leadership development.

We safely, constructively and deliberately take future officers to the outer edge of their comfort zone and we set them up for longer-term success as junior leaders; indeed, this is where we grow our leaders. We lecture theory and listen as OCdts articulate considered words; but we must stretch and then reflect, to enable self-learning to set the conditions for sustainable leadership development. Chief Instructor Old College is one of those unique posts where one can identify and resolve issues. The ability to positively develop a hectic training programme, work in a stunning setting, and share it with colleagues who want to work in the same arena creates a rewarding job and a sense of profound career satisfaction.'

THE LOUTS
Captain Ed Aitken

Amongst the stamping, soldiering and studying that goes on in a normal day at Sandhurst, the cadets could be forgiven for thinking that the permanent staff who deliver such excellent training might have superhuman powers. The ability to appear anywhere, at any time, to catch an officer cadet off-guard and to know the answer to every question whilst being immaculately turned-out, even after a week on exercise, might require a few tricks of the trade. However, the frenetic pace of life and the challenge of quenching the cadet's thirst for knowledge is quite exhausting for the young captains who work at the Academy.

Despite their appearance, these captains are actually very normal human beings who crave the socialising and good times that are such an important part of Army life. At Sandhurst this essential aspect of maintaining a work–life balance lies with an organisation called the 'Louts'. All captains at Sandhurst are automatically part of the Louts and wear the putrid three-coloured tie of burgundy red, champagne yellow and rosé pink

with great pride. The majors have the 'Taipans', the colonels have the 'Cardinals', but the life and soul of the party at the Academy belongs to the Louts. 'The Louts' is both the name of the club to which they belong and the phrase which collectively refers to all captains who work at the Academy.

The Louts was formed in the early 1980s initially as a club for giving a good send-off to fellow captains who were departing for pastures new. It has, in the past, attracted guest speakers such as Ken Livingstone and the Duke of Westminster. The beauty of the club is that its ambitions and forms of entertainment change with the generations of Louts who pass through the Academy, but always with the focus of ensuring its members can let off some steam.

Some of the traditions have lasted the test of time, the quirkiest of which is the termly signing of the ceiling in the Officers' Mess. Each term an elected Chief Lout, who is responsible for leading the charge with extra-curricular entertainment, has the honour of signing his name on the ceiling of the Officers' Mess. This is traditionally enabled by a three-tiered human pyramid constructed by his fellow Louts over whom the Chief has to scramble to reach the ceiling. This goes a little way to explaining some of the more wobbly signatures. Occasional redecoration eradicates history momentarily, but there have been some famous, and infamous, names which have adorned the ceiling of the Anteroom in the Sandhurst Officers' Mess.

Termly outings, or 'Loutings', usually involve the Louts getting into the Chief Lout's chosen form of fancy dress and partaking in activities away from the Academy. The huge Louts flag in the colours aforementioned is always taken on these expeditions and has been displayed in some extraordinary places over the years.

The most recent addition to the Louts repertoire is the Louts band 'Loutish Behaviour'. This draws its talent from the current crop of Captains who cover songs by bands such as The Killers and Electric Six. Loutish Behaviour play to the discriminating audience at any party organised by the Louts and have even been known to have the Commandant singing along to their set.

The Louts are a good example of how to have fun whilst showing that having a few drinks and a good time is all part of being a good young officer and demonstrates the careful balance that officer cadets should note.

chapter twenty-four:

Academics

DUNCAN ANDERSON

Tim Bean in full flight in the Woolwich Hall.

ritish officers have a reputation of being men of action. Long evenings in libraries studying military history and theory is not for them. A well-known cartoon from the late nineteenth century depicting gentlemen cadets struggling to answer examination questions epitomises this belief. On a shelf above them is a suit of armour, from the helmet of which appears a caption bubble: 'Gentlemen, we did not know much science, but we hit hard.' Enough said, many would say. This attitude has been reinforced by reminiscences of the academics themselves, of cadets asleep in their lectures, of colleagues' eccentricities, of nights spent drinking vodka with the Soviet Studies Research Centre, and of lecturers forgetting to turn up to their classes to the delight of their students. The foibles of any academic institution can make hugely comic reading, as novelists from Max Beerbohm to Tom Sharpe have discovered, and yet Britain's universities are amongst the best in the world. As with Oxford and Cambridge, there has been a great deal of fun at Woolwich and Sandhurst these past two and a half centuries, but there have also been immense achievements in both the sciences and the humanities.

The academic heart of Sandhurst lies in two buildings, a magnificent library, and the Faraday Hall, a long flat-roofed early 1960s construction, reminiscent of Grange Hill Comprehensive School. It was given the name Faraday Hall because it was originally a science block, and it serves to remind people that the present academy is the result of the fusion of Woolwich and Sandhurst, which took place in 1947. Today Professor Michael Faraday is the only Woolwich academic most people have heard about, but from the time of its foundation in 1741, until its merger with Sandhurst more than 200 years later, Woolwich was the British power-house for experiments for research and experiments in mathematics, geometry, chemistry, physics, ballistics, indeed, in virtually every field of scientific endeavour, in the eighteenth and early nineteenth centuries easily outclassing Oxford and Cambridge, and even the four excellent Scottish universities.

Woolwich academics were exemplars of research-led teaching. The books they produced were designed to make mathematics and science accessible to cadets destined for the engineers and artillery. Thomas Simpson, one of the first lecturers in mathematics, published *The Nature of the Law of Chance* in 1740 and *A Treatise on Algebra* in 1745. These were followed by Charles Hutton's *A course of Mathematics for the use of Academies* and Olinthus Gregory's *Mathematics for Practical Men*. A little later, concerned that engineers and gunners might make mistakes when making calculations when under pressure Peter Barlow produced *New Mathematical Tables*, which covered every conceivable calculation and were still being used as late as the Falklands campaign.

Woolwich pioneered the practical application of disciplines which could seem abstract. Paul Sandby, for example, is remembered as a landscape painter and drawing master, but his skills, which were essentially those of a draughtsman, could be

The names of gentlemen cadets carved into tables in the Academy library.

applied to the construction of roads, bridges and fortifications, which was the role he played in the late 1740s in the 'stabilisation' of the Highlands after the Jacobite uprising of 1745. Samuel Hunter Christie taught mathematics, researched the magnetic and electrical properties of metals, and the Earth's magnetic field, and gave the army an early version of the prismatic compass. Another mathematician, Francis Bashforth, experimented with ballistics, and invented the first effective ballistic chronograph, which could accurately measure the velocity of a round. Alfred George Greenhill applied his mathematical skills to calculating the optimal twist rate for lead core bullets, which found expression in the 'Greenhill Formula', which is still in use today, and which earned him a knighthood. Frederick Abel, a lecturer in chemistry, developed a safe way to manufacture gun-cotton, went on to develop cordite, and then to design electrical fuses to detonate explosives, for which he too was knighted.

Woolwich was an academic hothouse, an environment in which men of talent could pursue their researches, the sum of which always being greater than its parts. Would Michael Faraday have achieved all that he did in another environment? Given what we know about the state of the sciences in universities in the early nineteenth century it seems unlikely. Faraday's work on the composition of gases, on electro-magnetism and on optics all had immediate practical military applications, but apart from being a brilliant research scientist he was also an inspiring teacher. He outlined his technique in *Chemical Manipulation, Being Instructions to Students in Chemistry*. Faraday was a showman, who could keep a class of cadets enthralled by burning sulphur under water or by igniting a balloon filled with hydrogen.

By the early nineteenth century the scientific education given to the cadet officers of the engineers and artillery at Woolwich

was amongst the best in the world. The same could not be said of the infantry and cavalry, whose level of competence left much to be desired, as evidenced by the disastrous campaigns in the Low Countries between 1793 and 1795 and in 1799, both of which ended in humiliating evacuations. Appalled at the lack of professional competence displayed by many officers, a veteran of the 1793–95 campaign, Lt Col John Gaspard Le Marchant, managed to secure the government's agreement to establish military colleges for infantry and cavalry officers in Great Marlow and High Wycombe in 1801.

Le Marchant's academic curriculum was designed to give young officers a basic competence in mathematics, cartography, drawing and languages. With Britain facing invasion less than eighteen months after the establishment of the colleges, he was fortunate to be able to secure the services of Isaac Dalby, who although employed as a professor of mathematics was also a gifted cartographer. Between 1784 and 1796 Dalby had played a leading role in the production of the first ordnance survey maps of the south of England, skills which he now imparted to the first generation of cadets. Another of Le Marchant's early appointments, William Delamotte, famous as a landscape artist, stayed for forty-seven years as the College's drawing master. The influence of both men can be seen in the excellent maps and sketches of the Peninsula and other campaigns produced by the first generations of Sandhurst-educated officers.

When the colleges moved from High Wycombe and Great Marlow to Sandhurst in 1812, the academic staff accompanied them, lured in part by magnificent accommodation offered to them in the houses of 'Tea Caddy Row'. One of the first academics appointed after the move to Sandhurst, John Narrien, a thirty-two-year-old mathematician, was to spend forty-four years at the College, becoming an institution in his own right, today memorialised in the Narrien Library. In addition to mathematics Narrien was an astronomer, whose charts of the night sky proved invaluable aids to night-time navigation.

Some of the academic instruction mirrored that of Woolwich, but Sandhurst diverged in one respect, that of the study of military history, which was to become increasingly important. For nearly seventy years after the foundation of the College, commandants, governors and most members of the members of the directing staff were veterans of the wars Britain had fought from the middle of the eighteenth century until Waterloo. William Harcourt, the first commandant, had begun his military career with the capture of Havana in 1762, and had fought in the American War of Independence. George Murray, governor of the College between 1819 and 1824, had achieved fame as Wellington's brilliant quartermaster-general, George Scovell, commandant between 1837 and 1856, had played a vital role in the Peninsula as Wellington's chief of intelligence, and Harry Jones, commandant between 1856 and 1866, had fought at Badajoz, Vittoria and Nivelle, and had been wounded leading the forlorn hope during the first assault on San Sebastian. These men had made history and at least some of them wrote history, in contributions to military journals and quarterlies like *Blackwoods* and the *Edinburgh Review*, and sometimes in monographs, like Major General Charles Rochfort Scott, the Lieutenant Governor of Sandhurst in the late 1850s who added his *The Military Life of Field Marshal the Duke of Wellington* to an already substantial collection of Wellington memorabilia.

The establishment of the staff college only a mile from the cadet academy in 1858 gave a considerable impetus to academic study at Sandhurst, allowing a degree of cross-fertilisation. In that year a thirty-two-year-old officer of the Royal Engineers, Captain Charles Chesney, was appointed as the first professor of military history at Sandhurst, a position which allowed him to research and write his *Waterloo Lectures*, based on matching interviews with surviving veterans with a detailed survey of the battlefield. Chesney was the first operational military historian, whose devotion to academic objectivity impelled him to discredit a large number of regimental histories, be critical of Wellington's conduct of the battle, and attribute the final victory to the timely arrival of the Prussians. In 1859 an officer of the Royal Artillery, Captain Edward Bruce Hamley, was appointed the staff college's first professor of military history, and at Chesney's invitation also gave lectures at the cadet college, while his magnum opus, *The Operations of War*, became essential reading at both institutions. When he left in 1866, Chesney replaced him at the staff college.

The best known of Sandhurst's military historians in the nineteenth century was Major George Henderson, an officer of the 84th Regiment, who had served in Wolseley's Egyptian campaign of 1882, and who was appointed to Sandhurst in 1889 as an Instructor in Tactics, Military Law and Administration. Henderson's real interest was military history, as evidenced in the publication shortly after he arrived at Sandhurst of his first book, *The Campaign of Fredericksburg*, which began his life-long interest in Stonewall Jackson and his search for the fundamentals of what is today termed the 'manoeuverist approach'. Like Chesney before him, Henderson moved on to the staff college, though he maintained a close relationship with the cadet college, having formed an intellectual relationship with Sandhurst's commandant for most of the 1890s, Major General Sir Cecil James East. A veteran of the Crimea, the Indian Mutiny, the Zulu War of 1879 and the Third Anglo–Burmese War, East was an academic as well as a distinguished soldier. With Britain and France at the brink of war over the Fashoda Incident in 1898, East produced a timely analysis of the enemy's capabilities, *The Armed Strength of France*, which looked not just at the strength of the navy and the army but also at communications, industry, demographics, culture, education and political stability, and provided the model for all subsequent studies. East's greatest contribution to Sandhurst, however, was to translate into English General Ruprecht von Arnim's *Extracts from an Infantry Captain's Journal*, a brilliant guide to maintaining the effectiveness of an infantry company on operations, which was employed as a training manual at Sandhurst and many other cadet colleges, including RMC Kingston and West Point, in the years before the First World War.

An exam in 1893.

The existence of a group of soldier-scholars in Sandhurst did not, of course, indicate a high general level of education in the College. In 1869 the report of Lord Dufferin's committee on military education found that many cadets were idle, and that military instruction predominated too much over education proper. A third of a century later, after the lamentable performance of the army in the Second Boer War, the Akers Douglas Committee on military education produced evidence which was very much the same. Many cadets were found to be ignorant of basic facts of history and geography, some were functionally illiterate, while others were innumerate – while a few were both. The members of the committee identified the problem as the excessive attention devoted to sport at the public schools, which was producing a generation of physically fit ignoramuses. With the course having been reduced from eighteen months to one year the committee concluded that the civilian staff were too few in number and had too little time to repair the damage produced by a defective system of public school education.

Coming after the humiliating reverses of the first months of the Boer War, the report of the Akers Douglas committee had the effect of improving academic education at Sandhurst. The number of civilian instructors was increased, the course was lengthened, and more time was devoted to academic subjects. In a remarkable innovation the teaching of the academic subjects was linked increasingly to their possible military applications. The examination papers sat by Sandhurst's senior cadets in June 1914 bear testimony to the general success of this process. One of the exercises set by the modern languages department asked cadets to translate a lengthy hand-written despatch from German to English, and then translate it from

English into French. Mathematics, trigonometry and geometry were particularly testing, with cadets asked to solve a number of practical problems. One question, for example, required cadets to calculate the angle of elevation at which a tripod-mounted Vickers medium machine gun could produce the most effective 'beaten zone'. It seemed an easy enough question if one had mastered trigonometry, but there were complications. The calculations had to include the effect of the wind, coming in at different speeds and different directions. On the military history paper, a question asked the cadets not merely to analyse the difficulties Wellington faced in his withdrawal from Spain the autumn of 1812, but to put themselves in his quartermaster-general's situation, and suggest possible solutions.

Thanks to the Akers Douglas committee, by the summer of 1914 the academic courses at Sandhurst had achieved a level of sophistication which would do credit to a modern institution, but with eighteen months they had disappeared, and were not to be re-established for almost a third of a century. The massive expansion of the army meant that the intake was doubled and then quadrupled, the courses were shortened, and concentrated on what was immediately vital in making a junior officer effective on the Western Front. All but one of the academic staff were dismissed, some finding work in other educational institutions, many volunteering for the armed forces. Sandhurst ceased to be a college and became a training camp.

Spending priorities in the 1920s and 1930s saw the army starved of funds, which prevented the re-establishment of the academic staff on anything approaching the pre-1914 level. Cadets of this period like David Niven and Peter Carrington recalled the complete absence of anything other than subjects directly related to junior command. The training objectives published in February 1930 stipulated physical fitness, leadership and character, making no mention of the development of intellect. Gentleman Cadet Edward Bell wrote to his mother on 31 January 1937 that he was practising drill and studying tactics, but that 'there are tons of societies and, as for sport, I have put my name down for soccer. I hope to play tennis and have been told that one can swim this term … I have also entered for a pentathlon. You have to do five things. Riding, swimming, fencing, revolver shooting and running.'

Training of this sort did not necessarily produce junior officers of limited effectiveness, but there was nothing in the courses that could be considered remotely intellectually challenging. The catastrophes which overwhelmed the British Army in the first years of the Second World War led to a complete overhaul of the system for selecting and training officers during the course of 1942, a reform process which had the full support of the Chief of the Imperial General Staff (CIGS) Alan Brooke, and his protégé Bernard Montgomery.

The situation for the army in 1945 was very different from that of 1919. Britain faced a huge Soviet Army in central Europe and disorder and insurgencies throughout the empire. When he took over as CIGS in 1946 Montgomery pressed ahead with plans, first promulgated in 1875, to merge Woolwich and Sandhurst into a single academy, and to re-establish a broad range of academic education, without which officers would be ill-equipped to deal with the complex problems of the post-war era.

Montgomery chose Major General Francis Matthews, who had been director of military training for the Middle East during the war, as the first commandant for the new academy. To make the new academy a success, he needed an academic who could work in harmony with Matthews, one who understood what military training entailed, and who would be able to adapt academic courses to military requirements. An added complication was that the new academic staff would no longer be employees of Sandhurst per se, but civil servants, who would enjoy both the advantages and disadvantages that this new status would confer.

In the course of discussions in the War Office one name kept coming up, that of Henry Harrison Hardy, the recently retired headmaster of Shrewsbury. Like the great majority of his generation Hardy had considerable military experience, serving in the Rifle Brigade during the First World War, rising to the rank of major, and being awarded the MBE. As headmaster first of Cheltenham College and then of Shrewsbury, Hardy had been an enthusiastic supporter of Officer Cadet Training Units (OCTUs), and in the late 1930s had been the headmaster's conference representative on the War Office committee tasked with maintaining and expanding school cadet forces. His work had impressed the senior civil servants involved, and had earned him elevation to the CBE. Hardy also had a deep interest in military history, one which he was able to transmit to his son, the actor Robert Hardy.

Hardy fitted the bill – an academic, an administrator of a famous public school, a decorated soldier, and a 'Whitehall Warrior' of undoubted skill. On 21 October 1946 Montgomery wrote to Hardy outlining his plans. 'Our objective is an institution which, while preserving the necessary military bias, will ensure that the officer of the future has a deeper and more liberal educational foundation than was previously provided at Woolwich and Sandhurst. I believe that such an education is essential if we are to produce the type of officer we need and if we are to get the best out of our human potential.' Montgomery wanted Hardy 'to act as head of the civilian teaching staff, to correlate their activities and to maintain a proper balance between such studies as history, modern languages, political science on the one hand and the natural sciences on the other. I am most anxious to enlist for this purpose a man of distinction in the academic world whose vision and experience can help and guide us at the outset in the creation of a sound and invigorating educational tradition. I regard this work as of the greatest national importance.'

The merger of the College and the Academy brought a large part of Woolwich's excellent library to Sandhurst, giving the new institution a major resource for original research, particularly in military history. Over the next few years the civilian academic staff grew in numbers, and as their careers developed created new departments, better designed to meet the requirements of military education. Peter Horst Vigor, who arrived in 1948 to establish the department of modern languages, was a thirty-year-old wartime lieutenant colonel with a degree in Russian from Cambridge. He had survived the disastrous Norwegian campaign in 1940, had been wounded at Gazala in 1941 when serving as a signaller in 7th armoured division, and finally, thanks to his skill as a linguist, had been attached as a liaison officer to Konev's 1st Ukrainian Front, which allowed him to observe the battle for Berlin.

Vigor's experience with the Soviets left him with a profound distrust of Communism, to which he gave full vent in *A Guide to Marxism and its Effect on Soviet Development* (1966). In 1972 with the support of the CDS and the Foreign Office, he established a Soviet Studies Research Centre in a group of huts dating from the First World War in woodland north of the Faraday Hall. By the late 1970s Soviet Studies comprised some of the best analysts of the Soviet armed forces in the western world, whose reports were eagerly consumed by NATO high command, the US chiefs of staff, and the CIA. In the process Soviet Studies bequeathed to Sandhurst a Russian language library, second only to that of the School of Slavonic Studies.

Philip Warner arrived in Sandhurst at the same time as Peter Vigor. He, too, was a veteran of the war, having become a prisoner of the Japanese at the surrender of Singapore. Almost starved to death while working on the Burma railway, Warner was sufficiently recovered by 1946 to complete a degree in history at Cambridge. Joining the department of modern studies, at first Warner lectured in military history, while researching and writing biographies of leaders who had managed to cope with disaster, like Kitchener, Haig and Auchinleck.

Warner's interest in the subject of leadership was shared by John Adair, another Cambridge graduate who came to Sandhurst in 1961 after a period as a national service officer serving as an adjutant with the Arab Legion. Adair's researches resulted in *Effective Teambuilding* (1968), the first of what was to become a corpus of works on the study of leadership. Adair's work on leadership was reinforced by the arrival in 1965 of Richard Snailham, a twenty-five-year-old Oxford graduate who was a friend of the explorer Colonel Blashford-Snell, with whom he began a programme of adventure training. One of their first expeditions, a hugely testing white-water rafting adventure down some 500 miles of the hitherto unexplored upper reaches of the Blue Nile, provided the material for Snailham's first book, *The Blue Nile Revealed* (1970), the first of a series of adventures which took him and the cadets of Sandhurst down the Congo, the Amazon, and to many other potentially dangerous environments.

Snailham's adventures provided the raw material for Adair's studies of leadership which resulted in his famous three balls model, today used throughout the world. Realising that the existing academic departments dealt with the subject only peripherally, in 1973 Warner proposed to the commandant, Major General Robert Ford, that a new academic department be formed, that of communications and leadership studies. The

timing was propitious. Ford had just relinquished command in Northern Ireland, where the 'Bloody Sunday' massacre had been the result, at least in part, of garbled orders and a confused chain of command. With Ford's full support, Warner began transferring academics like Snailham to the new Communication and Leadership Studies Department. One of the most prominent early recruits was Dr Tony Clayton, who had arrived at Sandhurst in 1965, after serving as a colonial office official in Kenya, during which time he had participated in the suppression of the Mau Mau insurgency. Clayton's first book, *Counter-Insurgency in Kenya: A Study of Military Operations against the Mau Mau*, is still essential reading for those who wish to understand this campaign. Direct experience of this controversial campaign and the years spent educating cadets enabled Clayton to write his magnum opus, *The British Officer: Leading the Army from 1660 to the Present*, which has become required reading in military academies throughout the world.

The Communications Department is now the Department of Communications and Applied Behavioural Science, a change of emphasis introduced by Dr Ian Stewart, a behavioural psychologist who arrived at Sandhurst in 1990 and became head of the department in 2006. Having worked in Ministry of Defence public relations Stewart was very much aware that a junior officer who mishandled an interview with the media could do untold damage to the conduct of a campaign. To obviate this danger Stewart increased the amount of time cadets spent engaged in realistic hostile interviews. Stewart left in 2011 to join Inspirational Development Group, an international tutorial agency offering seminar programmes on leadership and business management. He was succeeded by Dr Deborah Goodwin, whose expertise in the field of negotiations proved invaluable to junior officers conducting shuras in Afghanistan, and has earned Dr Goodwin worldwide recognition.

In his letter of instruction to Hardy, Montgomery had mentioned the need to teach junior officers political science, a discipline which in Britain in the mid 1940s was scarcely twenty years old, and at that time taught by only a handful of universities, notably Balliol College at Oxford, which had pioneered the degree of politics, philosophy and economics in the mid 1920s. One of the first academics employed to teach this new discipline was William Glynn Jenkins, who arrived in Sandhurst in 1956 with appropriate degrees from Oxford and Yale. Still only 30 years old, Jenkins had served in the war as a subaltern in the Royal Marine Commandos. Shortly after his twentieth birthday in 1945, Jenkins had single-handedly stormed a series of German strong points which had been holding up 8th Army's advance into the Po Valley, actions for which he received the DSO, the youngest officer ever awarded this medal in the history of the British armed forces. An inspiring teacher, Jenkins was for many years the living embodiment of the ideal junior officer, his memoir of his own experiences, *A Commando Subaltern at War*, serving as a guide to future generations.

By the late 1970s Political Science had become the Department of International Affairs. Under its new head, Dr John Sweetman, who had earned a doctorate at Oxford on British military administration in the mid-nineteenth century, the academics still introduced the cadets to the evolution of the British state, and the position of the army within it, but the emphasis turned increasingly towards Britain's position within alliance systems. Thanks to the employment of a new generation of academics like James Higgs, Rosemary Durward and Martin Smith, the department gained unrivalled expertise on the development of NATO, expertise which was maintained and expanded thanks to regular visits to Brussels and Mons.

With the dissolution of the USSR and the collapse of the Warsaw Pact the new head of department, Dr Francis Toase, shifted the focus of the department towards the Balkans, the Middle East, and Central and South Asia. Having studied counter-insurgency operations in Southern Africa, particularly Zimbabwe and Namibia, Toase was very aware of the problems the British army would very likely experience handling large numbers of detainees in the operations in Sierra Leone and Bosnia and a little later, in Afghanistan and Iraq. In order to obviate the difficulties he foresaw, Toase introduced a new course on the Law of Armed Conflict, though this was only achieved in the teeth of considerable resistance from some elements in the army and the MoD, who considered it unnecessary. It turned out to be providential, when the difficulties Toase had foreseen actually emerged in the first months of the army's deployment to Iraq. One of the academics employed to introduce this new course, Dr Page Wilson, an Australian with a doctorate in international law from The London School of Economics, actually participated in the prosecution at the Hague of some of the most notorious warlords captured in the Balkans.

Montgomery's letter to Hardy had also stressed the need to teach the cadets history. The commandant in the late 1950s, Major General Ronald Urquhart, a graduate of Pembroke College Oxford, believed that greater specialisation was required, with the cadets being introduced to military history geared to their requirements. Urquhart, who had been awarded the DSO during the Normandy campaign, and had become Director of Combined Operations, believed he knew a man ideally suited to establish a department specialising in operational military history, Brigadier Peter Young, a graduate of Keeble College Oxford, who had recently retired as commander of one of the battalions of the Arab Legion. To everyone in Combined Operations Young was a legend. As a commander of an infantry platoon, Young had been wounded at Dunkirk, had recovered and become one of the founders of the Commandos. He had taken part in virtually every major raid in North West Europe, from Norway to the coast of France, including Dieppe and Normandy. Young had also raided along the Mediterranean littoral, and after the surrender of Germany, had raided along the Japanese-controlled coast of Burma. The normally acerbic Evelyn Waugh, who in his diaries dripped literary vitriol on many of his fellow commando officers, had nothing but admiration for Young. So, too, had the Director of Combined Operations who ensured that Young was awarded the DSO and the MC with two bars.

Arriving at Sandhurst in 1959, Young immediately began to recruit his department. One of his first appointees was Antony Brett-James, a Cambridge graduate who had served as a signaller in 5th Indian Division in North Africa, and subsequently in all the major operations of the Burma campaign, during which he was mentioned in despatches. Brett-James became Young's deputy, and when Young retired in 1969, became head of the department until his own retirement in 1979. Both men wrote of their wartime experiences, Young producing *Storm from the Sea* and *The Arab Legion* and Brett-James publishing *Ball of Fire: the Fifth Indian Division* and *The Battle of Imphal.*

By the early 1960s universities were beginning to produce the first graduates who had specialised in military history, hitherto largely the preserve of retired officers. Young and Brett-James had almost a sixth sense of who had the potential to make a substantial contribution to the new discipline. The staff of the War Studies Department, as it was soon to be named, became the foundation on which the study of war became academically respectable. Amongst the first appointees were two young men from Oxford, John Keegan and David Chandler, the former the author of *The Face of Battle*, which revolutionised the study of the behaviour of men in combat, the latter the author of *The Campaigns of Napoleon*, which the then president of France, Charles de Gaulle, described as the definitive analysis of Europe's greatest general. Both men achieved high honours, Keegan becoming defence correspondent of the *Daily Telegraph*, and being knighted in 1991, Chandler succeeding Brett-James as head of department in 1979, and receiving a D Litt. in 1992, the highest academic distinction Oxford University could bestow.

During the 1960s the department grew steadily in strength. Another Oxford graduate, Christopher Duffy, a gifted linguist, fluent in French and German, and with a working knowledge of Russian, arrived in 1963. Duffy quickly established himself as one of the leading historians of European military history, his studies of Frederick the Great, the army of Prussia and the army of the Austrian Empire becoming definitive texts. Passionate in his belief that one should not write about campaigns until one had actually walked the ground, Duffy also surveyed and wrote about the fortress zones of Europe, and, adopting the personae of an Austrian analyst, wrote extensively on the routes which the Soviets might take if they were to invade Western Europe.

By the end of the decade Duffy had been joined by Ned Willmott, who was to become one of Britain's leading naval historians, and take several visiting professorships in the United States, and Richard Holmes, a Cambridge graduate who was an enthusiastic Territorial Army soldier. Holmes eventually rose to the rank of brigadier, at that time the highest rank in the Territorial Army, was awarded the CBE, and left for a professorship at Cranfield University. Deeply impressed by *The Face of Battle*, Holmes produced his own study of the realities of combat, *Firing Line*, which developed many of the ideas in Keegan's earlier work.

The 1970s saw the arrival of John Pimlott and Ian Beckett, who produced a pioneering study of British counter-insurgency; Paddy Griffith; who introduced war gaming and the concept of the 'empty battlefield'; Nigel de Lee, who embarked on a programme of recording the reminiscences of veterans of the First and Second World Wars, laying down a resource which will be of incalculable value to future generations; Michael Orr, a Russian specialist who moved on to Soviet Studies; Keith Simpson, who was to specialise in studies of the Waffen SS, and left to work in Conservative Central Office under Margaret Thatcher, in time becoming the MP for Norfolk Central; and Hew Strachan, who became the Chichele Professor of the History of War at Oxford and was knighted in 2013.

The concentration of so many military historians in one department has helped War Studies to be uniquely productive. Two of its academics, John Keegan and Hew Strachan, received knighthoods. Three have been awarded the Templer Medal, military history's equivalent of the Booker Prize: Hew Strachan for a study of the reform of the British Army in the nineteenth century; Dan Marston for his account of the training of the Indian Army during the Second World War; and Paul Harris for his definitive biography of Douglas Haig. Eight accepted professorships: Richard Holmes at Cranfield; Ned Willmott at Annapolis; Ian Beckett at Kent; Dan Marston at the Australian Defence Force Academy; Gary Sheffield, the author of a major study of the Somme, at Birmingham, Andrew Lambert, a naval historian, at Kings; Colin McInnes, the historian of Britain's nuclear deterrent at Aberystwyth; and Stephen Badsey, an expert on media operations and author of the concept of the 'media flank' at Wolverhampton. Several more have taken jobs in which they can develop their specialisms more fully: Dan Todman, editor of the Alanbrooke diaries, at Queen Mary College; Kristian Gustafson, an expert on the CIA, at Brunel; Peter Lieb, the author of a ground-breaking study of the German occupation of France, at the German military history institute in Potsdam; Garth Pratten, the author of a widely acclaimed study of Australian Army junior leadership during the Second World War, at the Australian National University; Stuart Gordon, one of the architects of the 'Helmand Road Map', at the London School of Economics; and Chris Pugsley, formerly a lieutenant colonel in the New Zealand army, and an acknowledged expert on Gallipoli, back in his homeland to become the official historian of the 2nd New Zealand Division in the Second World War. These departures should not be seen as a loss; rather, they mark the spread of the department's influence throughout the academic world.

As the 'New World Dis-Order' of the 1990s morphed into the 'Forever War' of the 2000s, the demands on the academic departments became ever greater and more complex. In 1946 Sandhurst had been fortunate to acquire the services of a director of studies who was skilled both as an academic and a Whitehall bureaucratic. In the intervening years directors had frequently been able to give very little direction; those who were bureaucrats lacked educational vision, while those who were educationalists lacked the skills to handle the complexities of military and civil service administrative procedures. In 2006, exactly sixty years after Hardy's appointment, Sandhurst got a director who combined both abilities. Sean McKnight, a graduate of Oxford and King's, joined the War Studies Department in 1989, but had left to join the civil service mainstream, becoming director of the military court service at a particularly testing time.

It would seem axiomatic that a staff like that at Sandhurst would be employed to support operations, but suggestions that highly educated Sandhurst academics should be enlisted as political advisors or as operational military historians embedded with units, a practice adopted by every other western country, ran into considerable opposition from a variety of quarters within the civil service and the army. That such opposition was eventually overcome owed much to McKnight's abilities as a twenty-first-century 'Whitehall Warrior'. Dr Stuart Gordon of DIA and Ronnie McCourt of CABS, both Territorial Army Lieutenant Colonels, participated in the invasion of Iraq in 2003, Gordon as a political advisor and McCourt as commander of a media support team. Subsequently James Higgs of DIA served for more than a year as a political advisor to the British commander in Basra, while Duncan Anderson, the head of the War Studies Department, deployed to Baghdad in 2005 and 2006 as part of a small British army team tasked with rebuilding the Iraqi Military Academy at Ar Rustamiyah. While in Iraq Anderson was also able to operate as an operational military historian, embedding with the US Marines in Fallujah and the US Army in Ramadi, during which he was able to observe the beginning of the 'Al Anbar Awakening'.

The army's need to staff Military Analysis modules, the educational courses for promotion from captain to higher ranks, meant that Sandhurst academics were deployed to wherever the army was operating. By the time British forces had withdrawn from Basra and from Helmand five academics had taught in Iraq, Drs Harris, Strohn, Fremont-Barnes, Marston and Metcalfe, while Drs Anderson, Metcalfe, Strohn and Flint had taught in either Kandahar or Bastion. In addition, Dr Strohn, a lieutenant colonel in the Bundeswehr Reserve, deployed to Kunduz as part of a German Army training team, while Dr Marston, holding dual American and British citizenship, was seconded to the US Army's counter-insurgency training team at Tadji, to the north of Baghdad, and was subsequently seconded to the staff of General Petraeus, where he helped in the writing of American counter-insurgency doctrine. Subsequently Marston made regular trips to Afghanistan, reporting directly to Petraeus on the progress of the campaign. Two academics who also held commissions in the Territorial Army, Dr Kristian Gustafson, a Canadian, and Dr Garth Pratten, an Australian, also served in Afghanistan, Gustafson training Afghan special forces and Pratten deploying to Kandahar as a military historian, tasked with recording the campaign in the south east. Meanwhile Dr Anderson was able to reprise his role as an operational military historian, embedding in 2007 and

2012 with British units operating in Sangin, Garmsir, and Nad-e Ali, experiences he was able to incorporate into his teaching at Sandhurst, particularly his survival of two IED strikes in his earlier deployment to Al Anbar and of two more in Helmand. Dr Stuart Gordon also served in Afghanistan, reporting on the progress of the campaign for his work designing both the 'Helmand Road Map', during which he narrowly survived an ambush in Kabul. The effectiveness of a counter-insurgency campaign is notoriously difficult to measure, but Dr Björn Müller-Wille of DIA was able to give the government some idea of progress, thanks to lengthy deployments to Helmand, during which he conducted surveys of local attitudes.

When Sandhurst academics went to Iraq and Afghanistan, they believed that they were the first civilian staff since the formation of the modern academy to deploy to an operational zone, but they weren't. Half a century earlier, a team of Sandhurst academics had gone to the Federation Military Academy in Malaya, helping their military colleagues establish a programme of training and education which would produce the junior officers for the new army of an independent Malaya. This deployment, today almost entirely forgotten, was hugely successful, giving Malaysia one of the most effective corps of officers in South East Asia.

In 2012 the British government decided to try to repeat the experiment in Afghanistan, establishing the Afghan National Army Officer Academy at Qargha, to the west of Kabul. Sandhurst academics had already produced a number of studies of Afghan military history. Foremost amongst these was Dr Tony Heathcote, a graduate of the School of Oriental and African Studies, who had come to Sandhurst in 1965 as the curator of the Sandhurst Museum. Having only recently retired, Heathcote made his expertise freely available to his former colleagues. Two members of the War Studies Department, Dr Ed Yorke and Dr Fremont-Barnes, had also written extensively on Britain's involvement in all three Afghan wars, on the Russian War, and on the post-2001 conflict. Having already worked to re-establish the Iraqi officer academy, Anderson was the logical choice to lead the mission, deploying for twenty-two months, January 2013 to October 2014, to Qargha. He was soon joined by Dr Mike Rennie of CABS and Dr Ed Flint of DIA, both of whom served for more than eighteen months. The Afghan National Army Officer Academy is an on-going commitment. The academic deployed there for 2015 and 2016, Dr Fremont-Barnes of War Studies, has managed to create a library of more than 10,000 books in both Dari and Pashto, which is now the second largest in Afghanistan. Fremont-Barnes is due to return to Sandurst in the spring of 2017 after a deployment of nearly two years, when he will be replaced by another War Studies academic, Dr Stephen Hart.

As a by-product of his work in media operations during the invasion of Iraq, Lt Col McCourt began to run short defence diplomacy courses on leadership, communications and associated subjects at the behest of the Foreign and Commonwealth Office. Over the last ten years the number of these courses has expanded considerably, leading to Lt Col McCourt forming a new department, Academic Outreach. The areas covered, too, have grown in scope and complexity, and now include counter-terrorism, counter-insurgency, negotiation skills, aid to the civil power, the demands of civilian and military leadership, and the law of armed conflict. The academics of all three departments have now run courses in many troubled countries, including South Sudan, Uganda, the Democratic Republic of the Congo, Sierra Leone, Gambia, Kenya, Namibia, Ethiopia, Sudan, Algeria, Tunisia, the West Bank (Palestine), Bahrain, Qatar, Kuwait, Oman, the UAE, Saudi Arabia, Uzbekistan, Tajikistan, Nepal, Sri Lanka, Bangladesh, Burma, Colombia, Ecuador, Peru, Albania, Kosovo, Bosnia and Macedonia. Short deployments of this type have helped the academic staff expand their expertise, giving them first-hand experience of large areas of the world where British assistance can be of real value to governments under considerable strain. The experience gained in these deployments has been fed back into teaching at Sandhurst, the cadets' interest being stimulated by first-hand accounts of the operations of Maoist guerrillas in Nepal, of fighting between the Nuer and the Dinka in South Sudan, or preventing Hamas or Hezbollah terrorist attacks in Fatah-controlled territory on the West Bank.

The academic departments of Sandhurst are now regarded as an important reservoir of expertise, upon which the MoD, the army, other departments of state, and occasionally the armed forces of allied nations, can draw. Two academics have worked in the Cabinet Office – Sarah Oliver of CABS and Catherine Sowerby of DIA; Jenny Metcalfe of DIA has been seconded to the FCO, Page Wilson of DIA to the European Court of Human Rights; Rosemary Durward of DIA to the Council of Europe, Lloyd Clark of War Studies to the new Army Leadership Centre; and Deborah Goodwin of CABS to a UN agency, where she ran training courses in negotiation skills.

The army has made particularly heavy demands on War Studies. The department has unrivalled expertise in organising and conducting staff rides, so that scarcely a day goes by without a request for assistance being received. There are very few battlefields that some member of the department has not studied, from Christopher Duffy tracing the campaigns of Frederick the Great or the march of the 'Young Pretender' in 1745; Lt Col Peter McCutcheon surveying the Falklands battles of 1982; Chris Mann shepherding cadets through the complexities of Narvik in 1940; Garth Pratten cycling along the route of the Japanese advance down the Malayan Peninsula in 1942; Paul Harris and Ed Flint of DIA trudging along the Ho Chi Minh Trail; Chris Pugsley climbing the slopes of Anzac Cove on the Gallipoli Peninsula; Steve Walsh taking cadets across the Volga into Stalingrad; or Matthias Strohn introducing British officers to the Soviet assault on Berlin 1945. Beginning in 1995 the American Army also sought assistance, this time to provide expertise for the Alam el Halfa and El Alamein Battles of 1942, which HQ CENTCOM and US 3rd Army studied as part of the bi-annual Bright Star Operation. The Turkish army, too, has

Cadets on Exercise NORMANDY SCHOLAR.

sought assistance, Chris Mann taking Turkish generals through the siege of Malta and the Tunisian campaign of 1942–43. With the anniversary of the First World War, War Studies provided a team of three experts on the conflict, Matthias Strohn, James Kitchen and Stu Mitchell, to work with Operation Reflect, the British government's programme of commemoration.

In 1947 the Sandhurst academics were entirely British, the great majority had MA degrees from Oxford or Cambridge, and most had served in the First or Second World War, often with great distinction. Seventy years on, only a handful of academics have served in the regular army, though the experience they bring to their colleagues is invaluable. Ronnie McCourt of Academic Outreach, Peter McCutcheon and Chris Pugsley of War Studies, and Dennis Vincent and Chris Jacobs of CABS all left the army as lieutenant colonels, several having been awarded military MBEs, with a combined record of service which include Malaya, Northern Ireland, Sierra Leone, the Balkans, Iraq and Afghanistan. Other academics have served in the Territorial Army, some of whom have been on operations in Iraq and Afghanistan.

A major difference with the generation of 1947 is that nearly half the academic faculty are from overseas, the old commonwealth of Canada, Australia, New Zealand and South Africa being strongly represented, but with powerful contingents from the United States and Germany, and individuals from Sweden, Norway, the Netherlands and Italy. Today all but a handful of academics hold a doctorate, and although Oxford and Cambridge are still very much in evidence, their dominance is no longer crushing. Some academics have multiple identities. Dr Gregory Fremont-Barnes of War Studies for example, born in the United States, holds degrees from Chicago, UCLA and Oxford, has taught in Japan, and today holds a British passport. Like Fremont-Barnes, Dr Paul Latawski, also of War Studies,

was born in America and became a British citizen, but also has strong family connections with Poland. Latawski's fluency in Polish has proved an enormous boon, not just for Sandhurst but for the army as a whole. From 1907 onwards the British army produced numerous publications on various operations of war, but failed to archive them systematically, so that the majority were lost. Thanks to his researches on 1st Polish Armoured Division, Dr Latawski discovered a complete set of British doctrine pamphlets in Polish, meaning that the evolution of doctrine can now be traced with considerable accuracy, at least by a speaker of Polish. Now seconded to Land Command, Dr Latawski has been engaged in the task of translating and interpreting these documents, providing future generations of historians with a valuable resource.

The best example so far of the advantages which can be gained by recruiting academics from a variety of backgrounds was the research conducted over a ten-year period by War Studies into the Normandy Campaign, which allowed the creation of Exercise NORMANDY SCHOLAR. The department's four German lecturers, Drs Claus Telp, Klaus Schmider, Peter Lieb and Matthias Strohn, worked in the archives in Freiburg; their Canadian colleague, Dr Kristian Gustafson, researched in Ottawa; the Americans, Dr Dan Marston and Dr Gregory Fremont-Barnes, trawled the archives in Washington and Carlisle; while their British colleagues, Dr Simon Trew, Dr Stephen Hart, Professor Lloyd Clark and Tim Bean worked their way through the National Archives in London, all groups researching platoon-level actions, which allowed them subsequently to match up German and Allied accounts of the same actions. In addition, Dr Paul Latawski researched the Polish contribution, Dr Peter Lieb, fluent in French, looked at the effect of the battles on the civilian population, while Dr Chris Pugsley, reprising his career as an infantry officer, walked the battlefields, matching the accounts of war diaries to the ground. The result of these labours was an exercise in which cadets are placed in a situation which was the same as that faced by a platoon commander, Allied or German, in the summer of 1944. They are given just as much information as that platoon commander had in his possession in 1944, and the cadets are then required to use seven questions to arrive at a solution to the problem, a process which is then critiqued by their military and academic instructors. Exercise NORMANDY SCHOLAR is the most effective means of 'hard-wiring' the seven questions into the young officers' consciousness that has yet been devised, and was the product of a collective effort of Sandhurst academics of four nationalities working in German, Canadian, British, American, Polish and French archives.

Exercise NORMANDY SCHOLAR is an indication of another major difference between the Sandhurst of 1947 and the Academy today. Seventy years ago cadets attended lectures, participated in seminars and gave presentations. All this is done today, but learning in the classroom is reinforced by exercises in which the academic and military merge seamlessly, such as AGILE INFLUENCE, run by CABS, in which cadets

learn how to run a shura, or TEMPLER'S TRIUMPH, run by DIA, which tests the cadets' ability to conduct effective counter-insurgency operations.

For many years it has been clear that the skills in leadership and management cadets acquire at Sandhurst was worthy of academic recognition at tertiary or post-graduate level. Unlike 1947, when the great majority of cadets arrived straight from high school, the average age of cadets today is twenty-three, of whom around 84% already have a degree. The Academy has now entered into a partnership with both the Open University and Cranfield University, the former to give credits for an undergraduate teaching stream, the latter to give credits for a post-graduate certificate which will lead to a MA degree.

But Sandhurst is not, and never can be, a military university. Its purpose is to produce militarily effective platoon commanders and it is very good at doing this. The academics understand this, just as those who have worked at both the Academy and the College in previous centuries have understood this. The key to being an effective academic at Sandhurst is, to paraphrase Le Marchant, to have the ability to light the fire of enthusiasm for learning within the cadet. Michael Faraday could do this in the 1820s, delighting cadets with his displays of pyrotechnics, and Peter Young did this in the 1960s, discharging a Brown Bess in a lecture on Napoleonic warfare. Health and safety legislation prohibits such displays today, but Faraday and Young would recognise a kindred spirits if they could return to the second decade of the twenty-first century to witness Peter Lieb stripping and assembling a MG42 before a platoon of intrigued cadets, or sit with cadets to watch a camcorder video of Duncan Anderson being blown up by an IED in the streets of Ramadi. Like the character of war, the character of academic teaching at Sandhurst will change, but like the nature of war, the nature of academic teaching at Sandhurst is immutable.

THE LIBRARY

The Library has been an integral part of cadet education at Sandhurst ever since the Royal Military College was opened on this site in 1812. Originally located in the anteroom directly above the Grand Entrance, the Library was supervised by the Chaplain, the Reverend W. Wheeler, who was tasked with acquiring a collection of books 'requisite to form a military library … and arranged in order of matter'.

Officers attending the Senior Department (later to become the Staff College) paid a subscription of £2, whilst gentlemen cadets, in addition to purchasing their own basic textbooks, were expected to pay 10 shillings per year towards the cost of books and journals. In 1842 a librarian was appointed, at a salary of £20 per year, to assist the Chaplain, and by 1880 the collection had grown sufficiently in size to necessitate a move to the former chapel (now the Indian Army Memorial Room).

The Library's first printed catalogue was produced in 1904, and in 1907 a new set of rules was created to deal with the increase in use of Library facilities. Readers were to be restricted to borrowing one book at a time, with a maximum loan of

*The vaulted ceiling of
the Library betrays its
origins as the Academy
gymnasium.*

fouteen days, and fines of threepence per day were imposed on transgressors. A sign was erected, warning that: 'The library is intended for quiet conversation and reading. Loud talking and skylarking will not be tolerated.'

In 1913 the Library moved again, this time to the central section of the recently completed New College, and during the First World War more than 1,500 books were added, bringing total holdings to 7,000 volumes. The quality of the collection, however, still left much to be desired. A report in 1919 concluded that: 'The Library is still poor in standard works, and its space is much encumbered by obsolete and third rate fiction.' Little improvement seems to have been made during the 1920s, but in 1931 the Library was merged with the Museum, and moved to its present site in the former College gymnasium.

In 1939 the Royal Military College closed its doors for the last time, and for the duration of the Second World War became one of several Officer Cadet Training Units. In 1946 it was decided that the role of the College should be amalgamated with that of the Royal Military Academy at Woolwich, which had also closed in 1939, to form the Royal Military Academy Sandhurst. The new Academy opened in 1947, and a new Librarian, Lt Col G.A. Shepperd, was appointed. Lt Col Shepperd, who had lost both his legs in the Normandy campaign in 1944, set about his task with enormous energy, and by judicious purchase of both new and second-hand material, had added more than 100,000 volumes by the time of his retirement in 1976. Among the works that he was able to acquire were complete sets of Wellington's

dispatches and Napoleon's correspondence, along with many rare regimental histories.

Over the past thirty years the Library has been threatened with closure on a number of occasions, but it still survives, now enhanced by computerised catalogues and electronic access to books and journals. At its heart, however, remains the collection of more than 180,000 volumes so carefully brought together by Alan Shepperd and his successor John Hunt, forming a unique resource for future generations of cadets.

SANDHURST BY THE BOOK
Andrew Orgill

One might be forgiven for assuming that Sandhurst cadets have had little to offer the literary world beyond the confines of military memoirs and worthy texts on the operations of war. However, even a cursory glance through the cadet registers reveals the names of a wide range of literary figures, including poets, novelists, playwrights and journalists, who have paraded, with varying degrees of enthusiasm, on Old College Square.

It has to be admitted that one characteristic shared by several Sandhurst authors is that they failed to complete their training. An early example of this trait was the poet Robert Horne (1802–84), who was 'withdrawn by his friends' in 1819. Sadly Horne is remembered today less for his own work than for his friendship with figures such as Dickens and the Brownings. He is, however, almost certainly the only Sandhurst cadet ever to have thrown a snowball at John Keats. Another whose military career ended without a commission was Ian Fleming (1908–64), who arrived at Sandhurst in the autumn of 1926 as the proud recipient of a prize cadetship. For fans of James Bond it may seem entirely appropriate that Fleming's time in the Army should be cut short following an incident in which he was discovered climbing back into the grounds after an evening with a girlfriend in Camberley.

For sheer variety of literary styles and subject matter, few Sandhurst intakes can match the 140 gentlemen cadets who were commissioned in May 1882. Of these no fewer than twelve became published authors, producing books with titles ranging from *My Fifty Years with Dogs* (E.H. Richardson) and *Notes on South African Hunting* (A. J. Bethell) to *Man Outside Himself: Methods of Astral Projection* (Prevost Battersby). The intake's three most successful writers, the novelist Egerton Castle, the novelist and playwright Horace Vachell and the adventurer and mystic Francis Younghusband, sold hundreds of thousands of copies of their works on both sides of the Atlantic. Castle, many of whose romantic adventure stories were written in collaboration with his wife Agnes, managed to combine his literary activities with captaincy of the British Olympic fencing team in 1908.

Alec Waugh, the brother of Evelyn, was himself a successful writer, whose first novel had achieved considerable notoriety even before he was commissioned from Sandhurst in 1917. *The Loom of Youth*, written when Waugh was only 17, was considered shocking in its day because of its frank treatment of homosexuality at an English public school. By the time that it became apparent that the novel was a best-seller, Waugh was a POW, having been captured at Passchendaele while serving with the Dorsetshire Regiment. Waugh left the Army in 1919 to pursue his writing career, but rejoined the Dorsets in 1939 and retired with the rank of major in 1945.

Like Ian Fleming, John Masters also won a prize cadetship, but went on to enjoy a far more distinguished Army career, culminating in the award of a DSO for his command of 111th Indian Infantry Brigade in Burma in 1944, brilliantly narrated in *The Road Past Mandalay*. Masters wrote a superb account of soldiering in India in his memoir *Bugles and a Tiger*, but remains best known for his novels *The Nightrunners of Bengal* and *Bhowani Junction*. The latter was the basis of a very successful film starring Stewart Grainger and Ava Gardner.

Sandhurst's role as an Officer Cadet Training Unit during the Second World War inevitably brought an influx of literary talent, though tragically some of it was to be only partially fulfilled. Keith Douglas, who was killed in Normandy in 1944, has been described by Jon Stallworthy as 'the most individual and accomplished poet of his generation'. Another poet who promised much was Drummond Allison, who was killed in action at the Garigliano River in 1943. His posthumous collection, *The Yellow Night*, has been much anthologised in recent years.

It is often forgotten that some Sandhurst graduates find that military life is not for them and go on to highly successful alternative careers. Michael Morpurgo, author of the highly acclaimed *War Horse*, was a cadet in the 1960s as was celebrity chef and bon viveur, Keith Floyd, author of almost thirty cookbooks.

More recently the wars in Iraq and Afghanistan have been documented in personal accounts by a large number of former cadets. Of these, the one which has most caught the public's imagination is *The Junior Officers' Reading Club* by Patrick Hennessey, described by Boyd Tonkin in the *Independent* as; 'the most accomplished work of military witness to emerge from British war-fighting since 1945'.

In terms of the impact of his words on the world around him there is, of course, one Sandhurst cadet who towers above all others. It is easy to forget that Winston Churchill was awarded his Nobel Prize not for his achievements as a statesman, but for his contribution to literature. In their citation to his award, the Nobel Academicians highlighted Churchill's 'mastery of historical and biographical description and his brilliant oratory in defending exalted human values', an assessment that certainly will make him a hard act for future generations of Sandhurst writers to follow.

The entrance to the Library and the carved wooden cypher of Edward VIII.

chapter twenty-five:

Nursing Them Through

COLONEL BRUCE BAKER

*T*he surgeon is to examine every Candidate for admission to the Royal Military Academy and to certify whether he appears to have any difficulty in his articulation, or any mental, organic or bodily defect, that may disqualify him from Military Service.
'Duties of the Surgeon', 1840

Now as then on arrival at the Academy all officer cadets have an initial medical. Everyone hopes to get through Sandhurst without injury or illness but 90% will need medical advice at some time during the Commissioning Course. The RMC Hospital was originally the east wing of Old College, between the main building and the Superintendent's quarters that is now Old College Headquarters. An isolation hospital was built in the area of what is now known as Zayed Lines (formerly The Redoubt), and this became the main hospital in 1878 when the completion of the East Trident Block forced the move of the hospital out of Old College. For many years The Redoubt was known as Hospital Hill. In those days, cholera, smallpox and influenza threatened even the young and fit. The present Medical Reception Station (MRS) was built as the new hospital in 1913, and a further isolation hospital was built during the First World War where the Slim Officers' Mess now stands.

The MRS provides primary healthcare for up to 3,000 patients including families, officer cadets, permanent staff and to independent units either on site such as the General Staff Centre or nearby such as the Cadet Training Centre, Frimley Park. Health care includes the full spectrum of General Practice (GP) such as emergency care, routine clinics, midwifery, health visiting, baby clinics, nursing services and a dispensary. It is also a GP training practice, training two to four military GP trainees a year but also supervising military doctors not yet in specialist training, military nurses and combat medics. Almost every age range is covered from birth to, currently, two octogenarians.

The three military doctors and six Combat Medical Technicians deploy on various exercises and training to

Left: A Russian cannon, captured at Fort Bomarsund, during the Crimean War in 1854, stands guard over the original RMC Hospital.

Below: The current Medical Reception Station, completed in 1913.

Welcome to the MRS.

provide primary healthcare to officer cadets in the field. The Regimental Aid Post can be in a building or tent with four military ambulances at our disposal. Highlights include public order training and the overseas final exercises.

Officer cadets wishing to 'report sick' attend clinic at 0730 for medical assessment and treatment. They may require 'light duties' (excused various activities) or they may need to be admitted to one of the twelve beds.

In times gone by, if an officer cadet was admitted to the Hospital, a certificate was taken by one of the medical staff to the Colour Sergeant 'in order that the bedding may be properly aired'. These days, email is quicker.

On one occasion, an overseas cadet was bedded down in the Hospital and unable to go on the Academy leave weekend. He requested that he be allowed a take-away meal in the medical centre with his friends to get over the disappointment. The duty nurse gave permission but was somewhat taken aback when a large van arrived with a take-away meal for the cadet and his friends from a Lebanese restaurant in Mayfair, complete with waiter. Soon, the ward was temporarily host to a Bedouin feast, with the guests wearing traditional costumes.

REHABILITATION
Captain Sally Williams RAMC

I am nearly at the end of my phase 2 training and I am handed a piece of paper with my first posting … I'm off back to RMAS to be OC Rehabilitation, having only left Camberley a short time ago! In a few weeks' time I will be part of the notorious Directing Staff (DS).

I started work at RMAS in March 2013. I was met by the warm smile of Mrs Keeling and Ms Alberts. They must have over forty-five years' experience at RMAS between them. There is nothing that they have not seen. My predecessor, Major Pete Holton, was about to leave and with that, I was in the driving seat.

Initially, working at RMAS is an intimidating experience. There is history, legacy and tradition around every corner. Having last been there as a cadet a mere six months previously, my Colour Sergeant was still there teaching. The PTI who saw me up (and down) the high wire was still making cadets run in the gym and the

Staff Sergeants who helped me differentiate my firing pin from my rifle sling were still reeling off rifle lesson after rifle lesson! Things had changed though; I was no longer Miss Williams – I was Ma'am.

I quickly settled in to life at RMAS. The department is a busy place with a steady stream of patients, but with Mrs Keeling at the helm the department is a well-oiled machine. My job was to command the Rehabilitation Department. I had an office and a gym, and two very capable Exercise Rehabilitation Instructors (ERIs). At any given time we would have around twenty-five to thirty officer cadets who had become injured, and were transferred into full-time rehab. The stakes are high; we have only three months to get those injured, fit and back on course. The ERIs were an asset to the team. With a soldiering and physical training background, they cover a six-month course in injury rehabilitation. They not only offer a varied military experience but become specialists in physical training and exercise rehabilitation. The facilities at the academy are superb, and the cadets' every need is catered for to aid rehabilitation. We have our own rehab gym, full of a variety of equipment to suit all needs. Between the main gym and the swimming pool, there is no escape for the injured cadets!

Life at RMAS is hectic for everyone. The raft of captains in the mess can often liken itself to passing ships in the night, but if you make the walk over to the Officers' Mess, there will always be a friendly face around. Tradition at RMAS made me a 'Lout'; week 6 and week 14 parties saw thirty-plus young officers, dressed in fancy dress, trying to dodge the cadets as we head off camp on yet another jolly day out. Friday of week 14 was always a proud day. I'd stand in my uniform, whatever the weather, and watch another intake gain their commission. I took great pride in the part I had played in helping some of those cadets overcome injury to complete the course and embark on their new career as an officer in British army.

After two years at RMAS my time is almost over. RMAS is a huge beast; it no longer intimidates me, but excites me. RMAS will always hold a fondness in my heart as the place where I grew from a civilian into an officer.

LUCKNOW PLATOON
Major Richard Grimsdell RHA

Lucknow Platoon is unique within the Royal Military Academy Sandhurst. It supports both Colleges and exists to rehabilitate cadets who have suffered injuries whilst on the course. Although it is the platoon that nobody wishes to join, it is perhaps the one that they are most proud of serving in.

The main effort of the platoon is to fix and rehabilitate each cadet and then reintegrate them back into the Commissioning Course, at the same point in which they left. Lucknow sets the benchmark in this domain, boasting the greatest return to training statistics of any training establishment in the Army. There are many elements that contribute to such great success – the world-class rehabilitation facilities, the unwavering professionalism and dedication of the staff – but above all is the determination of the officer cadets. The platoon does carry an undeserved stigma. However, the drive and resolve shown by each cadet to get fit, commission and have the privilege to command soldiers is inspiring.

Alongside rehabilitation, the platoon runs an exceptional Professional Development package. This is demanding due to the plethora of injuries and mixed abilities within the platoon. Pleasingly, every cadet that returns back to the course is professionally more competent than when they arrived and has a depth of knowledge unrivalled by their new peers. The platoon embraces innovation and creativity. The cadets are encouraged to think for themselves and the Permanent Staff work tirelessly to create an environment that embraces lateral thought, producing an inclusive learning environment whilst empowering the cadets, encouraging them to thrive rather than merely survive.

The end product is exceptional. The platoon has proudly produced Sword of Honour winners, Queen's Medal winners and numerous JUOs. The cadets that return to training are better officers than when they arrived, both professionally and personally. The untold story of Lucknow is the shared battle.

Lucknow Platoon cadets travel around the Academy via electric buggy.

Each cadet experiences emotional setbacks due to their injury; they are proud and yet frustrated as they see their original course commission and have to ponder the prospect of not being able to achieve their dream of serving as an officer in the British Army. This shared hardship breeds empathy and humility and lays such a strong foundation for their future. After all, 'you are only your strongest when you have a weakness for other people'.

The confrontational nature of Public Order training requires a medical team to be on hand.

chapter twenty-six:

Always There

CAPTAIN ED AITKEN

Servants are warned against spitting over the Balasters into the Basement and also against shaking Rugs and Mats from the Dormitories into the Basement.

Orders to Servants, 29 October 1930, RMAS Archive

At Sandhurst we all had soldier servants, one between two or three Gentlemen Cadets. My servant was 'uncle' Bob Bartlett. 'Uncle was a real character, almost a "monument",' wrote Francis Ingall in 1927. 'Uncle', like so many Sandhurst servants before and since, became a legend in his lifetime. 'He had an enormous paunch and to support this vast overhang he wore his belt well below his navel. In his mouth at almost all times was a little cut-off clay pipe, generally smoked upside down.'

Quirkiness, rigid views and an absolute commitment to the institution defined many a Sandhurst servant. In 1950, John Gilmour recalled his batman Joe Vokes (by then shared between

fifteen cadets): 'He was a former trombonist in the Sandhurst band and a very likeable old codger with flat feet and waxed moustaches. He lives in Yorktown on the London Road just in front of the gasworks. Joe was a fearful snob and rather looked down on young men from grammar schools. He expected all his gentlemen to take a dinner jacket and tennis racket with them when they went away for the weekend. I think we each paid him the going rate of two shillings a week; our pay at the time was thirty-three shillings a week.'

With its own tailors, bootmakers, hatters, laundry and its mechanics, locksmiths gardeners, grooms, storemen and so many other trades, Sandhurst at its most self-sufficient resembled a vibrant town in miniature. Since its beginning, a dedicated workforce, some unseen, others highly visible like 'Uncle' Bob Bartlett and Joe Vokes, seamlessly held the place together. Typically they stayed for most, if not all their working

Right: After Sovereign's Parade, the Adjutant's charger is led along the corridors of Old College back to the stables.

Far right: A college servant in the 1930s.

CIVIL STAFF, 1878

2 Clerks	1 Housekeeper
2 Assistant Housekeepers	1 Nurse
1 Armourer	1 Messenger
2 Cleaning Arms	1 Hospital Servant
1 Clerk of the Kitchen	1 Cook
1 Under Cook	1 Kitchen Man
6 Scullions	10 Mess Waiters
6 Hall of Study Servants	1 Recreation Room
1 Cellar Storeman	42 Room Servants
1 Commandant's Orderly	1 Organist
1 Barrack/Artillery Storeman	1 Lamplighter
1 Turncock	5 Gatekeepers
1 Woodman in Charge	2 Estate Carpenters
6 Estate Labourers	

Left: The RMC Butchery, 1930s.

Below: Bottling in the RMC mineral water factory, 1930s.

lives, serving many generations of cadets. In 1919 Gatekeeper Charles Henry Shott died after fifty-six years at the RMC and was buried in the cemetery with full military honours. In 1947 the first *Wish Stream* noted there were nearly one hundred men who had been employed at Sandhurst for over twenty-five years.

There were over a hundred civilian staff paid according to a strict scale with annual, weekly and daily rates of pay. Thus the Housekeeper was paid £60 a year, the Estate Labourers 15 shillings a week (£39 a year) and the Commandant's Orderly one shilling and sixpence a day (about £27 a year).

Traditionally jobs were passed if not from father to son, then at least kept within the family. For nearly a hundred years the grounds were lovingly tended by three generations of the Clark family. 'Topper' Brown, after whom a bar in Old College is named, was one of a pair of brothers who worked for many years in the Academy. In 1937, Douglas 'Douggie' Coombes, aged fourteen, was 'dragged by the ear' by his father to work in the grounds, continuing a tradition of several generations both of his and his future wife's families. His grandfather was a batman from the 1890s until his death in 1926, as was his father. On his mother's side, his grandfather was a carpenter at Sandhurst and his uncle, Bert Garrett, was a dormitory attendant from 1946 until 1976. Douggie's wife June had a family history just as interwoven with Sandhurst connections. Her brother Les was Head Groundsman, and on one side of the family their grandfather was the Commandant's orderly for many years and their other grandfather was the famous 'Admiral' Harry Husted. The Husted family were renowned boatbuilders and oarsmen; the Admiral looked after the RMC boats and was a much-loved rowing coach for many years. Like Charles Shott, he was buried in the Sandhurst cemetery, his coffin carried by the College Eight in rowing flannels and red-and-white blazers, fresh from winning the Marlow Challenge Cup, a few days earlier.

When Douggie came in from the grounds to work in the kitchens he washed up in long troughs: 'There were no dishwashing machines, no mod cons.' Glasses and knives were washed in buckets by butlers and all the food had to be carried up and down stairs on trays. 'In those days we knew the cadets much better and there was a real loyalty when batmen used to serve their cadets and often save them from trouble.' He recalled the time when cadets had china 'jerry pots' under their beds; one evening he came back to work to see hundreds of them floating on the lake, like 'a carpet of lilies'. Another time he came in to serve breakfast to find that each of the 300 cups laid out in the Dining Room concealed a small live frog. Douggie left in 1987 when contractors took over the domestic staff.

John Sweetman, the long-serving Sandhurst academic and author, recalled that when he joined the teaching staff in 1969, officers on exercise were preceded by staff from the Officers' Mess, who set themselves up in lay-bys and handed out coffee and refreshments whenever needed. It was, he pointed out, a different era. Ken Massey joined the staff in 1964 as a silverman. 'We had our own little gimmicks for getting the silver up to scratch. We used to get a jam tin (jam came in seven-pound tins) and collect the officers' aluminium cigar tubes, put them in the jam tin with a handful of soda, fill it up with knives and forks, cover them with water which then fizzed and took off all the brown bits. We used to call it 'pickling'.' He also had to polish the tables, which he did by climbing onto them: 'We took our shoes off, of course, got the old beeswax polish and waxed away.' Ken was soon on other dining room duties. His day began at six with breakfast and went on through lunch, tea and dinner. 'The cadets looked on tea as the best meal. It was only a half hour but they could relax. Each cadet had three pats of butter and then you put out jam, syrup,

peanut butter, cheese and biscuits and bread.' In those days of the two-year course, Ken got to know the cadets quite well, always working in the same pantry. Each of the four pantries catered for a company. Ken graduated from butler to the cellar as storeman where he taught himself all about wine. He later became College Supervisor of Victory College.

Today, many of the civilian staff are Nepalese. Changes to Gurkha terms and conditions resulted in many wives joining their husbands on what were previously unaccompanied tours and settling in the UK after retirement. The employment of Gurkha families has brought their menfolk's hard work and cheerful nature to the corridors of Sandhurst and to quote one manager 'we could not function without their willingness to work unsociable hours'. When the next edition of this book is compiled there will, no doubt, be a raft of long-serving Nepalese staff to feature.

There are still staff who have been at Sandhurst for decades. Chris Massingham joined in 1979 as a Trainee Chef. Typically he joined the family 'firm', his father being an Army chef at the Academy and his mother a cleaner. Making his way up the promotion ladder he became Executive Chef for RMAS from 1989–93 before joining the management team first in New College and, from 1996, the Mess Manager of Old College. He met his wife, Sharon, currently New College Deputy Mess Manager, at Sandhurst thereby carrying the family tradition into the twenty-first century.

Douggie Coombes (fourth from the right) with outdoor staff, 1938.

Above: Preparing the Long Jump 1937 – Douggie Coombes, far right.

Above right: The Admiral on the Lower Lake.

Right: The Admiral's funeral, 27 June 1922.

Rose Mitchell in the Silver Vault working on a cup presented in August 2016 by members of Waterloo Company 1960–64 in memory of their CSM, Reg Page.

Chris remembers the end of the 'dinosaurs' as many of the older chefs were unable to cope with modern catering methods. 'When I arrived, food was steamed to within an inch of its life with variety provided by different flavoured gravy.' Anyone who passed through Sandhurst pre-1980 will undoubtedly agree!

Rose Mitchell arrived as a cleaner in 1995 to join her husband who was a storeman. She remained after she was widowed and, in 2009, became the Silver Keeper responsible for the cleaning and upkeep of the vast collection of silver at the Academy. Previous employment in a jewellers undoubtedly helped but she learned most of her trade on the job. Gone are the melting aluminium cigar tubes of Ken Massey's day with modern commercial products the order of the day although plenty of elbow grease is still required. The silver is an eclectic mixture of RMC and RMAS acquisitions and Regimental and individual presentations. Indeed, items of silver are still presented today. Rose prepares sporting trophies for the relevant fixtures and ensures that the tables are laden with silver for dinner nights with most cadets and staff blissfully unaware of her efforts in the troglodyte world of the silver vault. She reflects that although she has worked for several different contractors during her time the friendly camaraderie amongst the civilian staff is unchanged. 'It's a lovely place to work, not just with the people but I love the way the seasons change reflected in the trees around the lake.' Undoubtedly, 'Uncle' Bob Bartlett would have expressed the same sentiments.

John Archibald, on the other hand, has been highly visible for the last sixteen years, 'portraying a friendly and welcoming attitude' as Hall Porter of Old College. He likes the variety of it, organising rooms for conferences, even for children's parties, making sure the place is secure, seeing different people coming in and out, 'watching fresh-faced change during the year and emerge fully fledged at the end of their training'. Like so many of the civilian staff, he has willingly taken on other duties and now acts as announcer, toast master and corporate host for visitors to Old College. There is a timeless quality in the way John speaks of his job, an echo of earlier generations of Sandhurst servants and a clue perhaps to why so many stay so long.

John Archibald presides while HRH The Crown Prince of Bahrain signs the visitors' book.

chapter twenty-seven:

Governors and Commandants

MAJOR MARTYN COOK

Major General Paul Nanson escorts HRH The Prince of Wales to the Sovereign's Parade.

There is a tendency always to look at the governors and commandants of Sandhurst as distant figures remote from everyday affairs, ensconced in Government House, leaving the day-to-day business of the Academy in subordinate hands. To today's officer cadets the commandant of RMAS can seem an equally remote figure, as their world revolves around the Platoon Commander and Company Commander, and anything further up the chain of command suggests trouble. However the reality has always been that most governors did get involved in the development of the course in the face of financial stringencies and the regular surges in demand for young officers to meet the ongoing crises of Empire, usually followed by cutbacks in numbers to balance the financial cost. Harcourt, Hope, Scovell, Jones, Cameron et al., forgotten names that grace the Memorial Chapel or whose portraits are found in the corridors of Old College, all left their mark and had a view on how the course should be structured and what talents an officer needed to make his way in the Army of the day.

Right: Lieutenant General The Hon. Sir George Murray GCB. Governor RMC 1819–24. Oil on canvas by Sir Thomas Lawrence.

COMMANDANTS OF RMAS REMEMBER

Major General Andrew Ritchie, Commandant 2003–06

It is a surreal experience to return to Sandhurst thirty years on from being a cadet. The sights and the sounds, even the smells, are evocatively the same. I can never cross Old College Parade Square without expecting to be shouted at by some distant colour sergeant for not swinging my arms ('Mr Ritchie Sir, you look like Humphrey Bogart pulling the *African Queen*').

Of course many things have changed – and generally for the better. The cadets are older (average age twenty-three) and more educated (85% graduates) with significant numbers of women and members of the British minority ethnic communities. I find them to be more mature and better balanced than my generation. They also ask a lot more questions. The core Army values of integrity, loyalty and teamwork are not so familiar to them when they arrive, but during their year at Sandhurst they quickly became socialised into the military culture.

Much of what we teach the cadets has also changed. The Commissioning Course is more intensive, and in many ways more comprehensive, than in my day. Soldiering has become an increasingly complex business and there is a greater need for today's young officers

IN MEMORY OF
GENERAL THE RIGHT HON.
SIR GEORGE MURRAY
G.C.B. G.C.H.
COLONEL 1ST ROYAL REGT OF FOOT
DIED 28TH JULY 1846 AGED 74
HE SERVED IN HOLLAND EGYPT SYRIA THE WEST INDIES
DENMARK AND SWEDEN WAS Q.M.G. IN THE PENINSULA
COMMANDER IN CHIEF IN CANADA
CHIEF OF THE STAFF OF THE ARMY OF OCCUPATION IN FRANCE
COMMANDER OF THE FORCES IN IRELAND
AND TWICE MASTER GENERAL OF THE ORDNANCE
HE WAS GOVERNOR OF THIS COLLEGE
FROM 1819 TO 1824

Inset: Memorial to Sir George Murray in the Royal Memorial Chapel.

161

Left: Major General Andrew Ritchie with the royal party on the steps of the Grand Entrance following the commissioning of HRH Prince Henry of Wales.

Below left: Painting by Sergei Pavlenko which hangs in the Grand Entrance. The State Trumpeters were added later on the suggestion of Her Majesty The Queen to add perspective.

to understand the environment in which they will operate. Commanding twenty-first-century soldiers is arguably a more demanding challenge and there is an increased focus on the softer skills of communication and management.

But continuity is equally important. 'Sandhurst is about standards' was a phrase coined by Academy Sergeant Major Huggins when I was a cadet and it remains just as relevant today. Those enduring standards of character and behaviour are central to the teaching of our future officers. They also continue to be well trained in the traditional military disciplines and the development of leadership potential runs through the whole course. These high standards have not changed; nor must they if the Army is to continue to be operationally successful.

**Lieutenant General Peter Pearson,
Commandant April 2006–07**

As I told the parents of the newly arrived cadets, 'the course is designed to be tough. The cadets must know what it is like to be tired, wet, hungry and frightened, if they are to be ready to lead their soldiers in difficult and dangerous circumstances. They must be able to think under pressure, to organise themselves under pressure and, most importantly, to inspire their soldiers under pressure. They will not always enjoy the experience, so be prepared for the odd anguished phone call. But, we must be confident that they are properly trained for their future roles as officers. For our part, we will provide them with the necessary tools in terms of military skills and professional knowledge, and this involves a trinity of moral, physical and intellectual elements. The academic staff here have as important a role as the military staff, and the chaplains also play a vital part.'

So, many things have not changed over the years. Given that the British Army was at war in the Middle East and despite mounting pressure from the cadets in their reviews, who wished that the instruction on the course was directed almost entirely to carry out the operations there, we maintained our emphasis on developing leadership and the cadets' intellect in the widest sense; on how to deliberate and act, rather than on what to think and do specifically. Commanding officers remained overwhelmingly satisfied with their young officers.

With all elements of the Army officer selection and initial leader training (including the TA and LE), as well as leadership in general up to the rank of lieutenant colonel, coming under the Commandant, it made for a rich and varied appointment. My lasting memories are of an academy brimming with varying talent and potential; a wide mix of races and creeds, of gender and ability, of strengths and weaknesses; in a wonderfully inspirational establishment that exudes history and is vital in so many ways. Long may its name be synonymous with excellence.

Major General David Rutherford-Jones, Commandant 2007–09

It is a strange thing that I cannot recall much of the detail of my time as an officer cadet in training at Sandhurst. The course was six months long and simply flashed past in a blur of activity, bordering on chaos. I do however recall Philip Ward, the commandant in 1977; he was often around us cadets – his visits always had a calming effect! But then we were teenage boys, I nineteen years old, with no experience of real life behind me. It seems hardly surprising that the experience of Sandhurst back then came and went in a dash. Today's young men and women are in so many ways different.

Returning to the Academy, literally for the first time since 1977, to take up the appointment of commandant was frankly surreal. Yet I sensed a remarkable familiarity about it all. The best and most necessary aspects of the culture and curriculum were intact, yet the Academy had evolved appropriately with change; the training and education was still relevant. It was pleasing to see that the Royal Memorial Chapel was still a part of the curriculum, so to speak, and that for the sake of new ways

Right: Major General David Rutherford-Jones with Malaysian General Ismail.

Below: Lieutenant General Peter Pearson with members of Sittang Company.

of developing leaders we had not lost sight of the experience of our great forebears. Slim was right, it is about 'you' (the leader); indeed, after thirty years of soldiering up to the point of becoming commandant, I had concluded that in the end, it really does boil down to the leader's personality and that individual's ability to inspire. Sandhurst's role in developing character is paramount.

The curriculum at Sandhurst will ebb and flow, change with the Army, and with evolving threats and challenges. The people change too. Society changes. But the fundamentals that underscore soldiering in the British Army endure, as do the principles of strong leadership, good character and exemplary behaviour among British officers. As long as the Army Officer Selection Board and Sandhurst never lose sight of these principles, the Academy will continue to flourish, and the Army too. Being commandant, responsible for developing tomorrow's leaders for the Army, and guardian of one of the nation's most important institutions was privilege indeed.

Major General Patrick Marriott, Commandant 2009–12

I arrived at Sandhurst in the summer of 2009 at the height of operations in Afghanistan. For the entire previous decade I had spent all my time either on operations or working on them in PJHQ. So, Sandhurst came as a welcome pause from the 'J3 wheel'. But I had been sent there for a reason. The CGS, Sir Richard Dannatt, was worried that young officers were arriving in theatre with only the bare minimum of focused, gritty training: nearly all those commissioning were finding themselves in the grist of fighting in 'Afghan' within six months of commissioning.

So, my task was to use what I'd learnt during that last decade (and more) and 'operationalise Sandhurst'. The words 'war footing' were used. Essentially, the focus had to shift. The 'constants of Sandhurst' were to be held (and quite right too) but the 'variables' were to be updated, 'grittified' and, above all else, made relevant to the fight. My boss, Paul Newton, called it

Major General Patrick Marriott with OCdt Sheikh Abdullah Al Khalifa from Bahrain.

I did just under three years and commissioned 1,831 cadets on the main commissioning course. Sadly, not all of them came back from Afghanistan. Those names are in the Royal Memorial Chapel, that spiritual epicentre of our Officer Corps; that heart from which our purpose is sourced. I changed not a jot of that. Like *Serve to Lead*, some things are rightly immutable – and wonderful too.

'the quiet revolution' which was kind but really all we did was accelerate very sharply the good work of our predecessors. My team was outstanding; every 'lout' knew Afghanistan; quite a few had been deservedly decorated. A few carried the scars. They and their superb colour sergeants were the operational exemplars. They inspired. I merely gently guided the tiller.

But we re-introduced much that had been lost since, perhaps, the Second World War – not as pre-deployment training per se but as to complement it. So, we either introduced or reintroduced: 'training through fear' (teaching cadets to lead scared people – including themselves); section weapons including live fire (where had they gone – we had six types of weapons in my platoon at Sandhurst in 1976 – now cadets just had one?); risk-taking (yes, judge it and go and take it); counter-IED training; more range time – shooting straight; battlefield health; a mock-up Forward Operating Base on Barossa (FOB William is still there – it should have been built in 1969); training for 'embedded partnering'; and a new final exercise focused on operations in Afghanistan. Above all else we started to educate and train 'wider leadership' – how to lead civilians, agencies and others over whom you might have no command relationship. I wish I'd had that. We enhanced media training and introduced moral dilemmas to training. The whole topic of 'key leader engagement' was brought in. There was much more. My old notes, from my time in PJHQ and my many, many visits to Afghanistan, were well thumbed.

But it was not all the variables. We reintroduced the cadet government thus recognising a greater number of cadets from across the senior intake. We brought the junior intake back on parade; 'at last', they said! We brought CCF and ACF cadets to the Sovereign's Parades to help with programmes and seating. They are still there but six years on, a few have marched up those steps. We all know why. For CGS I formed and led the team that wrote 'Developing Leaders'. It is humbling to hear even now my three phrases, taught to everyone under my wing since 1989, repeated by the generation that passed through Sandhurst 2009–12. I do hope they're still helping those who learnt them as cadets – *think to the finish; all of one company; do as you ought, not as you want.*

Lieutenant General Tim Evans, Commandant 2012–13

It was a real pleasure and a privilege to return to the Royal Military Academy Sandhurst as the commandant; it was not an appointment I had previously considered doing but I found it fascinating and very professionally rewarding. To train the next generation of young officers in the art of leadership against the backdrop of operations in Afghanistan concentrated all our minds. I adopted many of the embryonic initiatives that my predecessor, Patrick Marriot, had started, particularly those measures that were trying to bring the Academy into the twenty-first century and the information age. It was interesting to see that many of our teaching practices had not kept pace with the way our cadets were being taught at school and university and were markedly different from the methods that we were used to. We also reviewed the exercises to ensure our training objectives were still relevant, especially as the Afghanistan campaign started to wane. For although the exercises and infantry tactics were a vehicle for educating, training and assessing leadership skills, it was also important to provide the cadets with a basic understanding of possible future conflicts, whether it be counter-insurgency, hybrid or conventional warfare.

The Sandhurst Group was also expanding. The commandant was now responsible for the nineteen University Officer' Training Corps (UOTCs), the Young Officer Reservist training as well as Officer Selection at Westbury. There was synergy in

Lieutenant General Tim Evans planting a tree to commemorate the Diamond Jubilee of HM The Queen.

bringing these aspects under the Sandhurst banner as many of our cadets came from the OTCs. We were able to standardise training across the country, with the Sandhurst trademark and quality assurance. Sandhurst provided the OTC students a beacon on which to focus. We also started to train Reservist Young Officers alongside the OTC cadets, which encouraged the cross-fertilisation of ideas and provided an effective training platform that could be moulded to suit their needs. We also designed the first pilot course to train Reservist Officers at Sandhurst in eight weeks, from flash to bang; it was intense but worked extremely well and is now an option for the OTC cadets and Reservists. It placed aspiring young officers back with their units or OTCs in a fraction of the time, having been trained and commissioned, which helped generate interest in the other cadets or students as well as raising the standard of the training in the OTCs and the number of young officers in the Reserve Units.

Overall, I have very fond memories of my time at Sandhurst, both as a cadet in 1982 and as commandant in 2012; it is an institution that has such history and a worldwide reputation for excellence, which was important to protect. I was very impressed with the standard, drive and enthusiasm of our young officers and I was proud to be their commandant.

Major General Stuart Skeates, Commandant 2013–15
The title of this book captures the essence of Sandhurst through the ages. I suspect it was at the forefront of John Gaspard Le Marchant's mind during the Flanders Campaign in 1794–95. Leadership has always been about context and the greatness of Sandhurst is founded on its ability to adapt to the circumstances of a new era whilst retaining the ethos of the British Army Officer. 'Serve to Lead' is much quoted but rarely understood in the depth that stand an officer in good stead throughout a military career, or indeed a lifetime. Modern leadership theory would describe this as 'servant leadership', perhaps 'authentic leadership'. Both are apt labels for the Academy's philosophy and, most importantly, describe how the staff develop their officer cadets, our future leaders. Indeed, it is a mark of the strength of the institution that whether prince or pauper, man or woman, regular or reserve, British or foreign, all officer cadets are equal under the baleful gaze of the Sandhurst colour sergeant. When addressing the families on 'Ironing Board Sunday' on my very first day as commandant I recalled my first day as an officer cadet, twenty-five years before (to the day). As a somewhat jumped-up graduate and Junior Under Officer in the Officers' Training Corps, I rather took exception to my colour sergeant's assessment of my sartorial elegance shortly after arriving. The fact that this was followed by my first experience of a changing parade, conducted at lightning speed, will surprise nobody who has gone before me or since.

The meritocracy of the Commissioning Courses has always been based solely on an officer cadet's ability as a leader: that intangible quality that inspires others through personal example and a combination of character, professional competence and intellect. It is also why Sandhurst is so widely emulated and so important to the nation's fabric; and why Sandhurst will become ever-more important to the Army in future. The character of conflict in the world as it is turning out no longer just threatens our people, interests and territory; it threatens our values. So developing leaders who do not just abide by, but live by, the Army's values and genuinely 'Serve to Lead' assumes ever greater significance. So Sandhurst must remain a lodestar for all who have marched up the steps of Old College, the cardinal point for military leadership and at the heart of the British Army.

Major General Paul Nanson, Commandant 2015–present
Having not served at Sandhurst since I marched up the steps in 1986, returning has been a real voyage of discovery. On the one hand I have been hugely impressed by how much has changed and, in particular, how effective the new commissioning course is at preparing our young men and women for the next challenge. But I have also been comforted by what hasn't changed. The tone, ethos and atmosphere of Sandhurst remains the same as I remember thirty years ago – indeed I suggest the same as it has been for 204 years. And the quality of the permanent staff remains as impressive as it ever was. As I travel around the world, I am amazed at just how high the Sandhurst stock is, and that is absolutely down to the professionalism of those who work here, civilians and military alike.

I mentioned that we are about preparing our young men and women for the next challenge. The Academy is now but one part of the Sandhurst Group, an organisation designed to manage leader development from the moment a young person decides to become an Army officer to when they arrive at the front door of the Staff College. The Academy continues to provide the strongest of foundations, based on developing courage, competence and character, but it remains all about the journey. We never stop learning about leadership, even thirty years on, which is why I am so delighted to have the privilege of serving at this amazing institution once more.

Right: Major General Stuart Skeates with members of 44 Support Squadron RLC.

part four:
A TRADITION OF LEADERSHIP

chapter twenty-eight:

The Colours

WO1 Ryan Bowness

The first set of colours was presented to the Royal Military Academy Sandhurst by King George VI on 14 June 1947. The Queen and both the Princesses accompanied him. The colours were consecrated on the square in front of the officer cadets. The King in addressing the cadets concluded with the following words:

Above all, remember that the career which you have undertaken is one of great unselfishness. Your colours by their consecration may remind you of the supreme example of unselfishness which the world has seen, and your motto 'Serve to Lead' may teach you that only by emulating such an example can you each hope to play your part as a leader of men.

The colours of infantry regiments and the standards and guidons of the cavalry symbolise the loyalty of the regiment to the Crown and the honours that have been earned in that service, with the names of the battle honours emblazoned on them. They are the traditional rallying point in battle, and now that they are only paraded on ceremonial occasions they represent the history of the regiment and serve as a symbol of that tradition for the soldiers on parade.

Walk into the Royal Memorial Chapel and immediately above the door and flanking you on either side of the western aisle hang the colours of the RMAS and the RMC. By the late nineteenth century it had become the custom for colours to be laid up in a consecrated place of significance to the regiment, where they could disintegrate to dust above those who continued to serve. So it is with the colours of the Royal Military College and Royal Military Academy Sandhurst. The earliest colours have gone, but some 150 years of parades and traditions can still be read into the tattered silk that is hung there, silently crumbling through its own weight.

On the left facing the altar are the first colours presented by George VI alongside those presented by Her Majesty Queen Elizabeth in 1957 and 1974. On the right are the 1858 colours presented by Queen Victoria and the two sets of colours of George V. The most recent colours of 1991 replaced by those presented on 21 June 2005 are hung immediately above the main entrance.

Far left: Silently crumbling – the colours of RMC and RMAS in the Royal Memorial Chapel.

Left: The laying up of the colours of the RMAS, 7 August 2005.

The colours on parade.

The first colours of the Royal Military Academy presented by HM King George VI set the pattern for the three sets of colours presented by his daughter, the present Queen. The detailed design of both colours can be seen in the George VI windows above the main entrance to the Chapel. Here the link between the Crown and the Academy symbolised by the consecration and presentation of Colours is depicted with the Regimental Colour of the Academy on the left, the King's Colour in the centre under the profile of King George V and the Sovereign's Banner on the right. This was first presented by His Majesty King George V in 1918 and was continued by King George VI when taking the passing out parade in 1948. The colours are paraded by the Academy on all formal occasions, and in particular for each Sovereign's Parade that marks the commissioning of each graduating intake at the end of each term.

The existence of the Royal Military College at Sandhurst was due to royal patronage, and the awarding of colours to a training establishment remains unique in the Army and was a visible sign of the importance of the link between the College and the Crown. Queen Charlotte presented the first colours to the Royal Military College on Thursday 12 August 1813, the Prince Regent's fifty-first birthday, and *The Times* reported the following day:

The colours we understand, were wrought and embroidered by the hands of the QUEEN and PRINCESSES and were presented by her Majesty. The cabinet ministers left town on Wednesday evening and yesterday morning, to be present on the occasion. The Duke of YORK also left town early for Sandhurst. The PRINCE REGENT left Brighton on Wednesday … Yesterday morning, at ten o'clock, his Royal Highness, accompanied by the

Princess Charlotte, the QUEEN and Princess AUGUSTA ELIZABETH and MARY, and the Duke of CAMBRIDGE, with a number of attendants, left Windsor in their travelling carriages to proceed to the military College. After the ceremony of Her MAJESTY presenting the colours to the youths, the Royal Party were entertained with a sumptuous dinner by General HOPE, the Governor, at his house in the College.

William IV, accompanied by the Duke of Wellington, presented the second set of colours on 14 September 1835:

We were drawn up in line to receive him with our colours flying. Of course we presented arms, the band at the same time playing 'God Save the King', and close inspection commenced. The King walked slowly down the front rank, and up the rear rank which stepped back two or three paces so as to allow His Majesty plenty of space to have a good look at us. The inspection being over, we broke into open column, marched past in slow and quick time, and performed a variety of evolutions, including how to form square and receive cavalry, for which we had been drilled almost daily by Major Wright for some time previously. It was a grand sight and attracted a large attendance of the surrounding residents.
Gentleman Cadet John F. Mann, 1835

Queen Victoria and the Prince Consort, accompanied by the Queen's half-brother the Prince of Leiningen and the Princess, drove over from Windsor to Sandhurst on the morning of 6 November 1858 and 'inspected the Royal Military College, and, with the Royal Party, honoured the Governor, Major General Sir Harry Jones, with her company at luncheon, and afterwards returned to Windsor Castle'. Victoria would present a second set of colours on 22 April 1880.

*HM Queen Elizabeth II presents colours to the
Royal Military Academy, 27 June 1957, detail of
a painting in oils by Major Peter Hutchens (then
commanding Marne Company).*

On Saturday 10 May 1913 King George V presented 'new colours to the battalion of Gentlemen Cadets at the Royal Military College'. It was held during the week that the King was in residence at Aldershot where he witnessed the Army's preparedness for war. The old colours were laid up in the RMC chapel on 15 June 1913.

On 8 June 1933 a second set of colours carrying George V's insignia was presented by Field Marshall HRH The Duke of Connaught, brother of the King, and a graduate of RMA Woolwich of 1868.

Following the presentation of colours to the RMAS in 1947 Her Majesty Queen Elizabeth II presented a new set of colours on 27 June 1957, then again in 1974 and 1991. General Sir Michael Walker, Chief of The General Staff, presented the current set on 21 June 2005 on her behalf. In her presentation speeches, Her Majesty referred to the great traditions of which the cadets were heirs, 'built by those who served and studied here before you upon the firm foundations of unselfishness heroism and self-sacrifice'; and again, of the importance of strength of character, integrity, and moral and physical courage, and as a reminder 'that to succeed in the greatest tasks requires the greatest self-sacrifice'.

The Presentation of Colours parades continue to be ones of great pageantry, so it was with the parade on 21 June 2005. The old colours march on for the last time, and after the inspection march off, never to be formally paraded again. The parade then forms a hollow square and the regimental drums are stacked forming what was once the standard wartime altar. The new colours are placed on the stacked drums and consecrated by the Chaplain General. Following the speeches the colours are received by the Academy with a general salute and are then trooped along the ranks of the Academy so that each cadet may see them. Three cheers are given for Her Majesty The Queen and the Royal Military Academy Sandhurst marches past and off the parade ground.

THE SOVEREIGN'S BANNER

On 7 November 1918 a Guard of Honour accompanied by Under Officer J. O'Doyle was presented by His Majesty at Buckingham Palace with the King George V Banner, which could be in the custody of the Champion Company at Arms of the Royal Military College. The banner was presented to the Banner Ensign, Under Officer the Earl of Brecknock and was then trooped, with the Guard of Honour marching past in slow time in column of divisions and in quick time in close columns, followed by an advance in review order, Royal Salute and three cheers for The King. It was a London pea-soup of a day as evidenced by the short surviving Pathé newsreel and the painting of the presentation by Captain French, son of Field Marshall Viscount French.

The title 'Champion Company' was awarded to the best company in a series of military and athletic competitions, with the winner becoming the right flank company of the cadet battalion on parade. The competition was discontinued from 1914 until 1917 and was revived after the First World War with the Champion Company parading the King's Banner. After being laid up in the Royal Memorial Chapel during the Second World War, the Banner was presented again to the Champion Company by HRH the Duke of Gloucester on 14 November 1947. The presentation of the Sovereign's Banner by HM Queen Elizabeth II on 27 October 1978 in the forecourt of Buckingham Palace led to the King George V Banner being laid up in the Royal Memorial Chapel. In 1999 a new Sovereign's Banner was presented.

'In 1918 my grandfather King George V presented to Sandhurst a banner which was always to be carried by the Champion Company on parade … my grandfather's banner has been carried on every major parade since it was presented. More recently it has been the privilege of the Champion Platoon to carry the banner. From today I would like this platoon to be

Above: King George V Banner.

Right: The presentation of the Sovereign's Banner, 27 October 1978.

Below: The Sovereign's Banner is paraded.

known as the Sovereign's Platoon, in keeping with the custom started by my father in 1948.'

The nature of the competition has changed several times since its inception, and from 1993 it has been for the platoon that scores the highest in a series of military skills with individual academic performance also counting towards the final score. The Sovereign's Banner Parade is held in Week 10 of each term.

chapter twenty-nine:

The Sovereign's Parade

MAJOR PETE MIDDLEMISS

Perhaps my most vivid memory of Sandhurst is of a battalion parade before the King. Imagine 600 cadets, buttons and brasses shining in the sun, lined up along the length of the parade-ground in file, the scarlet-clad college band behind them on the steps of the Old Buildings. Under-officers, their swords glittering, stand to the fore; the adjutant, mounted on a charger, faces the parade. The edge of the parade-ground is lined with spectators – soldiers and civilians; in the near distance is the lake, fringed with trees. The King advances slowly down the straight white drive between the spectators; slightly ahead of him, on either hand, march cadet stick-orderlies wearing broad white cross-belts and swinging silver-mounted canes. Suddenly the adjutant rises in his stirrups and, throwing back his head, roars to us to slope arms. Six hundred men move as one: crash-two-three, crash-two-three

The finale to the Sovereign's Parade: the Adjutant rides his charger into the Grand Entrance, Old College.

– than the swift, silent third movement as the right hand cuts away to the side. The King has reached the saluting-base; the stick-orderlies, twenty yards apart, move on a few paces and come to a halt with almost mechanical synchronisation. Then: 'Batt-al-ion, Roy-al Sal-ute! Pres-enttt Arms!' Moving again as one, each right arm crashes against the butt of the rifle, and the rifle is swung in front of the body, bayonets sparkling like diamonds in the sun. A crash as the right foot is raised and smashed behind the heel of the left; then the deep roll of drums, and the first soft notes, rising in a crescendo, of the National Anthem.

Anon, 1938 *Infantry Officer: A Personal Record*

The Sovereign's Parade marks the end of each term with the commissioning parade of the current intake of officer cadets. Originally called Inspection Day – it was the day when the Commander-in-Chief or his representative inspected the cadets and confirmed that the senior class was of a suitable standard to be commissioned.

One of the first images we have of the Royal Military College at Marlow is of Inspection Day in 1804, with the cadets on parade ready to march past and show their skill at all the drill movements. This was not simply pomp and circumstance but a test of tactical skill, because the march past in slow and quick time and the advance in review order with all of the changes in formations and drill evolutions involved were the tactical drills of the day. The cadets' performance, with the senior cadets holding command and supernumerary appointments, was proof that they could fulfil the same appointments when they joined their regiments and could fill every appointment from soldier to CO if the need arose in battle. Each term the cadets were put through their paces by an inspection team usually lead by HRH The 2nd Duke of Cambridge who became General Commanding-in-Chief of the British Army and remained at its head for the next thirty-nine years, finally reluctantly retiring on 31 October 1895. Inspection Day became known as the Duke's Day.

It was a day of careful examination as witnessed by *The Times* in 1872:

At the conclusion of the inspection the students paraded a second time with arms and accoutrements, and went through a few evolutions in a creditable manner … the inspecting general proceeded to the Riding School, where a class of students, under the command of Captain Brooke, the Riding Master, were tested in riding drill … The gymnasium was afterwards visited, in order to witness some of the students going through various exercises.

This form of inspection occurred each passing out parade for most of the life of both the Royal Military College Sandhurst and the Royal Military Academy Woolwich. The year 1948 saw the first and last passing out parade at the Royal Military Academy Sandhurst. At the passing out parade for Intake 1, HM King George VI decided that he wished to mark the occasion by naming the parade in future the Sovereign's Parade and renaming the Champion Company the Sovereign's Company. So it has been ever since, the only change being the introduction of the Sovereign's Platoon.

Dr Tony Clayton recalls the one occasion in his long career as an academic at Sandhurst that the weather prevented a Sovereign's Parade:

It snowed, cadets were ordered to clear the Square, it snowed again. Wet weather was ordered and all trudged to the Churchill Hall. There was then a power cut. Preparation had been thorough; diesel generators were brought up to the side of the Hall. They then broke down for which no preparation had been made. The ceremony was held in a hall lit by candelabra from the Chapel, with the Chief of Staff of the time guiding the Sovereign's representative, an Admiral of the Fleet, to his place with the aid of a pocket electric torch!

It is a day of pomp and circumstance and celebration. For the graduating class who march up the steps and through the doors of the Grand Entrance to Old College it is the end of the beginning.

A SOVEREIGN'S PARADE
Officer Cadet Iain Powrie, 1967

Term 2 also culminated in our first Sovereign's Parade of which there were two each year in July and December. Being a junior intake we were, however, banished to the rear echelons of the Square where we were able to survive without too much scrutiny. In time, these Sovereign's Parades and the endless practices would become second nature, but one was always aware of the significance of slow marching up the steps into Old Building even though, at the time, such an event seemed a distant possibility. The parade always took the same form, the detail of which even now I can recall with some accuracy. We marched on in three ranks, usually to the stirring tune, 'Soldiers of the Queen', and having advanced formed two ranks on the inspection line. On the arrival of the Inspecting Officer there was a General Salute followed by the inspection throughout which would be entertained by the Academy Band with a musical miscellany.

Once the inspection was complete we formed threes, turned to our right and executed a march past in slow time. The most difficult manoeuvre took place as we turned left onto the line of the march past, executing a left turn and a change from three ranks to two. This placed each division at the advance in two ranks as we approached the dais. After the 'Eyes Right' we formed three ranks once again followed immediately by a left turn and two left wheels taking us back towards the inspection line. This corner of the Square was well named – 'Chaos Corner'! This was immediately repeated in quick time after which we reformed two ranks on the inspection line. After the trooping of the colours by the Sovereign's Company there then followed an Advance in Review Order, a General Salute, the Inspecting Officer's address and presentation of the Sword of Honour. The climax of the parade occurred during the march-off. The Senior Division, those being commissioned, preceded by the Colour Party, executed a slow-march up the steps of Old Building, followed by the Adjutant on his charger. The remainder dispersed. One of the more entertaining aspects of these parades was the ability of the Bandmaster to adapt popular tunes – two immediately spring to mind, 'Edelweiss' used as a slow-march and Sandie Shaw's 'Puppet on a String', a quick march. Although I can't recall them there were many others.

Gentleman Cadet Bernard Fergusson, 1930,
The Trumpet in the Hall

Passing-Out Day came at last. We marched past for the last time: the Sword of Honour was bestowed (by some oversight, not on me); we, the departing Senior Division, marched up the steps of the Grand Entrance to the strains of Auld Lang Syne, followed as tradition dictated by the Adjutant on his charger; and the great doors swung to behind us. The Adjutant now was Norman Gwatkin of the Coldstream, the only officer I have ever seen as smart as Boy Browning. He had been a wonderful friend and counsellor to us four SUOs, contriving to make us feel in our innocence that we really were helping him run the place; and we were as sad to say good-bye to him as to anybody.

Anon, 1938, *Infantry Officer: A Personal Record*

I will never forget our passing-out parade – my last experience of the glitter and panache of a peace-time army. The Seniors were lined up along the parade-ground; the colours flapped gently in the breeze. Then, to the roll of drums, we moved off in file at slow time, like a long caterpillar, towards the steps leading up to the main entrance. The head of the column mounted the steps, and, file by file, we disappeared into the interior. As I passed through the door I realised almost tearfully that Sandhurst was over and that I had become a man, with a man-sized job ahead of me. Suddenly I felt rather happy.

For the last time Harry, the two Johns, Jerry, Philip, Lionel, Bill and I went to the FGS for cups of coffee. We sat and talked cheerfully for a few minutes; then rushed off to change and be away, shouting good-byes. They were goodbyes too. The Japs hold Jerry; Lionel, Philip, and one of the Johns were killed in France.

Officer Cadet Iain Powrie, 1967

I can recall little of the parade less for the final slow march up the steps and out to the rear of Old Building by the Chapel where hats were tossed high in the air in celebration. The family had come down for the great day – little did they know that they would have to repeat the trip four years later to see brother Cameron commissioned into the Royal Army Ordnance Corps. The commissioning ball, to which we wore Mess Dress, was held that evening. At the stroke of midnight, I removed the black masking tape covering my solitary star and proudly realised that on this day, 20 December 1968, I had at last been commissioned. This was the culmination of about eight years of effort and I felt justly proud that I had achieved my goal and could return home to family and friends with my head held high at being accepted into the honourable profession of arms.

WO1 M. Gaunt, Academy Sergeant Major, 2002–05

The best moment for me each term is when I march past and salute the Sovereign's representative on the Sovereign's Parade with the RSM New College. Everybody grows an inch on that parade, both officer cadets and staff, and I know that when we march off we have done our job and now it is over to us to regenerate ourselves with the new intake and start again.

POLO MINTS AND PORT

Francis Hobbs

To the uninitiated the sight of gravestones outside Old College Headquarters may seem a bit disconcerting but, on closer inspection, names such as Alexander, Patrick, James Pigg, Dastur, and Blitz would, to most, indicate a link with animals. They would be right. These simple white stones under a single oak tree provide a lasting reminder of a silent but important participant in every officer's right of passage to commissioned rank.

The famous grey charger on which the Adjutant commands the Sovereign's Parade provides a unique and defining image of Sandhurst when it mounts the steps of the Grand Entrance following the last of the cadets who have just been commissioned. Until recently, the ceremonial chargers were stabled in East Mews, known for many years as Denton's Yard after Bill Denton, the longest-serving groom since 1945.

Over the years grooms and chargers have had to contend with adjutants possessing an extreme range of equestrian skills. Whether novice or competent horseman they have had to provide an immaculate mount, which not only reflects well on the excellence of Sandhurst, but establishes a calm focus for all those on parade, finishing with that long slow walk up the steps into the black void of the Grand Entrance and towards that single light beacon that is the great chandelier in the Indian Army Memorial Room.

To inexperienced riders this can be an alarming moment. No Adjutant wishes to be the first not (the author knows of none that have actually failed on parade) to mount the steps with aplomb in front of crowds which include so many guests, peers and seniors.

The origin of this rather unusual event is somewhat misty. There are accounts of an officer doing so in the late nineteenth century. However, the first to be recorded took place on 14 July 1926 when Captain Browning, the Academy Adjutant (later Lieutenant General 'Boy' Browning), a man reputedly concerned about his sartorial elegance, rode his own horse, the Vicar, into Old Building supposedly to stop him getting wet; others say it was simply a whim to show his equestrian prowess. Raining or not, on such weighty matters are traditions born!

However, when the great doors finally close, one small ceremony is not seen by the assembled crowds: that of the regular reward for another fine equestrian performance – the polo mint certain to pass from Adjutant to steed as thanks for another steady day; then Adjutant and stick orderlies will partake in a large glass of port or cherry brandy, to help revive the spirits following another hard parade.

THE VIEW FROM THE SADDLE

Major Pete Middlemiss, Scots Guards

Riding onto Old College Square at the head of 600 proud officer cadets for the first time was not only nerve-wracking but also tremendously exciting at the same time. The Sovereign's Parade encapsulates the hard year the officer cadets have had and is the moment to show off their discipline, teamwork and precision. As the Commander of the Parade you have to make it count to back this up. Of course the horse has a vote too! 'Coldstream' was immaculate for my first parade but decided on the day that he didn't like applause. Such are the vagaries of animals. Apart from that I couldn't fault him and the old stager guided me through the parade like the old professional that he is. Highlights of the parade are the first royal salute to the Sovereign's representative and the advance in review order. Both have enormous impact and leave a huge impression. Of course it is only many hard hours of training that achieve this. Officer cadets are put through their paces, colour sergeants

Opposite: Last-minute adjustments.

Below: Names of the Adjutants' chargers recorded in stone.

strain blood vessels, sergeant majors cajole and the mounted Adjutants try to remain serene. Everyone asks me about the horse climbing the Old College steps. It is a wonderful tradition and it is not an exaggeration to say it is an iconic moment. An experienced and well-trained charger knows that he earns his polo mints and a bit of tender loving care once he has done his duty and delivered the Academy Adjutant safely into the Grand Entrance. A wonderful moment and the glass of port that you share with the Stick Orderlies after dismounting has never tasted better.

THE SWORD OF HONOUR

Lieutenant F.W. Marshall wrote that in December 1881 he had passed out first at Sandhurst and obtained the regulation sword for general proficiency. He stated that he had been gazetted to the King's Own Borderers which wore the Claymore, and asked if he could get a Claymore in exchange for it with the inscription on the blade. A pencilled note above the Governor, General W.C.E. Napier's initials stated: 'This is the "Anson Sword" that Lieut Marshall has been presented with – write a letter to say that this cannot be done.'
Records of RMC, RMAS Archive, 10 July 1882

The Sword of Honour, originally called the Good Conduct Sword, was first awarded to a gentleman cadet at the Royal Military Academy Woolwich for 'the best-conducted cadet' in 1836. The 'Sword' was first won by C.A. Brooke who was commissioned into the Royal Engineers. Over the years the Sword almost invariably went to the Senior Under-Officer, of which there was only one at Woolwich.

There were awards of merit at the Royal Military College Sandhurst and the cadet could choose a sword or a revolver. The award of a 'regulation sword for general proficiency' was instituted with the award of the Anson Memorial Sword in memory of Captain Anson, VC. There is some debate about when this was first awarded, but the Anson Memorial Sword was given to the gentleman cadet who passed out first in the order of merit at Christmas, the gentleman cadet who came first in the summer term – there being two intakes a year – being given the more prosaically named General Proficiency Sword.

The first recorded winner was F.S. Maude, who joined the Coldstream Guards in 1883. Douglas Haig was the second person to win the Anson Memorial Sword, passing out on 21 December 1884, placed first of 129 gentlemen cadets in the order of merit, having scored 2,557 marks out of a possible 3,350.

Since the establishment of the Royal Military Academy Sandhurst in 1947, the Sword of Honour has been awarded to the individual cadet considered by the Commandant to be the best of his or her course.

The Queen's Medal was instituted by command of Queen Victoria in 1897, the year of the Queen's Diamond Jubilee. It was common to both RMA Woolwich and RMC Sandhurst, and at Sandhurst was always awarded to the cadet highest in the order of merit on passing out. Today it is awarded to the officer cadet who achieves the top place in combined military, academic and practical marks.

Far left: The Duchess of Cornwall presents the Sword of Honour to SUO Rosie Wild.

Left: SUO Kidane Cousland receives the Sword of Honour from HRH Prince Salman bin Hamad Al Khalifa of Bahrain.

THE BAND AT SANDHURST

[The Band] attend all marching past parades of the Students during the week; they also attend at the Sunday parades of the Riding Troop, the Royal Engineers and Serjeants. Two of the privates are employed daily as buglers to sound the necessary calls, being on duty at the Grand Entrance during the intervals. This tour of duty lasts 24 hours.

The Corporal and two Lance Corporals perform the duties of letter carriers in turn.

The Band forms the principal part of the Church Choir; they also form part of the fire brigade.

In addition to the above duties they add materially to the amusement of the Students by playing three times a week at Mess all the year round and twice a week in Summer at Cricket Matches etc. They are also used for the dances which are occasionally given by the Students with the Governor's sanction.

Memo to DGME. Records of RMC, RMAS Archive, 17 January 1876

The first record of an RMC band is in 1813; when on the move from Marlow to Sandhurst the establishment of the Band was fixed at a bandmaster and fourteen bandsmen. Its peculiar distinction is that it was organised as a separate corps and paid for by the War Office, thus becoming the smallest corps in the British Army. In 1863 band numbers were increased to eighteen, with the addition of a sergeant and another three bandsmen. It grew to twenty-five in 1914, and to a bandmaster and thirty in 1938. In 1948 the Bandmaster became Director of Music. The first Bandmaster of any record was Thomas Sullivan, whose son Arthur became one of Britain's best-known composers.

The RMA Band took its final parade on 3 August 1984, a victim to financial cutbacks and the whittling down of the Army: *It was a good parade and a fitting way to go. At the end of the parade, just after the newly commissioned cadets marched up the steps in slow time, the Band moved forward and halted facing the Sovereign's representative. The Drum Major asked for permission to march the Band off parade and received the reply 'With much reluctance, yes'. The Band then left the parade in slow time, marching up the Grand Entrance steps to 'Scipio', the Academy Slow March. The Grand Entrance doors closed slowly behind and the sounds of music died away, a final* mancante *or* decrescendo *to signify the end of the last act.*

Since then the Royal Military Academy has been served by the bands of the British Army attached to the Academy. They play in rotation at all the functions that were once the preserve of the RMA Band, providing order to the day with the bugle calls from Reveille to Lights Out.

The shrinking number of bands means that many of the directing staff's only experience of the role that a band plays in the life of a unit is here at the Royal Military Academy. Bands have played such an important part in Army life and the presence of a Band at RMAS is an essential element of an officer cadet's education. It shows them what a band is for and how different it is when your daily military life is regulated to music. The reduction in the number of bands means that they will not see that in their units, and it is here at Sandhurst that both officer cadets and the directing staff are educated in the important role that bands play in continuing our Army traditions.

WO1 M. Gaunt, Academy Sergeant Major 2002–5

Bottom: The RMC band, 1938.

Below: Trumpeters of the Heavy Cavalry & Cambrai Band.

Bottom right: The band of The Parachute Regiment play as the Colours are marched onto parade.

chapter thirty:

The Sandhurst Trust

Vaughan Kent-Payne

Guided tour for cadets from the French Military Academy St Cyr.

The Sandhurst Trust was started in 2003 as the charity of the Royal Military Academy Sandhurst and is the only specialist Army officer charity. Officer cadets and all serving and retired officers are encouraged to join in the knowledge that 100% of all membership donations are disbursed charitably.

The charity does the following:

It is the alumni organisation for all serving and retired Army officers and fosters esprit de corps by organising events and reunions.

Left: The Worshipful Company of Glovers visit RMAS.

Above: Sir David Reid (Former Chairman of Tesco) presents at RMAS.

On behalf of all those on Exercise CALEDONIAN CADET – 'Thank you to the Sandhurst Trust'.

It advances the education of officers and the public by holding leadership encounters with military and business leaders.

It helps to preserve the traditions of Sandhurst by organising guided tours and historical conferences.

It provides support to cadets and staff at Sandhurst.

The Trust also runs high-profile events at Sandhurst.

Finally, the Trust supports the retired Army officer community through partnership with the Officers' Association. Perhaps the last word on the work of the Sandhurst Trust should be from one of the many helped by the charity:

I wish to express my deep gratitude to the Sandhurst Trust for your grant to purchase a wheelchair hoist for me. This will enable me to once again leave the confines of my home and join my wife and friends in the wider outdoors. (Former captain, aged 88.)

Below left: The Sandhurst Trust Shop at the Academy Open Day.

Below: The Aston Martin Owners Club 80th Anniversary Concours.

To find out more, visit the website at:

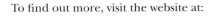

www.sandhursttrust.org

chapter thirty-one:

Alumni

Sᴜᴇ Hᴀᴛᴛᴏɴ

Sᴀɴᴅʜᴜʀꜱᴛ ᴀʟᴜᴍɴɪ ʀᴇꜰʟᴇᴄᴛ ᴏɴ ʜᴏᴡ ᴛʜᴇɪʀ
ᴛʀᴀɪɴɪɴɢ ᴘʀᴇᴘᴀʀᴇᴅ ᴛʜᴇᴍ ꜰᴏʀ ʟᴀᴛᴇʀ ʟɪꜰᴇ

Officer Cadet Mike Adler, Intake 35, 1965

Sandhurst taught me basic accounting, how to write appreciations and service papers, how to lecture and generally how to live in a world of commercialism but still maintain one's integrity. I remember the commandant (General John Mogg) telling us that the one thing that would guarantee our being thrown out of Sandhurst was a lack of integrity and that has remained with me for life.

Officer Cadet Tim O'Brien, CC95/1, 1995

The challenges presented at Sandhurst echoed throughout life – what I learnt was how to approach a problem, build a team, form a plan and lead its execution – maintaining flexibility, openness and humour throughout but in a resilient shell. What I realise now is the template is not confined to the military context but business, self-employment, humanitarian response and even parenting.

Officer Cadet Matt Fensom, SMC 36, 1984

It was an incredibly fast-paced Commissioning Course – only seven months at that time. I went off to face the 3rd Shock Army across the Inner German Border and, as I stood there in front of my first troop of soldiers, I remember well the feeling that, despite my knee-knocking nervousness, Sandhurst had prepared me well for this moment and all that followed in the ensuing thirty-two years.

Officer Cadet Arnison-Newgass, Intake 21, 1957

Did I perceive the benefits? I have often pondered this and have to admit that I find it hard to pin down just what I usefully

Alumni of Sandhurst look back on how their training prepared them for later life.

learned at Sandhurst in life- or military-skills. Today, however, I look with immense admiration at young officers at the front end, in Afghanistan, Iraq … and with wholly unjustifiable vicarious pride that I did once belong to the same tribe; and that has stood me well through life.

Officer Cadet Ray Pett, Intake 47, 1971
After thirty-seven years as a soldier, having had plenty of fun, interesting challenges and just enough excitement, I joined the NHS. Within a year I became Chief Executive of the largest NHS university hospital trust in the country. I subsequently joined the private sector as a director and then chairman of several companies. Throughout both civilian careers, what the Army taught me – starting at Sandhurst – about planning, organisation and, above all, leadership was directly relevant and greatly appreciated by thousands of staff.

Officer Cadet Kamal Sethi (Kenya), Intake 34, 1964
In some tribal cultures, leadership roles are entrenched based on age and hierarchical status regardless of knowledge, experience, education or rank.

Sandhurst had instilled in us various components of leadership – mission, knowledge, discipline, loyalty, courage, man-management, morale and teamwork. Despite this thorough preparation, I had to enlist support of an older experienced private to discipline a young troublesome corporal who regularly challenged authority with his own reasons why an assignment should be done differently in the presence of my platoon. Compliance and submission to authority was never a problem again. In the course, I balanced diplomacy, delegated enforcement and retained authority.

Officer Cadet Jonathan Gough, SGC 893, 1989
Over twenty-five years after Commissioning, I am still seeking advice from the friends I made during SGC 893. They instinctively know where I am coming from, understand why I have found that I need guidance and, crucially, they give me their counsel using Sandhurst-developed Terms of Reference.

Officer Cadet Richard Pawson, Intake 45, 1970
I learnt the following mantra at Sandhurst and it has served me well in business management: 'There is no such thing as "bad soldiers", just bad officers'. While not absolutely true as we all know, this idea that management is totally responsible for all aspects of training, improving, motivating and managing the workforce and their productivity is a fundamental tool of good business.

Officer Cadet Jonathan Ball, SMC 873, 1988
The skills I learnt, in particular leadership and diplomacy, set me up for life. The fellowship that being a Sandhurst graduate creates has served me well, as the unique experience that the Academy provides circumvents nationality, politics, religion and status, which has enabled me to achieve many things

around the globe during periods of natural disasters, warfare and civil unrest that may not have been possible without that connection.

Officer Cadet Gareth Evans, CC093, 1994
Possibly the most important base-value of being an officer that I have learned at Sandhurst was to be reliable – if you say you are going to do something then do it! That way soldiers and officers alike will be sure that they can trust you to carry out what you said you will do in a timely fashion.

Officer Cadet Ian Marshall, Intake 44, 1969
Serve to Lead: what a simple phrase. The motto has always been a guiding light and beacon during my full military career, my time in business and also now in my retirement. The motto is even more poignant now that I am fulfilling a management role with the Royal National Lifeboat Institution.

Officer Cadet Nigel Cairns, SGC 913, 1992
The thing that has really stuck with me from my commissioning course at RMAS, a quarter of a century ago, is *Serve to Lead*. Not just the words but the principle and the actions that entails. It underpins how I lead at all times. As the leader I am there to unlock potential and ensure those I am leading have the direction, environment and support they need to give of their best to achieve our objectives and their personal goals.

Officer Cadet William Hearnshaw, CC142, 2015
Sandhurst ensured that in every leadership situation I ask myself the question 'Why?' Why should my soldiers be doing this? Why do I need them to complete this task? Why is it important that it is done in this timeframe? This in turn led me to my belief that passage of information is key and the more people know, the more buy-in you have, and the more you will get from your soldiers and officers.

Officer Cadet Norman Butler, Intake 4, 1949
The unique challenge of Sandhurst certainly shaped my life for the better and the memories are indelible. I cannot resist commenting that one of the most useful and permanent lessons learned was how to change from any form of dress to any other in a couple of minutes.

Officer Cadet Don Irvine, Intake 35, 1965
The Sandhurst motto *Serve to Lead* was frequently traduced by many of us as *Rush to Wait*. In reality, however, I believe we did appreciate the true meaning of the motto even at the time. For myself, ordained as an Anglican priest many years later, I attempted to continue to honour the truly Christian sentiment of the motto in my service as 'the vicar', serving the Servant King. I did sometimes remark, not altogether flippantly, that in my military life I used to serve The Queen but now I serve The King!

Index

Locations that refer to illustrations or their accompanying text are entered in **bold**.

Individual Officer Cadets will be found alphabetically under 'Officer Cadets'.

Notes on Contributors

CHAPTER 1
Mr Sean McKnight, Director of Studies.

CHAPTER 2
Dr Duncan Anderson, Head of the War Studies Department.

CHAPTER 3
Dr Anthony Morton, curator of The Sandhurst Collection.

CHAPTER 4
Dr Duncan Anderson, Head of the War Studies Department.

CHAPTER 5
Dr Ed Flint, Deputy Head of the Defence and International Affairs Department.

CHAPTER 6
Dr Tony Heathcote, the Librarian when the first edition compiled.

CHAPTER 7
Dr Anthony Morton, curator of The Sandhurst Collection.

CHAPTER 8
Mr Robert Pellow, Post-Graduate Intern at RMAS.

CHAPTER 9
Mr Tim Bean, a senior lecturer in the Department of War Studies.

CHAPTER 10
Revd Mike Parker RAChD, Senior Chaplain at RMAS.

CHAPTER 11
Captain Richard Grimsdell RA, the commander of Lucknow Platoon.

CHAPTER 12
Captain Jeremy Satchell R Aus Arty, the Australian Liaison Officer.

CHAPTER 13
Lieutenant Colonel Lucy Giles RLC, the Commander of New College.

CHAPTER 14
Captain James Howlin COLDM Gds, the Adjutant of New College.

CHAPTER 15
Major Bob Whitaker RAPTC, the Staff Officer responsible for Physical Training.

CHAPTER 16
Major Ellis Harverson SASC ran the Dismounted Close Combat Wing.

CHAPTER 17
Mr Richard Anderson, a trustee of the Sandhurst Trust.

CHAPTER 18
Lieutenant Colonel Paul L'Estrange R IRISH, the Staff Officer responsible for training.

CHAPTER 19
Major Ollie Stead AAC, the Senior Major, New College.

CHAPTER 20
Lieutenant Colonel Geoff Weighell PARA, the Staff Officer responsible for Reserves.

CHAPTER 21
WO1 (SSM) Marie Ovenstone AGC (SPS), the Superintendent Clerk.

CHAPTER 22
WO1 (ACSM) David Macphee SG, the Academy Sergeant Major.

CHAPTER 23
Lieutenant Colonel Andrew Speed SG, the Commander of Old College.

CHAPTER 24
Dr Duncan Anderson, Head of the War Studies Department.

CHAPTER 25
Colonel Bruce Baker (late RAMC), the Senior Medical Officer.

CHAPTER 26
Captain Ed Aitken RL, the Adjutant of Old College.

CHAPTER 27
Major Martyn Cooke, Staff Officer in Academy Headquarters.

CHAPTER 28
WO1 Ryan Bowness YORKS, the Old College Sergeant Major.

CHAPTER 29
Major Pete Middlemiss SG, the Academy Adjutant.

CHAPTER 30
Mr Vaughan Kent-Payne, the Director of the Sandhurst Trust.

CHAPTER 31
Mrs Sue Hatton, the Membership Secretary of the Sandhurst Trust.

Picture Credits and Acknowledgements

This edition first published in Great Britain in 2017 by
Third Millennium Publishing, an imprint of Profile Books Ltd.

3 Holford Yard, Bevin Way
London WC1X 9HD
United Kingdom

www.tmbooks.com

ISBN 978 1 781258 23 1

Design: Matthew Wilson
Production: Simon Shelmerdine

Reprographics by Studio Fasoli, Italy
Printed and bound by Gorenjski tisk storitve, Slovenia
on acid-free paper from sustainable forestry

PICTURE CREDITS

(Key T-Top, B-Bottom, L-Left, R-Right, C-Centre)

Tim Graham/Alamy Front cover

Julian Andrews 2, BR32, B33, TL34, TR34, 52, TR53, 65, 68, 69, T75, 82, 83, TL84, L91, 124–5, 126, B133, L157, L168, 169, BL170, BC170, B171, 174–5, 184–5; **John Blashford-Snell** 99; **A. Bonner** B115; **D. Coombes** LC159, BL159, BR159; **Edward R. Flint** T25, C25, BL32; **Granger Historical Picture Archive/Alamy Stock Photo** R13; **Margaret Jones** 71, L72; **D.E. Langford** T78; **Steve Lister** 10, R35, **Annabel McEwan** 92, 93, 167, R168; **Old College Collection** R84; **Andrew Orgill** T21; **RMAS Archives** 7, 11, 12, 14, 15, 16, 17, 18, B20, 22, 23, 24–5, B25, 26, R27, 28, 29, 30, TR33, B34, C34, L35, 36, 37, TL38, TR38, BL38, BR38, T39, C39, 40, 41, 42, 44, 45, B46, 47, 48, 49, 50, L51, 52–3, TL53, 54, 55, 56, 57, 58, 59, 60, 61, 62–3, 64, B66, 66–7, 67, 70, 73, 74, B75, C75, 77, 78–9, 79, 80, 81, BL84, 85, 86 (TL-Cox Collection), 87, L88, 88–9, 89, 90, R91, 94, 95, 96, 97, 98, 100, 101, 102, 103, BL104, BR104, 105, 106, 107, 108, 109, 110, 111, 112, 113, T115, TL116, TR116, 117, 118, 119, 120, 121, 122, 123, 127, 128, 129, 130, 131, 132, 132–3, T133, 134, B135, 136, 137, 138–9, 140, 141, 144, 152, 153, 154, 155, 156, R157, 158, TR159, 160, 161, 162, 163, 164, 165, 166–7, 170–1, 172, 177, 178, 179, 180, 181, 182; **Sikorski Institute** 43; **Mike Smith** and **Dave Addison** 8–9, L13, 19, T20, L24, L27, 31, T32, TL33, CL38, T46, R51, T66, 76, BL88, T104, T135, 142, 143, T170; **Tempest Photography/Peter Dance** B21, B39, R72, 114, C116; **Jim Farrar** 173; **Patrick Ward** 176

ACKNOWLEDGEMENTS

When the Commandant asked me to examine the options of either reprinting or rewriting the 2005 edition of the book my first instinct was to simply commission a second edition. Aside from mere sloth on my part, the original was a masterpiece of both concise text and stunning photographs and I doubted if it could be bettered.

However, when I delved into the original in detail, it soon became apparent that much has changed in the last twelve years. Not only has the Army adopted a new combat uniform, thereby rendering some 30% of the original photographs out of date, but there have been some radical changes to the way in which training is conducted. Female cadets are totally integrated with their male counterparts in all aspects of training and, as this book goes to print, the first female officer cadet has been accepted into the Royal Armoured Corps. With the new Slim's Company Leadership Development Course and an ongoing commitment to the Afghan National Army Officer Academy, the original short courses chapter looked very dated. Finally, the Sandhurst Trust, in its infancy in 2005, is now a major aspect of life at RMAS. It was therefore obvious that, notwithstanding my initial instincts, a complete rewrite was required.

The original was given the resources commensurate with a new project whereas I was required to complete the rewrite as but one part of my 'day job'. Therefore I persuaded other people around Sandhurst to complete the various chapters as part of their extremely busy 'day jobs'. It is a tribute to the drive and professionalism of all the contributors that they succeeded in producing such quality material within the deadline. It is also a tribute to the even-more-busy Officer Cadets that they were willing to contribute quotes which do much to bring the text alive. Another revolution in the last ten years has been the improvement in the quality of mobile phone and tablet cameras. Whereas the original relied on images taken by professional photographers, many of the images in this volume were taken by cadets and staff and I am truly grateful for their diligence.

The original format has been retained, as to change it would be to change for the sake of change, but I hope that this edition has a fresh feel to it. If not, I have no doubt that, with the pace of change both within the wider British Army and at RMAS, somebody else will be tidying up my mistakes in another decade or so!

Vaughan Kent-Payne